UNDERSTANDING AND PREVENTING HIV RISK BEHAVIOR

 The Claremont Symposium on
Applied Social Psychology

This series of volumes highlights important new developments on the leading edge of applied social psychology. Each volume concentrates on one area in which social psychological knowledge is being applied to the resolution of social problems. Within that area, a distinguished group of authorities present chapters summarizing recent theoretical views and empirical findings, including the results of their own research and applied activities. An introductory chapter integrates this material, pointing out common themes and varied areas of practical applications. Thus each volume brings together trenchant new social psychological ideas, research results, and fruitful applications bearing on an area of current social interest. The volumes will be of value not only to practitioners and researchers but also to students and lay people interested in this vital and expanding area of psychology.

Books in the Series

Interpersonal Processes, *Stuart Oskamp and Shirlynn Spacapan, Editors*

The Social Psychology of Health, *Shirlynn Spacapan and Stuart Oskamp, Editors*

The Social Psychology of Aging, *Shirlynn Spacapan and Stuart Oskamp, Editors*

People's Reactions to Technology, *Stuart Oskamp and Shirlynn Spacapan, Editors*

Helping and Being Helped, *Shirlynn Spacapan and Stuart Oskamp, Editors*

Gender Issues in Contemporary Society, *Stuart Oskamp and Mark Costanzo, Editors*

Violence and the Law, *Mark Costanzo and Stuart Oskamp, Editors*

Diversity in Organizations, *Martin M. Chemers, Stuart Oskamp, and Mark Constanzo, Editors*

Understanding and Preventing HIV Risk Behavior, *Stuart Oskamp and Suzanne C. Thompson, Editors*

UNDERSTANDING AND PREVENTING HIV RISK BEHAVIOR
Safer Sex and Drug Use

STUART OSKAMP
SUZANNE C. THOMPSON
editors

The Claremont Symposium on
Applied Social Psychology

SAGE Publications
International Educational and Professional Publisher
Thousand Oaks   London   New Delhi

For information address:

SAGE Publications, Inc.
2455 Teller Road
Thousand Oaks, California 91320
E-mail: order@sagepub.com

SAGE Publications Ltd.
6 Bonhill Street
London EC2A 4PU
United Kingdom

SAGE Publications India Pvt. Ltd.
M-32 Market
Greater Kailash I
New Delhi 110 048 India

Printed in the United States of America

Library of Congress Cataloging-in-Publication Data

Main entry under title:

Understanding and preventing HIV risk behavior / editors, Stuart
  Oskamp, Suzanne C. Thompson.
      p. cm.
  Based on papers from the 12th Annual Claremont Symposium on
Applied Social Psychology, 1995.
    Includes bibliographical references and index.
    ISBN 0-8039-7424-8 (acid-free paper). — ISBN 0-8039-7425-6 (pbk.:
acid-free paper)
    1. AIDS (Disease) — Prevention—Congresses. 2. AIDS (Disease) in
adolescence—Prevention—Congresses. 3. Health behavior.
I. Oskamp, Stuart. II. Thompson, Suzanne Clare, 1944-
III. Claremont Symposium on Applied Social Psychology (12th: 1995:
Claremont, Calif.)
RA644.A25U224 1996
616.97′9205—dc20   96-10121

This book is printed on acid-free paper.

96 97 98 99 10 9 8 7 6 5 4 3 2 1

Sage Production Editor: Astrid Virding

Contents

1

Understanding and Preventing HIV Risk Behavior: An Overview

SUZANNE C. THOMPSON
STUART OSKAMP

Almost 20 years ago the first signs of the Acquired Immune Deficiency Syndrome epidemic were beginning to show themselves. Little was known about the disease at that time—what was the cause, how was it transmitted, how could it be stopped, who was at risk, could a vaccine or cure be developed? Today there are answers to some of those questions: The virus that causes AIDS has been identified (Human Immunodeficiency Virus) and much is known about routes of transmission. We also have learned that it will not be easy to develop a vaccine to stop the virus or a cure for those already infected; it may not even be possible. The solution to stopping the spread of HIV currently rests with individual behavior—safer sex, precautions in drug use, and decisions of women with HIV regarding pregnancy. If individual behavior is the key to containing the virus, then the critical question is how to influence individuals to take appropriate precautions.

AIDS is a frightening disease that leads to the wasting away of the body, vulnerability to a variety of debilitating infections, and an early death. That people would be highly motivated to protect themselves and their children from this fate is a reasonable expectation. Thus the early developers of interventions assumed that knowledge of the severity of the disease and how to take action to protect oneself would be sufficient grounds to impel individuals to take protective action. Undoubtedly much of this education had its intended effect on behavior for some people. Educated about the seriousness of the disease and how to protect themselves, many individuals have initiated a variety of protective behaviors—including abstinence, use of condoms, reduction in the number of sexual partners, reduced drug use, and use of bleach to clean needles. What is equally clear, though, is that knowledge and the desire to protect oneself, by themselves, do not provide a sufficient force to propel many people to make difficult behavioral changes consistently.

The behaviors that need to be changed to protect oneself are some of the most powerful reinforcers that humans encounter—sexual behavior and drug use. The satisfactions are multifaceted: physical pleasure, intimacy, affirmation of self, group membership, and escape from painful self-awareness. For many people living in poverty and despair, these may be their only consistent satisfactions, but even for people from more privileged circumstances, the power of the immediate situation may be more compelling than a distant threat. Thus, interventions to counter the spread of HIV need to draw on knowledge about the causes of behavior from social psychological theory and research in order to address the complexity of the motives and circumstances governing behavior.

Themes in This Volume

This volume brings together some of the most active and respected researchers in the area of promoting safer sex and drug use aimed at reducing the transmission of HIV. Several themes emerge from these chapters that characterize state-of-the-art research on safer sex and drug use. One feature that the chapters share is the use of social psychological theories and findings to help understand the causes of unsafe behavior and to develop interventions to encourage people to protect themselves. In common parlance, "theoretical" has come to mean an approach that lacks a practical application. In contrast, the authors in this volume give support to Kurt Lewin's view that "there is nothing so practical as a good theory" (Lewin, 1944/1951, p. 169). Theories provide a basis for selecting the factors that must be addressed to reach the goal of safer sex and drug use and the techniques that will induce behavioral change.

The researchers presented here have used theories in several different ways in their work. One approach involves the use of models that are designed to describe health protective behaviors in general. For instance, the chapter by Adler and Rosengard uses the Theory of Reasoned Action as a way of defining rationality in the area of adolescents' sexual decision-making, whereas the chapter by Jemmott shows the usefulness of the Theory of Planned Behavior in identifying ways to intervene with inner-city youth. The Health Belief Model (Rosenstock, 1974), the Theory of Reasoned Action (Fishbein & Ajzen, 1975), the Theory of Planned Behavior (Ajzen, 1991), and the Transtheoretical Model of Behavior Change (Prochaska, DiClemente, & Norcross, 1992) all aim to identify the cognitive, skill-related, environmental, and/or social factors that make it more likely that individuals will protect themselves.

Because many of these models have both common elements and unique ones, a popular approach is to combine ideas from several models in one study. Fishbein et al. (this volume), for example, use elements from the Health Belief Model, Social Cognitive Theory, Theory of Reasoned Action, and the Transtheoretical Model of Behavior Change in their community intervention, and they find that the variables in these theories are successful in predicting people's positions along a continuum of changes toward consistent condom use and consistent bleach use. Combining several models has the advantage of including a number of components that could lead to change. Rhodes and Malotte (this volume) and Fisher and Fisher (this volume) have taken this approach a step further, as each presents a new theory specific to HIV prevention. In these new theories the researchers have combined elements in the more general models that have proved to be particularly important loci for intervention with regard to HIV. Fisher and Fisher suggest that their broad theory, in turn, can be fruitfully applied to other health promotion behaviors, such as breast self-examination.

Another way to use theory to understand HIV protective behavior is to apply social psychological theories from traditional areas of study such as relationships, person perception, and cognitive dissonance to the issues that arise when individuals are deciding to use protection against HIV. In this vein, Clark et al. (this volume) use the rich theoretical underpinnings of research on attraction in relationships to shed light on women's perceptions of their partner's risk for HIV. Similarly, Morris and Swann (this volume) draw on the work on fear arousal and denial to suggest problems with using fear appeals to induce feelings of vulnerability to HIV. Both of these chapters illustrate the value of having a developed and tested theoretical model to suggest new ways to understand what seems like puzzling behavior—that is, failure to protect oneself against a frightening disease—and to propose empirically based interventions to combat it.

A second theme of this volume is that complex behaviors such as those involved in sexuality or drug use must be understood and addressed within their social and cultural framework. The chapters in this volume by Marín and by Adler and Rosengard are excellent examples of empirical work investigating the context for decisions made about sexuality. The chapter by Marín analyzes the cultural factors in the Latino community, such as traditional gender roles, sexual coercion, and discomfort with female sexuality, that make protecting themselves from HIV problematic for Latina women. Research findings show that these cultural factors can be changed because they vary with levels of acculturation. Adler and Rosengard draw on research on adolescent sexuality and contraceptive-use decisions as a context for understanding adolescents' HIV-protective behavior.

A number of other chapters also emphasize the theme that both understanding the reasons behind sexual decisions and planning appropriate intervention designs must be customized to specific cultural groups. In Fisher and Fisher's model, an important stage of intervention development is identification of the cognitions and behavioral patterns that may inhibit HIV prevention in a specific population, such as young gay men, minority adolescents, or college students. Rhodes and Malotte, and Fishbein et al., also make the point that influences on safe behavior may manifest themselves in different ways in groups that might seem similar, such as drug users who are in treatment programs versus those who are not. Furthermore, the same individuals may have different barriers to safe behavior depending on the situation. For example, different problems arise in condom use with a steady partner as opposed to a casual partner (Fishbein et al.). The idea that models of preventive behavior and interventions to induce change must be tailored to different groups and situations provides a counterpoint to the first theme of this volume, that theories provide the necessary framework for understanding and changing unsafe actions. Theoretical models identify the general cognitions, motivations, and environmental features that are important, whereas work on an individual population provides specific information about which aspect of these features needs to be addressed in that group.

A third theme in these chapters concerns social influences on individual behavior. Condom and bleach use occur because an individual acts to provide this self-protection, so in one sense they involve individual behavior. But those individual decisions can be strongly influenced by one's partner, friends, and social groups, so they also have a social component. Several chapters in this volume address the social nature of HIV-protective behavior. Both Jemmott and Fishbein et al. include perceived social norms in the community and social groups as part of their model of influence on intentions and behaviors. Fishbein et al.'s intervention addresses this social component by using role-model stories as presentation materials and peer networks for dissemination of the materials. Rhodes and Malotte recognize the importance of social support and social network characteristics for successful behavior change. The intervention they describe includes "support buddies" who help their peers to change, and supportive visits from outreach staff. In the Clark et al. chapter, individual HIV-protective behavior is viewed in the context of a romantic relationship. The authors make the important point that individuals' decisions to protect themselves are based, in part, on perceptions of their partner and on the nature of their relationship with that partner.

The chapter by Wierson and Bright takes an international perspective on the issue of social influences on behavior by comparing policy and programs for HIV-prevention education in the U.S. and Zimbabwe. They find that HIV education in Zimbabwe occurs in a relational context that emphasizes socially and personally relevant issues for students, whereas U.S. schools tend to focus just on increasing knowledge about AIDS and HIV. They suggest that interventions such as those in Zimbabwe, which integrate messages regarding condom use into discussions about more general personal concerns for students, are likely to be more effective than those that address only the cognitive domain. A similar point regarding adolescent sexuality is made by Adler and Rosengard, who indicate that information about contraception and protection against sexually transmitted diseases is often not sufficient to motivate behavior change if it is presented in isolation from the interpersonal challenges adolescents face in enacting those behaviors.

In a similar vein, Fisher and Fisher propose the next logical step by suggesting that interventions should be conducted with couples in relationships rather than trying to change the behavior of just one partner. The important point is that the social contexts in which individual behaviors take place need to be recognized and addressed to gain full understanding of HIV-preventive behavior and to maximize chances of increasing it.

A fourth theme in this volume is a focus on HIV prevention for adolescents and college students. Although the number of current AIDS cases is relatively low in these groups, several chapters provide evidence that this is not a reason for complacency. DiClemente's chapter details the epidemiological studies that examine the incidence of AIDS or HIV in young adult samples. He points out that, given the long latency before AIDS is identified, it is likely that rates of HIV infection in U.S. adolescents are alarmingly high, especially among African American youth. Adler and Rosengard discuss recent trends in adolescent sexual behavior that suggest that rates of HIV will continue to increase dramatically in this group. A similar note of concern is sounded by Wierson and Bright, who point out that current programs for HIV education in the U.S. are unlikely to have an effect on adolescents' sexual practices that would reduce the rate of spread of HIV.

Another theme that pervades many of these chapters is the importance of careful measurement. On the independent variable side, Clark et al. present data on a new scale of Partner Safety Beliefs that may be useful in predicting HIV risk behavior. Other chapters that use the various social psychological theories to predict health-protective behaviors have typically operationalized the key theoretical variables through precise questionnaire measures. On the dependent variable side, the studies by Fishbein et al. and by Rhodes and Malotte illustrate extremely careful procedures for sampling respondents and for measuring stages of change along continua of specific behaviors, such as consistency of condom use in vaginal intercourse with one's main partner.

Another important idea that is emphasized in these chapters is the need for broader and more complete research data. For instance, DiClemente points out that, even in the extensive epidemiological research, most of the available findings about the prevalence and incidence of HIV are based on special, homogeneous groups, such as Job Corps trainees or applicants for military service, not to mention even more atypical groups such as homeless people or patients attending sexually transmitted disease clinics. Thus, in the area of HIV risk behavior, it is valuable to have data from broader, less highly selected samples such as the high school students in Clark et al.'s first study, the general medical clinic adolescent patients in Adler and Rosengard's studies, or the inner-city youth in Jemmott's research. Fishbein et al. and Rhodes and Malotte also respond productively to this issue in a different way, by their careful geographic selection of community members in high-risk groups such as intravenous drug users, prostitutes, or sexually active street youth.

Many of the chapters have useful advice about types of interventions that should be effective in given situations or with particular kinds of target groups. For example, Adler and Rosengard offer suggestions about interventions with adolescent samples, as does Marín, whose focus is specifically on the difficulties of Latino parents in discussing sexuality with their teenagers. These two chapters agree that parents need help in dealing with such topics effectively. Morris and Swann add the point that use of fear motivation must be very carefully calibrated if it is not to cause denial and avoidance of relevant information. Fisher and Fisher point out that a potent personal motive, which may lead many sexually active individuals into HIV risk behavior, is to maintain their relationship with their partner. They conclude from this that intervention with both members of the couple is desirable and necessary to influence their joint risk-taking behavior, and Marín makes a similar point about the need for both males and females to be involved in training about effective condom use. However, concerning characteristics of the intervenor, Jemmott found that matching facilitators to participants by gender and ethnicity did not add to the success of the intervention, suggesting that a highly structured and culturally appropriate intervention program minimizes the importance of facilitator demographic characteristics.

A special aspect of interventions that is studied in a number of the following research reports is the use of special media, for instance, video presentations of interviews with "people like us" who have contracted HIV or AIDS, or peer-group members demonstrating successful negotiation of condom use or how to interrupt and leave unsafe sexual situations. Films of this sort were used as elements in broad-gauge intervention programs by Fisher and Fisher and Rhodes and Malotte. However, the findings of Morris and Swann raise a caution about material that strongly increases feelings of vulnerability to AIDS, showing that fear-inducing films can increase the chances of at-risk audience members denying the intended message of the film.

This potential problem can be circumvented if the media show models of successful risk-prevention behavior. This approach was emphasized in the community-level studies of Fishbein et al. and Rhodes and Malotte, which made use of less expensive "small media," such as brochures, newsletters, or even baseball cards, that told positive role-model stories of local individuals who were successfully reducing their HIV risk behaviors—social modeling in journalistic formats. The interventions used by Jemmott included games to teach knowledge about AIDS and exercises to increase familiarity with and correct use of condoms. In most of these studies, the effects of several different kinds of interventions were combined in a "big bang" approach and these combined interventions proved significantly effective in reducing unsafe behavior in the research of Fisher and Fisher, Jemmott, Fishbein et al., and Rhodes and Malotte.

A final common thread in this volume is the emphasis placed on careful evaluation of interventions that are intended to induce change. Fisher and Fisher, Fishbein et al., and Rhodes and Malotte all make the point that evaluation research needs to be an integral part of intervention studies. Good assessment of the effectiveness of interventions will promote the increasing ability to intervene successfully in future research as the components that work to induce change are identified and refined.

Varying Approaches

In addition to the common themes that appear throughout the book, the chapters also represent a rich variety of approaches to HIV-prevention behavior. The groups studied include inner-city youths, college students, gay men, Latinos, injecting drug users (IDU), female partners of IDUs, public high school students, Puerto Rican women at risk for HIV, prostitutes, street youth, men who have sex with men but do not gay-identify, and groups of adolescents in the U.S. and Zimbabwe.

The factors that are believed to play important positive or negative roles in preventive behavior also cover a wide area: denial processes

(Morris & Swann), feelings of susceptibility (Fishbein et al.), unwarranted confidence in judging partners' risk for HIV (Clark et al.; Fisher & Fisher), peer norms regarding preventive behavior (Fishbein et al.; Fisher & Fisher; Jemmott; Rhodes & Malotte), negative attitudes toward condoms (Fisher & Fisher; Jemmott; Adler & Rosengard), safe-sex behavioral skills (Fisher & Fisher), being passionately in love (Clark et al.), self-efficacy and behavioral control regarding condoms (Fishbein et al.; Jemmott; Rhodes & Malotte), social support for condom and bleach use (Rhodes & Malotte), perceived costs and benefits of preventive behavior (Fishbein et al.; Adler & Rosengard), environmental constraints (Fishbein et al.), traditional gender roles (Marín), sexual coercion (Marín), comfort with sexuality (Marín), the desire to become pregnant (Adler & Rosengard), and knowing someone with HIV (Wierson & Bright).

The intensity of the interventions described in this volume ranges from viewing a short AIDS-prevention film (Morris & Swann) through 6 hours of training involving information, motivation, and behavioral skills (Fisher & Fisher), or varied series of sessions extending over 4 months (Rhodes & Malotte), to a program involving personal contacts and dissemination of materials over several years (Fishbein et al.).

The AIDS epidemic continues to grow in this country and around the world. Currently, the only hope of stopping this tragedy is through interventions that change individual behavior. This book provides an excellent overview of current knowledge and research on how to promote the behaviors of safer sex and safer drug use that will slow down the spread of HIV. This book will be a useful resource for researchers who examine HIV prevention and for community workers and clinicians who wish to use sound, well-tested techniques for their intervention work. In addition, the book can serve as a thorough introduction for students who are new to the area of behavioral research on HIV and AIDS.

Acknowledgments

We are grateful for the financial support of this year's session of the Claremont Symposium on Applied Social Psychology from Claremont Graduate School, the other five Claremont Colleges, and the Society for the Psychological Study of Social Issues. We are indebted to the many people who helped make this conference a success, especially the authors of chapters in this volume. The help we received from Dr. Graydon Beeks of Pomona College and from the secretarial staff of Jane Gray, Gloria Leffer, and B. J. Reich was crucial, and the efforts of the CGS students who assisted on the day of the conference were much appreciated. We hope that the readers will benefit as much as we have from the combined efforts of all these contributors.

References

Ajzen, I. (1991). The theory of planned behavior. *Organizational Behavior and Human Decision Processes, 50,* 179-211.

Fishbein, M., & Ajzen, I. (1975). *Belief, attitude, intention, and behavior: An introduction to theory and research.* Redding, MA: Addison-Wesley.

Lewin, K. (1951). Problems of research in social psychology. In D. Cartwright (Ed.), *Field theory in social science: Selected theoretical papers* (pp. 155-169). New York: Harper. (Original work published 1944)

Prochaska, J. O., DiClemente, C. C., & Norcross, J. C. (1992). In search of how people change: Applications to addictive behaviors. *American Psychologist, 47,* 1102-1114.

Rosenstock, I. M. (1974). The health belief model and preventive health behavior. *Health Education Monographs, 2,* 354-385.

PART I

GENERAL PRINCIPLES

2

Adolescents at
Risk for AIDS:
AIDS Epidemiology,
and Prevalence and
Incidence of HIV

RALPH J. DiCLEMENTE

There is a growing awareness of the threat that HIV infection and AIDS pose for adolescents in the United States (DiClemente, 1990, 1993; Hein, 1992). Although the number of diagnosed cases of AIDS among adolescents remains relatively small compared with older age groups, there is ample cause for concern. Substantial epidemiologic data show the prevalence of high-risk behaviors among adolescents that increase the probability of HIV infection (DiClemente, 1992). Behaviors such as inconsistent condom use among sexually active adolescents, multiple sex partners, injection drug use (IDU), and the use of alcohol and other drugs that result in greater sexual disinhibition are associated with greater likelihood of exposure to HIV (Vermund et al., 1989). Each of these behaviors alone increases the probability of HIV infection, and they are often reported as occurring in combination (DiClemente, Hansen, & Ponton, 1996).

This chapter provides an overview of the epidemiology of AIDS, HIV prevalence, and HIV incidence among adolescents in the United States. However, a central tenet of this chapter is that relying on the number of AIDS cases to formulate prevention policies severely under-estimates the threat that HIV infection poses for adolescents. The following information describes cases of AIDS among adolescents but this is done primarily to establish a point of departure for presenting data on HIV prevalence and incidence among adolescents. Given the relatively long latency period from infection to clinical diagnosis of AIDS (Bacchetti & Moss, 1989), these epidemiologic measures of HIV are preferable to AIDS prevalence data for assessing the future threat of AIDS for adolescents. Because of the lengthy latency period, it is unlikely that AIDS rates *among adolescents* would demonstrate a sharp increase even with an increase in HIV infection rates. However, such an increase in HIV infection among adolescents would subsequently produce a greater number of diagnosed AIDS cases among older age groups, for instance among adults 20-24 or 25-29 years old.

As a detailed examination of the surveillance data will show, AIDS rates are not uniform among adolescents. Ethnic minority groups, espe-cially African Americans and Latinos, are disproportionately repre-sented among AIDS cases, even among adolescents in the 13-19 age group. HIV prevalence and incidence data also indicate that African American adolescents are at substantially higher risk than other ethnic groups.

Prevalence of AIDS Among Adolescents

As of June 30, 1994, there were 401,749 cases of AIDS reported to the U.S. Centers for Disease Control and Prevention (CDC, 1994). Of the total number of AIDS cases, 1,768 were adolescents aged 13-19. The proportion of adolescent cases between the ages of 13-19 was less than 1% of all diagnosed AIDS cases for males and approximately 1% of all diagnosed cases for females (see Figure 2.1). However, as men-tioned previously, the relatively small proportion of AIDS cases among adolescents should not be interpreted as an indicator of the low-risk status for this age group, due to the long latency period of AIDS. We need to consider also the proportion of diagnosed AIDS cases among young adults in the age groups 20-24 and 25-29.

Males diagnosed with AIDS in the age groups 20-24 and 25-29 account for 3% and 15% of the total number of male AIDS cases.

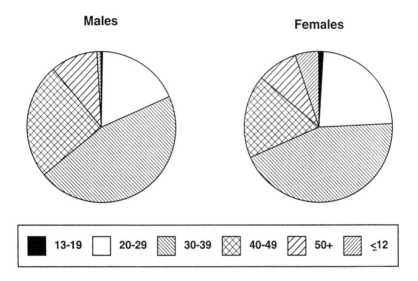

Males   **Females**

| 13-19 | 20-29 | 30-39 | 40-49 | 50+ | ≤12 |

Figure 2.1.   AIDS cases by age at diagnosis, reported through June 1994.

Similarly, females diagnosed with AIDS in the age groups 20-24 and 25-29 account for 6% and 17% of the total number of female AIDS cases. Combining the number of AIDS cases diagnosed within the age groups 13-19, 20-24, and 25-29, the proportion of cases is 18.5% of all male cases and 24.0% of all female cases (see Figure 2.1). Thus, although the proportion of adolescent cases is tiny, the proportion of young adults, an undetermined proportion of whom have contracted HIV infection as adolescents, is much larger.

As a footnote to Figure 2.1, the surprisingly large proportion of AIDS patients less than 13 years old is composed of pediatric AIDS cases. That proportion is strikingly higher among females than among males because the number of pediatric AIDS cases is similar for the two sexes but, at present, the total number of females with AIDS is much lower than the number of males with AIDS.

Ethnic Differences in AIDS Prevalence

Adolescents with AIDS are not uniformly distributed among ethnic groups. Most strikingly, African Americans and Latinos are markedly overrepresented among AIDS cases. Among males between the ages of 13-19, 1,203 cases of AIDS were reported—570 were whites, 368 were African Americans, 239 were Hispanics, and the remainder were Asian/ Pacific Islanders (14) or American Indians/Alaskan Natives (12). Thus, whites accounted for 47.4% of all AIDS cases among male adolescents, whereas African Americans and Hispanics accounted for 30.5% and 19.9%, respectively. In comparison, African Americans and Hispanics comprise only 13% and 6% of the U.S. population.

The data for female adolescents are substantially more skewed. Of the 565 cases of AIDS among 13-19 year-olds reported to the CDC through June 1994, 20% (113) were whites, whereas 63.4% (358) were African Americans, and 16.1% (91) were Hispanics. Clearly, the epidemiology indicates that these ethnic minorities are markedly over-represented among AIDS cases, and this is particularly true for females.

Differences Between Adult and Adolescent HIV Exposure Categories

There are also differences between adolescents and adults diagnosed with AIDS regarding the proportion of cases identified as falling in particular exposure categories—that is, as having particular risk factors for contracting HIV. Among adults, the preponderance of AIDS cases is reported in the exposure categories of male homosexual/bisexual contact and intravenous drug use. For adolescent males 13-19 years of age, only 32.1% and 6.4% of AIDS cases are reported in these exposure categories (shown in Figure 2.2 as MSM—male sex with male—and IDU, respectively). For adolescent females 13-19 years of age, the CDC does not report homosexual/bisexual contact as a risk exposure category, and 19% of AIDS cases are attributable to intravenous drug use.

For adults, heterosexual exposure accounts for 7% of AIDS cases, whereas among adolescents, heterosexual contact accounts for only 2.2% of AIDS cases among males, but 51.7% of AIDS cases among females (see Figure 2.2).

Though the number of adolescents with AIDS is small, the evidence indicates that heterosexual contact plays a very large role in HIV transmission among adolescent females, whereas for adolescent males, the hemophilia category is the largest risk factor (44%).

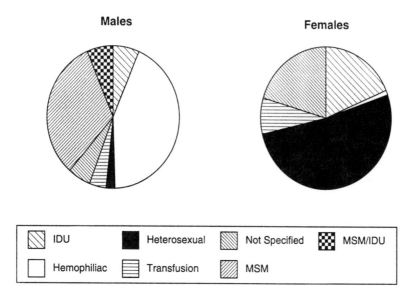

Figure 2.2. AIDS cases in adolescents aged 13-19 through June 1994, by exposure category.

HIV Seroprevalence Among Adolescents

Monitoring the evolving HIV epidemic has proven challenging because of the need to rely on surveillance data based on a clinical endpoint, that is, AIDS. Given the long latency period between infection with HIV and the eventual development of clinical symptoms, the number of clinical AIDS cases among adolescents not only severely underestimates the threat posed by HIV infection but also provides insufficient information for the allocation of health care and prevention resources. Back-calculation techniques can offer some insight into when adolescents may have been infected, but a more precise gauge of the threat of this epidemic for adolescents is provided by findings from HIV seroprevalence studies.

Currently, there are no representative population-based studies for estimating seroprevalence among adolescents. The absence of representative data limits assessment of the magnitude of risk for adolescents

Table 2.1
Prevalence of HIV Infection per 1,000 Adolescents for Selected Surveys, by Race/Ethnicity

		Race/Ethnicity		
Study	*Sample or Site*	*Black*	*Latino*	*White*
Burke et al., 1990	Military applicants	1.0	0.29	0.17
Kelley et al., 1990	Active-duty military[a]	5.1	4.0	1.25
St. Louis et al., 1991	Job Corps entrants	5.3	2.6	1.2
St. Louis et al., 1990	General hospital	8.3	4.9	2.7
Stricof et al., 1991	Homeless shelter	46	68	60
D'Angelo et al., 1991	Ambulatory clinics[b]	3.7	—	—
Ilegbodu et al., 1993	HIV test sites	12.9	5.2	6.2
Young et al., 1992	STD clinic	4.5	—	1.3
Lemp et al., 1994	Gay/bisexual youth[c]	212	95	81

NOTE: All findings have been converted and are presented as the rate of seropositive adolescents per 1,000 to permit comparability with other surveys.

a. Sample of active-duty military personnel was not exclusively comprised of adolescents.

b. This survey did not report ethnic comparisons; 88% of the sample was African Americans and 12% "Other." Due to their small proportion in the sample, "Other" ethnic groups are not shown in the above comparisons.

c. Adolescents ranged in age from 17 to 22.

and reduces the capability to monitor changes in infection rates over time and between geographic regions. However, numerous studies have been conducted with selected adolescent groups (Lindegren, Hanson, Miller, Byers, & Onorato, 1994; Sweeney, Lindegren, Buehler, Onorato, & Janssen, 1995). Much of the HIV seroprevalence data is derived from studies of applicants for military service or active-duty military personnel. Other studies have focused on disadvantaged youth receiving training in the Job Corps, homeless youth, adolescents seeking treatment in sexually transmitted disease (STD) clinics, and adolescents seeking medical care. The data from these subpopulation studies cannot be safely generalized to the adolescent population at large, but each study shows the effect of HIV on some specific group of adolescents. The best seroprevalence data that are available from a variety of adolescent surveys are summarized in Table 2.1.

In an HIV seroprevalence study of adolescent applicants for military duty, Burke and his colleagues (1990) focused exclusively on HIV infection among youths less than 20 years of age. After reviewing

1,141,164 serologic evaluations from adolescent applicants for U.S. military service between October 1985 and April 1989, they identified 393 teenagers as seropositive. Thus the overall HIV prevalence was 0.34 per 1,000 applicants. However, the seroprevalence varied markedly with ethnicity: It was 1.00 per 1,000 applicants among African Americans, compared to 0.17 among whites and 0.29 among Latinos. Separate analyses by gender showed that for males, prevalence for African Americans, whites, and Latinos was 1.06, 0.18, and 0.31, respectively, whereas for females the corresponding rates were 0.77, 0.12, and 0.16. To control for potential confounding factors, a maximum likelihood analysis was conducted that calculated adjusted odds ratios of being seropositive. This analysis indicated that African American applicants were 4.9 times as likely to be seropositive as whites, and Latino applicants were 1.1 times as likely to be seropositive as whites. With regard to gender, males were 1.4 times as likely to be seropositive as female applicants. However, the unrepresentative nature of the sample studied, especially the likelihood of HIV high-risk individuals not applying for military service, suggests that seroprevalence may be substantially higher in the overall U.S. adolescent population.

A study of U.S. Army active-duty personnel (Kelley et al., 1990) identified substantial variation in HIV seropositivity by ethnicity and age-group, somewhat similar to the preceding study of applicants for military service. Higher seroprevalence was found for African Americans (5.1 per 1,000) and Latinos (4.0 per 1,000) than for whites (1.25 per 1,000). Thus the HIV prevalence ratios compared to white soldiers were 4.0 for African Americans (95% confidence interval (CI) 3.6-4.4) and 3.2 for Latinos (95% CI 2.5-3.9). When only soldiers less than 20 years of age were considered, the overall prevalence was 0.5 per 1,000, with male and female figures being 0.4 and 0.9, respectively. When soldiers 20-24 years of age were considered, however, the overall prevalence increased to 1.8 per 1,000, with a sharp increase for males to 1.9 per 1,000, whereas females declined slightly to 0.7 per 1,000. The male-female ratio of 2.8 was markedly different in this age group, with males significantly more likely to be HIV positive than females.

To identify the determinants of seropositivity, Kelley et al. (1990) constructed a multivariate logistic model that controlled for the simultaneous effects of demographic and other potential confounding factors. After this statistical adjustment, the analysis showed that males were significantly more likely to be seropositive than females. African Americans and Latinos were 3.7 and 3.0 times as likely to be HIV positive as white active-duty personnel, a finding rather similar to seroprevalence studies of military applicants.

Since 1987, the CDC has serologically evaluated disadvantaged adolescents (aged 16-21) who were applying for Job Corps training, with over 137,000 entrants having been screened at sites throughout the United States (St. Louis et al., 1991). A major distinction between this evaluation and military data is that there are no exclusion criteria that would prevent application and entrance into the Job Corps for adolescents with a history of drug use or an alternative sexual orientation. Current drug addiction is an excluded condition, however. The Job Corps data collected between October 1, 1987 and February 28, 1990, indicate that disadvantaged adolescents, especially minority adolescents, are at increased risk of being HIV positive. Seroprevalence for the entire sample was 3.6 per 1,000—3.7 per 1,000 for males and 3.2 per 1,000 for females. Ethnic differences were substantial, as shown in Table 2.1. African American and Latino males had seroprevalence rates of 5.5 and 3.0 per 1,000, compared with 1.4 per 1,000 for white males. Similarly, African American females had higher seroprevalence (4.8 per 1,000) than Latino and white females (1.8 and 0.8 per 1,000, respectively).

Homeless youth are another adolescent subpopulation in which HIV prevalence rates have been examined. One study was conducted among adolescents receiving health care at Covenant House, a facility serving runaway and homeless youth in New York City (Stricof, Kennedy, Nattell, Weisfuse, & Novick, 1991). The sample was limited to adolescents aged 15-20 who were undergoing initial medical examination between October 1, 1987 and December 31, 1989. Over the course of the study, 2,667 individuals' blood samples were evaluated for the presence of HIV antibodies. Overall, HIV seroprevalence was high—53 per 1,000—with 6.8% of Latinos being HIV positive, 6.0% of whites, and 4.6% of African Americans. Males had higher rates than females— 6.0% versus 4.2%. Controlling for other demographic characteristics, ethnicity was found not to be significantly associated with HIV seroprevalence, whereas age was the only demographic characteristic that was differentially associated with being HIV positive. Older adolescents (19 and 20 years of age) were 2.7 and 3.7 times as likely to be seropositive as adolescents 15-16 years of age.

This report on homeless youth is one of the few studies that has not found a higher HIV prevalence among African American and Latino adolescents than among whites. Although this adolescent subgroup is clearly not representative of the adolescent population in general, it is a segment that is at high risk, as verified by the high HIV prevalence values found in relative contrast to other subpopulations that have been studied.

In another clinic sample, adolescents 13-20 years of age who were attending three ambulatory clinics at Children's Hospital Medical Center, Washington, DC, were studied (D'Angelo, Getson, Luban, & Gayle, 1991). For 15 months between 1987 and 1989, all such adolescents who had blood drawn for a medical test ($N = 3520$) were screened to identify presence of HIV antibodies. Most of the sample were African American (88.2%), and the mean age was 16.3 years. Of all blood specimens tested, 13 were seropositive, yielding an overall prevalence rate of 3.7 per 1,000. The HIV prevalence was higher in females than males (4.7 versus 1.7) and among adolescents 15-18 than those younger than 15 (4.9 versus 1.7). Of particular importance, among adolescents considered at high risk based on screening criteria, 41 per 1,000 were seropositive; however, the screening criteria used could correctly identify only 38% of those adolescents who were seropositive. This finding suggests that a large proportion of HIV-positive adolescents may be missed by using standard criteria and methods of identifying risk; in addition, many who are at high risk may be reluctant to be tested for HIV infection.

Sexually transmitted disease clinics provide another source of seroprevalence data. In an inner-city STD clinic, Quinn et al. (1988) found the HIV seroprevalence rate among adolescents aged 15-19 to be 22 per 1,000 (25 per 1,000 for females and 20 for males). In this sample 28% of the HIV-positive women were 20 years of age or younger. Results from this study have also shown that having an active sexually transmitted disease is an independent risk factor strongly associated with seropositive status. A review of seroprevalence studies conducted at STD clinics in the United States found the median HIV seroprevalence rate for persons less than 20 years of age was 11 per 1,000 with a range from 0 to 20. Persons aged 20-29, however, showed a substantially higher median seroprevalence of 45 per 1,000 with a range from 5 to 75 (Cannon, Schmid, Moore, & Papparoanou, 1989).

A more recent study of STD clinic patients by Young, Feldman, Bracklin, and Thompson (1992) examined the HIV seroprevalence rates among adolescents attending Mississippi State Department of Health STD clinics from 1988 to 1990. During this 2-year period, 9,855 adolescents aged 13 to 20 years attended the clinics and HIV antibodies were confirmed in 39—a rate of 4.0 per 1,000 (95% confidence interval 2.7-5.2 per 1,000). Seroprevalence rates were almost equal for males and females (4.1 versus 3.8) but they differed markedly by ethnicity. As shown in Table 2.1, rates among African Americans were 3.5 times higher than among whites (4.5 versus 1.3). The greatest difference was observed among females, with African American females having a rate of 4.7 versus 0 for white females; African American males had a rate of 4.5 versus 3.2 for white males.

Among hospital patients, a wide-ranging survey, the CDC Sentinel Hospital Surveillance Study (St. Louis et al., 1990), provided HIV seroprevalence data on patients, both adolescent and adult, seeking treatment at 26 hospitals across the U.S. To control for potential overrepresentation among patients infected with HIV and seeking medical care for conditions related to that infection, exclusion criteria were implemented that screened out patients whose reason for seeking care involved a condition often associated with HIV infection or HIV risk factors. To protect the patients' identities, blood specimens were evaluated anonymously. Thus, unlike HIV seroprevalence surveys conducted with applicants for military service, the findings from the Sentinel Hospital survey are not subject to self-selection or avoidance biases that may underestimate HIV prevalence rates. From January 1988 to June 1989, 89,547 blood specimens were evaluated for antibodies to HIV. The overall HIV prevalence rate was found to be 13 per 1,000. HIV seroprevalence was most prominent in the 25-44 year-old age group, although a sharp increase began in the mid-adolescent years. At two hospitals with the highest prevalence of AIDS, 1.1% and 3.8% of adolescents 15-19 years of age were identified as HIV positive. Ethnic comparison data shown in Table 2.1 indicate that for adolescents aged 13-19, African Americans had a substantially higher HIV rate (8.3 per 1,000) than Latinos (4.9) or whites (2.7).

Among adolescents specifically seeking HIV testing, a recent study by Ilegbodu, Frank, Poindexter, and Johnson (1994) examined the records of 4,017 adolescents receiving HIV counseling and testing services at a publicly supported site in Houston, Texas over a 3-year period (January 1990 to December 1992). An overall HIV seroprevalence rate of 10.2 per 1,000 was found, with males having a somewhat higher rate than females (11.2 vs. 9.7). Among males the ethnic differences were small (African Americans 11.8, Latinos 10.5, whites 9.9 per 1,000). However, among females, ethnic differences were pronounced (African Americans 13.5, Latinos 3.5, whites 4.5 per 1,000). The adolescents' age was strongly positively associated with seroprevalence; for example, adolescents age 14, 15, 16, and 17 had HIV prevalence rates of 6.8, 8.8, 9.1, and 12.9 per 1,000, respectively.

A recent study estimated the seroprevalence of HIV among young homosexual and bisexual men in San Francisco and Berkeley, California (Lemp et al., 1994). A total of 425 men between the ages of 17 and 22 were sampled from 26 diverse locations (i.e., bars, parks, dance clubs, street corners) during 1992 and 1993. The overall HIV prevalence was 94 per 1,000 (95% confidence interval 68-126). Seroprevalence was significantly higher among African Americans (211 per 1,000) than among other ethnic groups (Latinos 95, whites 81, and Asians/Pacific Islanders 42, $p<.002$). Not surprisingly, these young homosexual and bisexual men had the highest rates of HIV of any of the studies reported in Table 2.1.

In general, the findings from these diverse, though not representative, HIV seroprevalence surveys are clear: minority adolescents, in particular African American youth, are significantly more likely to be infected with HIV than are other adolescent racial/ethnic groups. With the exception of a few studies, the seroprevalence rate among African American adolescents far exceeds the rate for white and Latino adolescents.

CDC Job Corps Serosurveys

Although the previous data are informative, single-point-in-time HIV seroprevalence surveys do not allow observation of time trends. Thus, such data are limited in assisting policy and intervention planners in assessing changes in HIV infection rates, particularly among specific racial/ethnic and gender groups. However, one study has provided very useful data for monitoring changes in HIV infection over time— namely, the CDC Job Corps serosurveys.

As noted previously, applicants for Job Corps training are screened for HIV by the CDC. A recent follow-up study of HIV seroprevalence among Job Corps applicants aged 16-21 presented an assessment of time trends (Conway et al., 1993). Trends in seroprevalence by gender between 1988 and 1992, standardized for age, race, and Metropolitan Statistical Area, indicated a significantly rising rate among female applicants, whereas seroprevalence among males demonstrated a steady, significant decrease (see Figure 2.3).

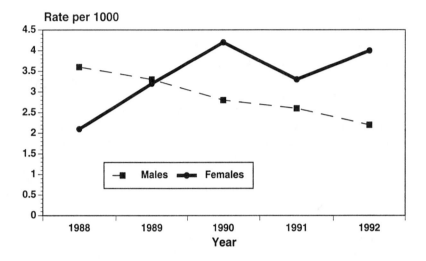

Figure 2.3.   Standardized HIV prevalence among students entering Job Corps training, January 1988 through December 1992.

Analyses of these adolescent Job Corps applicants were also conducted for racial/ethnic and gender groups, standardized for age and Metropolitan Statistical Area. The results indicated that in 1988, HIV seroprevalence was highest among African American males (5.6 per 1,000), but this group showed a substantial, significant decrease by 1992 to 3.4 per 1,000 ($p < .001$). In contrast, seroprevalence among Latino and white males remained relatively constant between 1988 and 1992, with the rate for Latinos being higher (1.9 versus 1.1). Similarly for females, HIV prevalence among Latina and white applicants did not change. However, among African American females the prevalence more than doubled between 1988 and 1992, from 3.2 to 6.6 per 1,000 ($p < .001$, see Figure 2.4). Thus, by 1992, African American women were almost twice as likely to be infected as were African American males.

The 1992 Job Corps data are displayed by age and gender in Figure 2.5. The graph clearly indicates that HIV rates are age dependent for both males and females. Seroprevalence for males, standardized for race and Metropolitan Statistical Area, rose from 1.3 per 1,000 for 16-year-olds to 4.3 for 21-year-olds. For females, the rates rose from 2.1 for 16-year-olds to 7.1 for 21-year-olds.

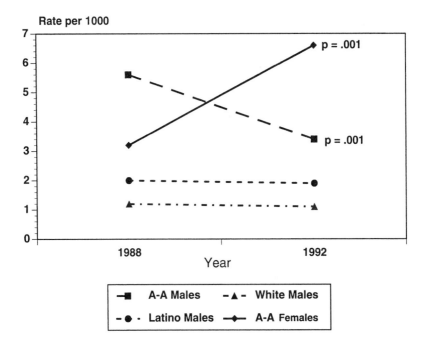

Figure 2.4. Changes in standardized HIV prevalence among students entering Job Corps training, 1988 to 1992.

HIV Incidence Among Adolescents

Although seroprevalence data are informative in identifying the currently existing number of HIV-infected individuals, it is also important to obtain incidence data—that is, the number of persons who are seronegative at one point but, on subsequent HIV testing, are found to be seropositive. Direct measurement of the incidence of new HIV infections greatly enhances our ability to track the evolving epidemic and it substantially improves the accuracy of epidemic forecasts. In view of the widespread dissemination of information about HIV and AIDS, incidence data also provide some insight into the effectiveness of prevention efforts. However, assessing HIV incidence is difficult because it can only be observed in persons who undergo repeated

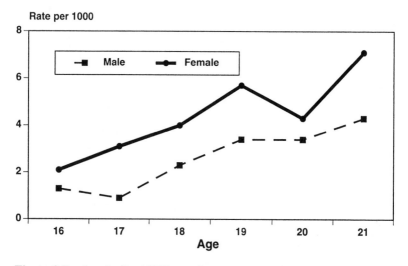

Figure 2.5.   Standardized HIV prevalence among students entering Job
Corps training in 1992, by age and gender.

serological evaluation for HIV (at two or more separate time points).
Fortunately, such information is available for adolescents and young
adults in the U.S. military (McNeil et al., 1991). Since 1985, soldiers
on active duty in the U.S. Army have been routinely tested for the
presence of HIV antibodies and are required to undergo repeated tests
every 2 years. This procedure has provided data on the incidence of new
HIV infections in previously HIV-negative soldiers.

Categorizing the U.S. Army data by age group, the findings for
soldiers under age 20 are of special interest for this chapter. However,
because two time points are required to evaluate incidence, and adolescents are first eligible to enlist at age 17, the data presented reflect
changes in HIV status only for this limited age group. Another caveat
is that the actual number of incident cases was low; only 22 whites and
26 African Americans seroconverted during the period of the study.
Nonetheless, the data provide valuable information on the frequency of
HIV infection in healthy populations of adolescents.

For these soldiers below age 20, the overall incidence was substantially different for African Americans and whites—0.76 and 0.22 per
1,000 person-years, respectively. When the data were divided into
period-specific rates to identify changes in the incidence of HIV infec-

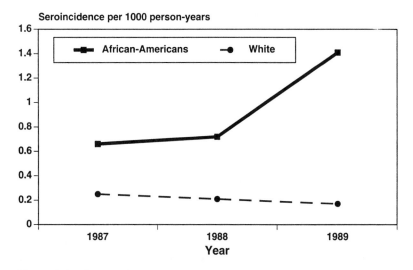

Figure 2.6.   Seroincidence rates among active-duty U.S. Army personnel less than age 20, by year and race.

tion over time, African Americans had higher period-specific incidence rates for all 3 years: 1987 (0.66 vs. 0.25), 1988 (0.72 vs. 0.21), and 1989 (1.41 vs. 0.17) (see Figure 2.6). Period-specific incidence rates declined significantly among white adolescents from 1987 to 1989. However, African American adolescents had sharply higher seroconversion rates in 1989 than in 1987, a period when HIV-prevention education programs and media campaign information were being disseminated rapidly. For 1989, the incidence rate for African Americans was 8 times greater than for whites. More alarming, for 1989 these African American adolescents below age 20 had the highest HIV incidence rate of any ethnic-age group in this study. Their sharp rise in HIV incidence indicates a need for more intensive HIV education targeted directly at this subgroup.

A similar study was conducted among military personnel in the U.S. Navy and Marine Corps (Garland et al., 1989). In this study, all active-duty personnel who had an enzyme-linked immunoabsorbent assay (ELISA) blood test for HIV with negative results were followed over time, as in the Army study. For Navy personnel aged 17-19, the incidence rate per 1,000 person-years was 0.22 for African Americans and 0.19 for whites. However, for the age group 20-24, the incidence rate among African Americans (1.90) was markedly higher than for whites (0.55). Incidence rates for white Marine Corps personnel aged 17-19 and 20-24 were 0.0 and 0.17, whereas the rates for African Americans were markedly higher—0.52 and 0.73. The overall findings were generally comparable to the Army data, except that the incidence rate for African Americans aged 17-19 was not as high.

Discussion

Clinically overt AIDS disease remains uncommon in adolescents, compared to older age groups. However, results from screening of applicants for military service, from seroprevalence studies of various adolescent samples, and from seroconversion (incidence) studies conducted with active-duty military personnel all indicate that subclinical HIV infections are not uncommon among U.S. adolescents. The seroprevalence data from the most recent survey of adolescent applicants for military service (Burke et al., 1990), indicate that 1 of every 3,000 teenage applicants was HIV positive. Moreover, AIDS and HIV infection are not uniformly distributed among ethnic groups. Data from prevalence and incidence studies indicate that African Americans are likely to have both higher prevalence rates of AIDS and HIV infection, and also markedly higher HIV incidence rates.

Of particular importance are the findings of Stricof et al. (1991) and Lemp et al. (1994), which identify adolescents in homeless shelters and homosexual and bisexual young males as having extremely high HIV prevalence rates compared to those for adolescents in other samples. In the latter study, as in most others, minority adolescents again had the highest HIV prevalence rates. The findings from research on AIDS and HIV summarized in this chapter suggest that adolescent groups have been both understudied and underserved, and that they may require additional prevention activities tailored to their particular needs. Clearly, one of the primary values of epidemiological monitoring is to identify subgroups at high risk of HIV infection and in need of greater allocation of resources for prevention.

Though adolescents applying for military service and the other selected samples that have been studied are not representative of the U.S. population in general, nonetheless the data are alarming and warrant serious attention from health educators, policy analysts, and public health officials. Although AIDS is less common among adolescents than among older age populations, serosurveys indicate that HIV infection is not uncommon among adolescents. Further monitoring of HIV infection is necessary to better gauge the magnitude and course of the HIV epidemic among adolescents and, ultimately, to assist in targeting prevention activities to reduce AIDS morbidity and transmission among the adolescent population.

References

Bacchetti, P., & Moss, A. R. (1989). Incubation period of AIDS in San Francisco. *Nature, 338*, 251-253.

Burke, D. S., Brundage, J. D., Goldenbaum, M. S., Gardner, L. I., Peterson, M., Visintine, R., & Redfield, R. R. (1990). Human immunodeficiency virus infections in teenagers: Seroprevalence among applicants for U.S. military service. *Journal of the American Medical Association, 263*, 2074-2077.

Cannon, R. O., Schmid, G. P., Moore, P. S., & Papparoanou, M. (1989). Human immunodeficiency virus (HIV) seroprevalence in persons attending STD clinics in the United States. *Sexually Transmitted Diseases, 16*, 184-189.

Centers for Disease Control. (1994, June). *HIV/AIDS surveillance report.* Atlanta, GA: Author.

Conway, G. A., Epstein, M. R., Hayman, C. R., Miller, C. A., Wenslell, D. A., Gwinn, M., Karon, J. M., & Peterson, L. R. (1993). Trends in HIV prevalence among disadvantaged youth: Survey results from a national job training program, 1988 through 1992. *Journal of the American Medical Association, 269*, 2887-2889.

D'Angelo, L. J., Getson, P. R., Luban, N. L. C., & Gayle, H. D. (1991). Human immunodeficiency virus infection in urban adolescents: Can we predict who is at risk? *Pediatrics, 88*, 982-986.

DiClemente, R. J. (1990). The emergence of adolescents as a risk group for human immunodeficiency virus infection. *Journal of Adolescent Research, 5*, 7-17.

DiClemente, R. J. (1992). Psychosocial determinants of condom use among adolescents. In R. J. DiClemente (Ed.), *Adolescents and AIDS: A generation in jeopardy* (pp. 34-51). Newbury Park, CA: Sage.

DiClemente, R. J. (1993). Confronting the challenge of AIDS among adolescents: Directions for future research. *Journal of Adolescent Research, 8*, 156-166.

DiClemente, R. J., Hansen, W., & Ponton, L. E. (1996). New directions for adolescent risk prevention and health promotion research and interventions. In R. J. DiClemente, W. Hansen, & L. E. Ponton (Eds.), *Handbook of adolescent health risk behavior.* New York: Plenum.

Garland, F. C., Mayers, D. L., Hickey, T. M., Miller, M. R., Shaw, E. K., Gorham, E. D., Bigbee, L. R., & McNally, M. M. (1989). Incidence of human immunodeficiency virus seroconversion in U.S. Navy and Marine Corps personnel, 1986 through 1988. *Journal of the American Medical Association, 262*, 3161-3165.

Hein, K. (1992). Adolescents at risk for HIV Infection. In R. J. DiClemente (Ed.), *Adolescents and AIDS: A generation in jeopardy* (pp. 3-18). Newbury Park, CA: Sage.

Ilegbodu, A. E., Frank, M. L., Poindexter, A. N., & Johnson, D. (1994). Characteristics of teens tested for HIV in a metropolitan area. *Journal of Adolescent Health, 15,* 479-484.

Kelley, P. W., Miller, R. N., Pomerantz, R., Wann, F., Brundage, J. F., & Burke, D. S. (1990). Human immunodeficiency virus seropositivity among members of the active duty U.S. Army, 85-89. *American Journal of Public Health, 80,* 405-410.

Lemp, G. F., Hirozawa, A. M., Givertz, D., Nieri, G. N., Anderson, L., Lindegren, M. L., Janssen, R. S., & Katz, M. (1994). Seroprevalence of HIV and risk behaviors among young homosexual and bisexual men. *Journal of the American Medical Association, 272,* 449-454.

Lindegren, M. L., Hanson, C., Miller, K., Byers, R. H., Jr., & Onorato, I. (1994). Epidemiology of human immunodeficiency virus infection in adolescents, United States. *Pediatric Infectious Disease Journal, 13,* 525-535.

McNeil, J. G., Brundage, J. F., Gardner, L. I., Wann, Z. F., Renzullo, P. O., Redfield, R. R., Burke, D. S., & Miller, R. N. (1991). Trends of HIV seroconversion among young adults in the U.S. Army, 85-89. *Journal of the American Medical Association, 265,* 1709-1714.

Quinn, T. C., Glasser, D., Cannon, R. O., Matuszak, D. L., Dunning, R. W., Kline, R. L., Campbell, C. H., Israel, E., Fauci, A. S., & Hook, E. W. (1988). Human immunodeficiency virus infection among patients attending clinics for sexually transmitted diseases. *New England Journal of Medicine, 318,* 197-203.

St. Louis, M. E., Conway, G. A., Hayman, C. R., Miller, C., Petersen, L. R., & Dondero, T. J. (1991). Human immunodeficiency virus infection in disadvantaged adolescents. *Journal of the American Medical Association, 266,* 2387-2391.

St. Louis, M. E., Rauch, K. J., Petersen, L. R., Anderson, J. E., Schable, C. A., & Sentinel Hospital Surveillance Group. (1990). Seroprevalence rates of human immunodeficiency virus infection at Sentinel Hospitals in the United States. *New England Journal of Medicine, 323,* 213-218.

Stricof, R. L., Kennedy, J. T., Nattell, T. C., Weisfuse, I. B., & Novick, L. F. (1991). HIV seroprevalence in a facility for runaway and homeless adolescents. *American Journal of Public Health, 81(Suppl.),* 50-53.

Sweeney, P., Lindegren, M. L., Buehler, J. W., Onorato, I. M., & Janssen, R. S. (1995). Teenagers at risk of human immunodeficiency virus type 1 infection. *Archives of Pediatrics and Adolescent Medicine, 149,* 521-528.

Vermund, S. H., Hein, K., Gayle, H. G., Cary, J. M., Thomas, P. A., & Drucker, E. (1989). Acquired immunodeficiency syndrome among adolescents: Case surveillance profiles in New York City and the rest of the United States. *American Journal of Diseases of Children, 143,* 1220-1225.

Young, R. A., Feldman, S., Bracklin, B. T., & Thompson, E. (1992). Seroprevalence of human immunodeficiency virus among adolescent attendees of Mississippi sexually transmitted disease clinics: A rural epidemic. *Southern Journal of Medicine, 85,* 460-463.

3

Adolescent Contraceptive Behavior: Raging Hormones or Rational Decision Making?

NANCY E. ADLER
CYNTHIA ROSENGARD

In a volume devoted to understanding and preventing AIDS risk behaviors, it is essential to identify sexual behavior patterns, to understand the context in which sexual decisions are made, and to address possible implications that these behaviors and decisions may have for interventions and for the social policies that underlie them. This chapter outlines the current trends in adolescent sexual behavior, places these trends within the context of the debate over the "rationality" of adolescent behavior, and discusses some intervention and policy implications of these perspectives.

AUTHORS' NOTE: The research reported in this chapter was supported by grants RO1 HD16137 and RO1 HD23880 from the National Institute of Child Health and Human Development. Dr. Rosengard was supported by the training program in Psychology and Medicine for the National Institute of Mental Health (MH 19391). We appreciate the helpful suggestions of A. J. Alejano, Marilee Coriell, Philip Moore, Crystal Park, and Lauri Pasch and the excellent support of Lauren Smith in surveying the literature.

The sexual behavior patterns of adolescents have changed dramatically during the last two decades. Earlier initiation of sexual intercourse, increasing rates of teenage pregnancy and sexually transmitted diseases, and use of drugs and alcohol in conjunction with sexual behavior are features of the changing landscape of adolescent sexual decision making. A closer examination of these recent trends will illuminate the context that influences adolescents' exposure to risk for sexually transmitted diseases, including AIDS.

Recent Trends in Adolescent Sexual Behavior

Initiation of sexual intercourse. Over the past 20 years, the age at which young people initiate sexual activity has decreased. A far larger proportion of teenagers are sexually active now than was the case up through the 1970s (Centers for Disease Control (CDC), 1991; Miller, Turner, & Moses, 1990; National Center for Health Statistics, 1991). Currently, 56% of young women and 73% of young men have had sexual intercourse by the time they reach 18 years of age, compared to 35% and 55% respectively in the early 1970s (Alan Guttmacher Institute, 1994). In one recent U.S. national survey, almost a quarter of 14-year-old males and nearly 40% of 15-year-old females reported having had sexual intercourse (Leigh, Morrison, Trocki, & Temple, 1994). The early initiation of sexual behavior has been associated with a number of negative outcomes and risky behaviors, including higher numbers of sexual partners (Miller et al., 1990), increased risk of pregnancy and sexually transmitted diseases, and greater use of substances such as alcohol and cocaine (Irwin & Shafer, 1992).

Rates of sexually transmitted diseases. Not surprisingly, with increasing numbers of adolescents being sexually active, rates of sexually transmitted diseases (STDs) have increased dramatically. By the late 1980s, one-fourth of all adolescents were infected with a STD before they graduated from high school (Millstein, 1989). Among sexually active teenagers, one in four acquire an STD every year—around 3 million teenagers (Alan Guttmacher Institute, 1994). Rates of gonorrhea among adolescents more than tripled in the 30 years from 1958 to 1988; there are now over 1,000 cases per 100,000 young women (Divi-

Table 3.1
Teen Pregnancy Rates in Industrialized Countries

Country	Pregnancy rates per 1,000 teenage females
United States	109.9
England & Wales	53.4
Norway	45.8
Canada	45.4
Denmark	34.0
Sweden	33.2
Netherlands	15.0

SOURCE: Jones et al. (1987).

sion of STD/HIV Prevention, CDC, 1993). As of 1990, adolescents accounted for one quarter of the total number of STDs reported in this country (Hingson, Strunin, Berlin, & Heeran, 1990). In view of these patterns of sexual behavior and of STDs, there is concern that adolescents are at high risk for exposure to HIV. Although a relatively small number of teenagers have been diagnosed with AIDS, a substantial number of young people in their 20s have developed AIDS. Given the long incubation period of HIV, this means that most of them actually contracted the virus during their teenage years.

Teenage pregnancy. Rates of teenage pregnancy are also high. Each year over one million U.S. adolescent girls become pregnant (Hayes, 1987)—11% of all females age 15 to 19. Almost one-fifth of teenage females who are sexually active conceive annually (National Center for Health Statistics, 1991). Both STDs and pregnancy rates are much higher in the U.S. than in other countries. Despite comparable rates of sexual activity across many industrialized countries, the United States has the highest teenage pregnancy rate of any developed country (see Table 3.1). The U.S. rate is triple that of the Scandinavian countries and more than double that of Canada and England (Jones et al., 1987).

Contraceptive practices. The type of contraceptive method used by adolescents is a function of their age, but changes associated with age may also reflect their amount of sexual experience. There have been shifts over time in the relative popularity of contraceptive methods among U.S. adolescents. In 1988, the method used most often by teens aged 15-19 was oral contraceptives, with condoms in second place. By 1990, the method used most often by teens aged 15-17 years old was condoms, whereas pills continued to be the most frequent choice of 18- and 19-year-olds (Brown & Eisenberg, 1995).

There is evidence that adolescents who are sexually active are not protecting themselves effectively from pregnancy or sexually transmitted diseases. The relatively high rates of STDs and of pregnancy provide evidence of this, as does research on contraceptive behavior. In a sample of college-age students, only one-third reported using any method of contraception and of those only one-quarter reported using condoms (Haffner, 1988). Similarly, in a 1991 survey, only 58% of adolescents aged 15 and 16 reported ever having used contraceptives (CDC, 1991). In a longitudinal study of adolescent males conducted from 1988 to 1991, the percentage reporting condom use at last intercourse decreased from 56% to 44%; because condom use also decreased with age, when age was controlled for, there was no significant drop in the use of condoms between 1988 and 1991 (Ku, Sonenstein, & Pleck, 1993). However, this finding followed a period of generally increasing condom use prior to 1988.

Alcohol and substance use. The use of psychoactive substances or alcohol is a potential risk factor in conjunction with sexual behavior (e.g., Robertson & Plant, 1988; Stall, McKusick, Wiley, Coates, & Ostrow, 1986). Studies have reported alcohol use rates as high as 66%, marijuana use rates around 50%, and rates of cocaine use close to 10% for U.S. high school students (Irwin & Shafer, 1992). In addition, between 1988 and 1991 there was an increase, from 0.5% to 1.6% in the number of adolescent males reporting intravenous (IV) drug use (Ku, Sonenstein, & Pleck, 1993).

Views Concerning the Rationality of Adolescent Behavior

Given the preceding statistics on adolescent risk behavior and its consequences, it is not surprising that many observers question teenagers' ability to make rational health decisions for themselves. One school of thought regarding adolescent behavior portrays adolescence as a discontinuous period in development—a time when young people are influenced by raging hormones to the point of being impulsive, rebellious, and continually preoccupied by sexual thoughts. A German term for this view is *Sturm und Drang* ("storm and stress"). Embracing this view of adolescence as a discontinuous period and of adolescents as risk takers who are lacking in judgment, particularly in relation to their sexual and reproductive behaviors, encourages social policies aimed at protecting adolescents from the negative consequences of their behavior. Policies limiting adolescents' rights to make independent decisions assume that adolescents lack the capacity to make reasoned choices. Some legislation (e.g., laws mandating parental consent for abortions) explicitly refers to limitations in adolescent decision making as the basis for restrictive policies. In addition, viewing adolescence as a time of irrationality limits the types of approaches that are considered and may inhibit the development of effective behavioral interventions for reducing risky behavior. For instance, if one assumes that adolescents lack the capacity for reasoning and decision making, one might consider interventions that focus on information and decision making to be irrelevant.

A second, more recent school of thought considers adolescence as a developmental period that is not necessarily discontinuous nor characterized by *Sturm und Drang*. This perspective views adolescents as exhibiting a continuity with what came before and with what will follow. Adolescents are seen to be struggling with issues of identity and separation from family, but this struggle occurs within reasonable bounds with no dramatic breaks either from family or from their earlier or later development. Because this view characterizes adolescence as a period of confusion rather than irrationality, it encourages the development of a broader range of interventions that are targeted at adolescents' sexual decision making.

To address this issue, we will discuss two studies that have examined the extent to which adolescents engage in rational decision making regarding contraceptive use. Using a value-expectancy model of decision making that defines rationality in terms of consistency of reasoning, we will argue that adolescents are reasonably "rational" in their contraceptive choices. However, we also note that the relationships are not perfect and that it is important to understand factors that may influence adolescents not to protect themselves from the risks associated with sexual activity.

What Is Rationality?

Rational Models of Behavior

In models of decision making and choice behavior that are referred to as "rational models," rationality means optimizing one's outcomes. These models have recently predominated in psychology in addition to economics and other social sciences. They assume that individuals act like lay economists, weighing the costs and benefits of various options open to them and choosing the one that provides the best ratio of benefits to costs.

The models specify that, to make the choice that is optimal, individuals need accurate information on (a) the range of options available, (b) the potential consequences that could result from selecting each option, (c) the likelihood of each consequence occurring if the option were chosen, and (d) the harm or benefit that would be experienced if the potential consequence did occur. These rational models are prescriptive, describing a process by which individuals "ought" to make decisions. In everyday life, however, there are many factors that can prevent individuals from acting in line with these models; hence, they will not always make the choice that economists or psychologists think they ought to make. Individuals may not have full or accurate information on the possible range of outcomes that could occur or on the likelihood of these outcomes resulting from a given choice. They also may not be able to predict how much they would benefit from or be harmed by a given outcome in the short or long term. There are also cognitive limitations and biases that create obstacles to making optimal choices. These include limitations on people's awareness of options and their ability to process and combine information, and heuristics that may systematically distort their perception of outcomes (Tversky & Kahneman, 1973).

These psychological models, it should be noted, are based on "subjective expected usefulness." The models define rationality in terms of choosing the option that will maximize the expected usefulness of a given choice based on the individual's subjective evaluation of likelihoods and values. The person's evaluations may not be accurate, but according to these models, individuals are acting rationally if they select the best option *based on their subjective evaluations.*

These rational models capture important aspects of what drives behavior. Individuals do try to anticipate the consequences of their actions and to make the choice that will be most gratifying. Even if they do not make the optimal choice, they strive to make the best choice given their understanding of the choices and the likely consequences. However, the models need to be modified to explain fully how people make choices and behave in everyday life. This is particularly true if we want to understand complex socially embedded behaviors such as contraceptive use or nonuse. Rather than abandoning these models, we should expand them to include additional variables that may influence behavior. Also important is to establish the extent to which the components of these rational models actually relate to behavior. To the extent that the rational components influence behavior, interventions that address them (e.g., interventions that alter perceptions of the likelihood and value of outcomes) should be effective in influencing behavior.

Here we describe one rational model and how it has been used to understand contraceptive behavior among adolescents.

The Theory of Reasoned Action

The Theory of Reasoned Action (Ajzen & Fishbein, 1980) posits that people's behavior is best predicted by their *intention* to engage in a given action. Intention, in turn, is influenced by their general *attitude* toward taking the action (i.e., whether engaging in the behavior is seen as good or bad), which is determined by specific beliefs about the likelihood and value of consequences that would result from taking the action; and their *social norms* regarding the behavior, which are determined by beliefs regarding what specific people who are important to them think that they should do with regard to the behavior.

In terms of adolescent contraception, the theory would predict that: (a) adolescents' intention to use a given method of contraception will predict their actual use; (b) their intention will depend on their general attitude toward using the method and on their perception of the extent to which significant others want them to use the method; and (c) their global attitude and global social norms will reflect their specific beliefs about the contraceptive method and about others' wishes. As previously discussed, the model uses *subjective* evaluations of likelihood and value. The model fits—and individuals are deemed to be rational—

insofar as their choices reflect their own expectations regarding the outcomes.

The Theory of Reasoned Action has been used to examine contraceptive use and safer-sex behavior in a number of populations (for a review, see Terry, Gallois, & McCamish, 1993). In the section following, we describe two studies in which the first author and her colleagues have used the model to understand adolescent contraceptive behavior.

Contraceptive Decision Making (Study One)

Our initial study (Adler, Kegeles, Irwin, & Wibbelsman, 1990) was designed to apply the Theory of Reasoned Action to adolescent decision making regarding contraception. We interviewed 345 female and 161 male adolescents who came to one of two adolescent medicine clinics for routine health care. One clinic was based in a university and the other was part of a large HMO. We oversampled females to ensure having sufficient statistical power to test the theoretical model in one group. The respondents were aged 14 to 19 (mean for females = 16.7, for males = 16.2); 32% of the females and 43% of the males had not initiated sexual activity at the initial interview (Time 1). For some of the respondents the clinic visit was related to reproductive health but for others it was not.

We had conducted earlier interviews with a smaller sample of adolescents ($N = 60$) to elicit beliefs about possible consequences of using four common methods of birth control: condoms, pills, diaphragms, and withdrawal. Although we did not consider withdrawal a method of birth control, we included it because it is commonly used by adolescents. From these interviews we defined 25 possible outcomes of using a contraceptive method (e.g., "allows sex on the spur of the moment," "will prevent pregnancy") that are listed in full in Table 3.2.

In the main study, the adolescents were asked to consider each of the 25 possible outcomes in relation to each of the four methods of contraception. They indicated how likely they thought it would be that they would experience each outcome if they were to use the method when they were having sex (e.g., how likely it would be that using a condom would allow for sex on the spur of the moment). They also rated how good or bad it would be if each outcome did occur to them (e.g., how

Table 3.2
Outcomes Related to Contraceptive Use

1. Makes me the one responsible for preventing pregnancy
2. Makes it easy to have sex on the spur of the moment
3. Makes it seem that I was planning to have sex
4. Is uncomfortable or painful to use
5. Affects my (my partner's) menstruation
6. Protects me from sexually transmitted diseases
7. Is easy to use
8. I (My partner) will get pregnant
9. Decreases sexual pleasure because of feel, taste, or smell
10. Is expensive
11. Is natural
12. Is immoral
13. Is inconvenient
14. Is clean
15. Is used by a lot of people my age
16. Can be used without having to go to a doctor
17. Can be used without parents knowing about it
18. Gives me guilt feeling
19. Requires me to have self-control
20. Requires my partner to have self-control
21. Requires putting chemicals into my (my partner's) body
22. Affects my physical appearance
23. Would have minor or immediate effects on *my* health
24. Would have minor or immediate effects on *my partner's* health
25. Would have major or long-term effects on my (my partner's) health

NOTE: On the items that were worded differently for males and females, the wording in parentheses was for males.

good or bad it would be to use a method that allowed for sex on the spur of the moment).

We contacted the adolescents again about a year after the initial interview and were able to reinterview two-thirds of them (234 females and 106 males). In the second interview we obtained detailed information about their sexual and contraceptive behavior in the intervening year. They indicated how frequently they had used each type of contraception during the year and the frequency with which they used other methods or had sex without using any contraceptive.

Table 3.3
Correlation of Intention to Use a Method With
Frequency of Its Use in the Subsequent Year

Method	Females	Males
Pill	0.42***	0.10
Condom	0.35***	0.25*
Diaphragm	0.27***	0.27*
Withdrawal	0.20**	0.46***

*p < .05; **p < .01; ***p < .001.
SOURCE: Adler et al. (1990).

Overall Results

One step in evaluating whether or not adolescent behavior is impulsive and nonrational is to examine if there is any association between adolescents' intention to use a given contraceptive method and their actual use of it in the next year. One would not expect a perfect (or even very high) correlation over such a long period, particularly because the circumstances of the adolescents' relationships changed substantially in the course of one year. Most of our respondents who were sexually active at the initial interview were not with the same partner one year later. Despite this, as can be seen in Table 3.3, intentions that were expressed in the context of one relationship related positively and significantly to behavior, even though it was often in the context of another relationship.

More importantly, the prediction of behavior from intention was better for methods over which the adolescent was likely to have the most control. The highest correlation between intention and behavior for females ($r = .42$, $p < .001$) was for their use of oral contraceptives, the one method that is coitus-independent and does not require cooperation of the male partner. This is the method whereby a woman can most easily translate her intentions into action. For males, the strongest correlation of intention and behavior occurred for withdrawal ($r = .46$, $p < .001$), the method over which they have the most control. Not surprisingly, the only method for which there was no significant association between intention and use during the next year was the male adolescent's intention that his partner use birth control pills.

Another aspect of rational decision making is whether a person's intention reflects his or her attitude toward taking the action and his or her perception of social normative expectations. To test this, we regressed the adolescents' behavioral intention to use a given method (BI) on their global attitude toward its use ($Aact$) and their global perception of social norms (SN). The results are shown in the first column for each sex in Table 3.4. For all methods, these two variables were significantly related to intention (multiple Rs ranged from .54 to .74 for females and from .33 to .82 for males; the relationships were lowest for the diaphragm, with which many adolescents were unfamiliar).

A final aspect of rationality is whether a person's global attitude reflects the specific beliefs and values the person holds about possible consequences, and whether a person's global perceived social norm reflects that person's beliefs about the desires of specific individuals in his or her social network. To test the former, we summed the products of each respondent's perceived likelihoods and values across the 25 beliefs—$\Sigma(B_i a_i)$—and found that the sums were significantly correlated with the respondent's global attitude for all but the diaphragm for males (correlations ranged from .21 to .42 for females and .08 to .36 for males—see the second column for each sex in Table 3.4). To test the latter, we summed the products of each respondent's normative beliefs about the expectations of specific individuals by his or her motivation to comply with those expectations, across the set of relevant referents—$\Sigma(NB_i MC_i)$. The sums were significantly correlated with global perceived social norms (correlations ranged from .58 to .79 for females and .59 to .81 for males—see the third column for each sex in Table 3.4).

Thus, the adolescents in our sample appeared to have been thinking and acting in accord with predictors of the decision-making model: Their intentions predicted their behavior and reflected their attitudes and perceived social norms. These latter variables, in turn, reflected their specific beliefs and values about possible outcomes and their beliefs about the expectations of specific individuals, respectively.

Beliefs Related to Intention to Use Condoms

A second purpose of the study was to examine which specific beliefs about a contraceptive method were related to intention to use the method. Such an analysis can suggest more proximal influences on

Table 3.4
Relationships Among Components of
Decision-Making Models for Sexually Active Adolescents

Method	Females			Males		
	Multiple R for BI regressed on Aact & SN	Correlation of $\Sigma(B_j a_i)$ with Aact	Correlation of $\Sigma(NB_j MC_i)$ with SN	Multiple R for BI regressed on Aact & SN	Correlation of $\Sigma(B_j a_i)$ with Aact	Correlation of $\Sigma(NB_j MC_i)$ with SN
Pill	.74	.42	.68	.43	.26	.71
Condom	.54	.26	.58	.45	.36	.59
Diaphragm	.54	.21	.67	.33	.08	.61
Withdrawal	.59	.27	.79	.82	.24	.81

SOURCE: Adler et al. (1990).

intention (and presumably on behavior) and provide insights into what beliefs should be addressed in an intervention designed to increase use of a given method.

For interventions aimed at safer-sex behaviors, it is particularly helpful to understand the determinants of intentions to use condoms. Of the 25 possible consequences that our respondents rated for each method, some consequences were more relevant for some methods of contraception than for others (e.g., putting chemicals into one's body is most relevant to oral contraceptives and would not be expected to relate to condom use). We examined the relationship between the respondents' perceived likelihood that a given consequence would occur if they were to use condoms and their intention to use condoms in the next year. These analyses included both adolescents who had initiated sexual activity and those who had not. For the latter, questions were framed in terms of their expectations and intentions if they were to have sex in the coming year. In analyzing the relationship between each belief and intention to use condoms, we controlled for ethnicity, whether or not the adolescents were sexually active, and whether or not they had used condoms before. This last variable was controlled to assure that the association of beliefs and intentions was not due to their joint associations with past behavior.

Of the 25 beliefs, somewhat different sets emerged for males and females as significant predictors of the intention to use condoms (see Table 3.5). The beliefs that were associated with intention to use condoms primarily had to do with the social and physical aspects of using them. For both males and females, the belief that condoms are popular with one's peers, that they are easy to use, and that they enable sex on the spur of the moment were significantly related to their intention to use condoms.

In addition, females who were more likely to intend to have their partner use condoms believed more strongly that condoms are clean, are not inconvenient to use, and require the male partner to have self-control. The fact that young women's intended condom use was related to the belief that using condoms required their partners to have self-control suggests something about the nature of teenage sexuality. Possibly, for young women, using a method that slows down the process of intercourse is desirable. This positive belief could be useful in encouraging females to urge their partners to use condoms because in designing interventions to influence sexual behavior it is helpful to

Table 3.5
Semipartial Correlation Coefficients
of Beliefs Associated with Intentions to
Use Condoms, Controlling for Sexual Activity,
Prior Condom Use, and Racial/Ethnic Background

Beliefs	Female Adolescents	Male Adolescents
Condoms enable one to have sex on the spur of the moment	.17**	.28**
Condoms are easy to use	.14*	.52**
Using condoms is popular with one's peers	.23**	.29**
Using condoms requires one's partner to have self-control	.17**	ns
Condoms are clean	.18**	ns
Condoms are inconvenient	−.19**	ns
Condoms are painful or uncomfortable to use	ns	−.31**
Using condoms makes the male adolescent responsible for contraception	ns	.29**

SOURCE: Kegeles et al. (1989)

NOTE: Coefficients are from multiple regression analyses between each belief and intentions to use condoms.

$*p < .01$; $**p < .001$; ns = not significant.

provide positive motives for using a contraceptive method and not to rely simply on fear of negative consequences from failure to use it.

Among males, those who were more likely to intend to use condoms believed more strongly that condoms would not be painful or uncomfortable to use and that using them made the male responsible for contraception. The latter belief might serve as a positive motivator for males to use condoms, and interventions might emphasize their responsibility as a way to boost their motivation and enhance their self-concept as a responsible partner.

Another interesting finding concerned which specific normative beliefs were linked to intentions to use or not to use condoms. For both male and female adolescents, the perceived wishes of their partner and of their father were positively related to their intentions—that is, the more favorable these individuals were perceived to be toward condom use, the greater was the adolescent's intention to use them. For males, no one else's opinions seemed to matter. Females, however, were also influenced by their mother's, doctor's, and friends' wishes. This suggests that condom use may be more subject to social influences for female adolescents than for males.

Beliefs Unrelated to Intention to Use Condoms

Many of the beliefs that were unrelated to condom use were not surprising because they had been included for their relevance to other methods. However, there were two outcomes that might have been expected to relate to intentions but that did not do so for either males or females: the belief that condoms would prevent pregnancy and that they would prevent STDs. On closer analysis, we found that most of the adolescents believed that using condoms would prevent pregnancy and STDs, and they believed this whether or not they intended to use them.

This result makes it clear that knowledge of these health effects of condoms is not a sufficient condition for their use. What is needed in addition is the belief that other consequences, more tied to the interpersonal issues in condom use, will follow from their use. This finding has implications for sex education. Traditional sex education courses tend to focus on the health advantages of condom use and may not address the most proximal influences on adolescents' intentions and behavior. The beliefs that relate more closely to intentions are, however, more difficult to discuss. To do so requires directly addressing the physical and interpersonal aspects of intercourse, whereas discussion of health risks can remain on a more abstract level. Yet if we are to encourage condom use, it may be important to discuss not just their health benefits but also how to put on a condom without it being inconvenient or uncomfortable to use, the advantages of slowing down the act of intercourse, and the value to one's relationship of being a responsible partner.

Motivation to Avoid Pregnancy (Study Two)

One important aspect was missing from the study of contraceptive decision making previously described. That research focused on evaluating the usefulness of the decision model in relation to contraceptive choice and on methods of measuring costs and benefits of contraceptive use. However, this approach neglected a critical factor that sets the context in which contraceptive choices are made: the motivation to avoid pregnancy. Although this volume is focused on understanding and preventing HIV risk behaviors, the issue of motivation to avoid pregnancy is a critical one to consider because it will also greatly influence decisions about contraceptive use.

In the year that we followed the adolescents in the contraceptive decision-making study, 20% of the sexually active females became pregnant. This is in line with national averages; about one-fifth of sexually active young women aged 15-19 conceive each year. Nonetheless, the pregnancy rate was surprising because, although our sample consisted of urban teens, they were all in health care systems in which contraception was not only available but was actively discussed and encouraged. Thus, lack of access could not explain their failure to use contraception. We realized that application of the decision model in Study One was based on the expectation that adolescents wanted to avoid pregnancy, and this approach ignored the important question of their level of motivation to avoid pregnancy as a contributor to contraceptive use. Therefore, Study Two addressed the extent to which sexually active female adolescents were motivated to seek or avoid pregnancy and the effect of this motivation on their contraceptive use. Because this study in many ways paralleled the previous one, it is described in less detail.

Participants in the second study were female adolescents who had initiated sexual activity at least six months prior to the initial interview. The 6-month period was chosen because it is a time of substantial risk of unwanted pregnancy, in part because risk may be tied to conflicts over acknowledging one's sexual activity. As in the initial study, respondents were recruited following their visit to an adolescent medicine clinic. Of the 290 who were initially interviewed, 272 were reinterviewed six months later, and 253 (87%) were interviewed for a third time a year after the initial interview.

The theoretical framework for this study was again the Theory of Reasoned Action but the behavioral focus was the act of becoming pregnant in the subsequent year. We assessed respondents' beliefs and evaluations regarding the various consequences that could be affected by becoming pregnant (e.g., "I would finish high school," "my relationship with my boyfriend would be better"), their perceptions of whether significant others wanted them to become or not to become pregnant, their motivation to comply with these wishes, and their intentions to become pregnant. Although it would have been most informative to have assessed these components with regard to use of each contraceptive method in addition to in relation to becoming pregnant, doing so would have made the interview prohibitively long. Thus, only the component of intentions was assessed in relation to the use of several forms of contraception.

The results of the study, like those of Study One, showed that the adolescents' decision making was consistent in the sense that it could be predicted from the components of the Theory of Reasoned Action. The strength of their intention regarding becoming pregnant in the coming year was significantly related to their attitude toward pregnancy and their perception of normative expectations (multiple $R = .51$). Attitudes, in turn, were significantly related to the specific beliefs held by the young women regarding the consequences of becoming pregnant and their evaluation of these consequences ($r = .45$). Similarly, their view of social normative expectations was related to their perceptions of the wishes of specific individuals and their motivation to comply with the wishes of those individuals ($r = .16$).

There was some variation in the young women's attitudes toward pregnancy and their intentions regarding conception in the next year. Although most of them held negative values regarding pregnancy during that period of their lives and thought it unlikely that they would conceive, about one-fifth viewed pregnancy positively (i.e., they indicated that it would be good to become pregnant in the next year). A positive view of pregnancy, in turn, predicted poorer contraceptive vigilance in the subsequent year ($r = -.20$) (Adler & Tschann, 1993).

Although adults may not consider it "rational" for these young women to desire pregnancy, they were acting in a consistent manner. They had an explicit set of beliefs about the consequences of pregnancy and these beliefs were linked to their intentions and influenced their subsequent behavior. They may, however, be misinformed or be distorting the likelihood of some of the outcomes. For example, an adolescent may well be wrong in her belief that pregnancy will improve her relationship with her boyfriend. Similarly, a young woman's expectation that a child will bring her love may not be realized. Nevertheless, it is important to appreciate that these expectations can guide behavior. If adolescents expect these results to stem from pregnancy then becoming pregnant may be a reasonable course of action, particularly if they do not perceive equally compelling disadvantages. In that case, given their perceptions of the contingencies in their personal world, they are making the choice that they think is best. If *we* believe that, in the long run, their choice is not the best one, then to bring about change we need to focus on these contingencies and on adolescents' perception of them.

Considering adolescents' motivation for pregnancy is also important in trying to influence their safer-sex behaviors. The behaviors recommended to reduce or eliminate the risk of HIV normally preclude the possibility of conceiving. If a young woman is motivated to become pregnant, she is not likely to respond positively to messages about abstinence or condom use. To influence her, more emphasis would need to be placed on assuring the HIV status of her partner or on developing options other than pregnancy to enhance her life goals (see the discussion following). In addition, young women may make trade-offs between the risk of pregnancy and the risk of an STD, even including AIDS. Those young women who are highly concerned about avoiding pregnancy may choose to use the pill or Norplant because these provide the best protection against pregnancy. Once they are using these methods, however, it may be more difficult to persuade them to add use of a condom to protect against STDs. In sex education and in communication from health care providers, it will be important to emphasize that intercourse holds risks of both pregnancy and STDs, and that protection is needed from both.

Irrationality of Adolescent Contraceptive Use?

The previous studies focused on the extent to which adolescents were consistent in their reasoning and behavior regarding contraceptive use. Although there were significant relationships among components of the Theory of Reasoned Action, as expected, including the prediction of behavior from intention, these adolescents were not completely "rational" in their choices and behavior. A large majority of the variance in behavior was not accounted for by the rational model.

However, it would be unreasonable to expect a perfect predictive relationship. First, as we noted earlier, the actual circumstances under which the contraceptive choice occurred were likely to have changed because many of these adolescents were not with the same partner six months or a year later. Second, a number of situational factors also influence behavior and may deflect an adolescent from acting consistently, and these factors must be taken into account for a full understanding of contraceptive behavior. Unlike many decisions, there is a major social component to the decision to use contraception and in its implementation—that is, the use of many contraceptive methods must be negotiated with another person. Negotiations over the use of a coitus-dependent method such as condoms often occur in situations that do not lend themselves to deliberate thought. Consistency with one's intentions may be particularly difficult in circumstances where alcohol or other substances may impair judgment (Jemmott & Jemmott, 1993).

The choice regarding contraceptive use is a complex one, not simply a matter of deciding to take a given action or not. Rather, there is a range of choices, each with a set of potential costs and benefits. There is no perfect method of contraception. Condoms provide the best protection against STDs but not against pregnancy, whereas the most effective contraceptives do not provide protection from STDs. Moreover, most methods of contraception are behaviorally demanding, requiring fore-thought well in advance of intercourse and multiple behaviors to assure effective protection.

In addition, motivation to use a contraceptive method is complicated by the nature of the benefits versus the costs of the behavior. In general, the benefits of using a contraceptive (or more accurately, the costs of *not* using a contraceptive) are probabilistic and in the future: If one doesn't use a method of contraception, one *may* get an STD or *may* get pregnant, but neither event is sure to occur. Unfortunately, the costs of using a method are immediate and obvious. There are financial and social costs involved in addition to possible unpleasantness: Methods of contraception can be costly, can interfere with the spontaneity and pleasure of sex, and can cause physical changes or reactions.

Implications for Interventions and Social Policies

Motivation

Adolescent sexual behavior can have serious negative consequences. As with many health risks, however, these consequences are uncertain, whereas the behaviors needed to avoid the risks have clear and imme-diate costs associated with them. Because of this, adolescents need to be strongly motivated to protect themselves from those risks. In addi-tion to addressing access and availability of methods, a comprehensive intervention should address all aspects of motivation, including motivation to use specific methods, to avoid STDs, and to avoid pregnancy. Interventions addressing the latter issue would focus on increasing options and life choices for young women so that pregnancy would not be seen as the only (or best) pathway to achieving status or self-esteem (e.g., Jorgensen, Potts, & Camp, 1993). Although much less research has been done on young men, it may be the case for them as well that the decision to avoid getting a partner pregnant can be facilitated by opportunities to build self-esteem, to plan their lives around goals other than "scoring" or fathering a baby, and to develop knowledge and skills to avoid pregnancy (Danielson, Marcy, Plunkett, Wiest, & Greenlick, 1990; Eisen, Zellman, & McAlister, 1990; Robinson & Frank, 1994).

Open Discussion of Sexuality

Addressing adolescent sexual activity in an open fashion is a key to effective efforts to reduce the frequency of teenage pregnancy and STDs. Despite some people's fears that providing sex education will encourage teenage sexual activity, there is no evidence that it increases the rates of such activity (Visser & van Bilsen, 1994). In some cases, it has been shown to reduce rates of intercourse and initiation of sexual activity (Howard & McCabe, 1990). Unfortunately, although sex education programs have been successful in increasing knowledge and some have raised rates of contraceptive use among sexually active adolescents, many programs have not been effective in reducing rates of teenage pregnancy or in increasing the use of birth control (Kirby, 1985). One reason for the lack of effect may be that many school courses focus exclusively on biology and health. Adolescents may be getting the health message from these courses but that information in isolation is often insufficient to motivate behavior.

Teenagers need to learn how to negotiate the physical and interpersonal challenges involved in effective contraceptive use—often the most immediate determinants of contraceptive usage (e.g., Barth, Leland, Kirby, & Fetro, 1992). Messages about contraception are complicated by the fact that adolescents are facing the risks of both pregnancy and STDs. At times, protection may require the use of two methods of contraception. Adolescents need to be highly motivated if they are to use these methods and we know relatively little about how they balance the risks of pregnancy versus STDs in selecting contraceptive methods. With increasing age and sexual experience, it is important to note that both males and females move from use of coitus-dependent methods (mainly condoms) to coitus-independent methods (mainly oral contraceptives). From the perspective of STD prevention, this is a troubling shift and we need to know more about the considerations that underlie this change. Also, we must design communications to both younger and older adolescents about their sexuality in such a way as to increase motivation to avoid both types of risk.

More open discussions also need to focus on what it means to have sex. Adolescents are bombarded in popular culture with messages about sex and sexuality. Educators' and parents' discussions with adolescents about sex tend to be clinical and biological. To help adolescents anticipate obstacles to contraceptive use and develop positive motivation for using birth control, they need to be able to discuss openly the physical, emotional, and social aspects of sex. Ideally, such discussions would happen in the context of the family, but for children whose parents are unable to do this, a combination of expanded sex education and available school-based services will be particularly important.

Sources of Contraceptive Information

Adolescents may be getting health messages from school and possibly from parents, but where are they getting information on the interpersonal aspects of contraceptive use? Most likely this type of information comes from their peers and from the entertainment media. The entertainment media are especially poor places to get information about social aspects of sexual activity because they typically portray irresponsible sex with no consequences. As Brown and Eisenberg (1995) concluded,

> all forms of mass media, from prime-time television to music videos, magazines, advertising, and the news media, include vivid portrayals of sexual behavior. Sexual activity is frequent and most often engaged in by unmarried partners who rarely appear to use contraception, yet rarely get pregnant. (p. 192)

Similarly, there is rarely an indication in the media that STDs may also result from intercourse.

Adolescents may find it difficult to obtain an accurate idea of the actual risk of pregnancy or of STDs from unprotected intercourse (see discussion in Adler, Moore, & Tschann, in press). Sex education courses that use fear messages may exaggerate the actual likelihood that pregnancy or STDs will result from one or even several acts of unprotected intercourse. In relation to pregnancy, for example, adolescents may initially develop a 100% expectation that pregnancy will result from unprotected sex. Despite that expectation, many teenagers do not use contraception the first time they have sex (Darling, Davidson, & Passarello, 1992). Fortunately, most of them do not get pregnant from this first encounter; but unfortunately, that first "dodging of the bullet" may suggest to them that their prior expectations about pregnancy resulting from intercourse were wrong. Based on the knowledge that they had intercourse and that "nothing happened," they may now move to the opposite extreme in their expectations. They may begin to feel that they cannot get pregnant, perhaps even that there is something physically wrong with them that prevents them from becoming pregnant. They will then have little motivation to use birth control until they find that they can, in fact, get pregnant. A similar process may happen concerning fear of sexually transmitted diseases because many programs stress that "it only takes once" to be infected. We need to do much more to teach adolescents about the *probabilistic nature* of pregnancy and other adverse consequences of unprotected sex.

Situational Influences in
Contraceptive Decision Making

We also need to consider the situational determinants of contraceptive use. Countries where issues of sexuality are more openly discussed and contraception is more readily available have much lower rates of teenage pregnancy than in the United States (Jones et al., 1987). School-based clinics that make contraception available to students have shown promising but mixed results in the U.S. (Kirby, Waszak, & Ziegler, 1991). Interesting to note is that a recent evaluation of school-based clinics found that adolescents who had health coverage that would allow them to obtain services elsewhere were as likely to use school-based clinics as were adolescents with no separate health care coverage (Brindis, Kapphahn, McCarter, & Wolfe, 1995). This finding suggests that the accessibility of the school-based clinics or other positive aspects encourage their use by students.

Gender Differences and
Couple Decision Making

Much of the research on sexual behavior has focused on adolescent females. Welcome exceptions to this are the National Survey of Adolescent Men (Pleck, Sonenstein, & Ku, 1993) and some evaluations of school-based programs (e.g., Eisen, Zellman, & McAlister, 1990). Our Study One, concerning contraceptive decision making, showed that both males and females are actively involved in making contraceptive choices. The intentions of the young men regarding contraceptive methods that they could control predicted their subsequent use of these methods, and their beliefs about the consequences of their use were consistent with their contraceptive attitudes.

An area of special ignorance concerns how adolescent partners interact over contraceptive choice and usage. In developing future research and interventions, it will be important to consider both the role of the male partner and how the *couple* acts to determine contraceptive choice.

Policies Related to Adolescent Sexuality

Our own research and other studies in adolescent decision making challenge the assumption that adolescents are irrational in their decision making (cf. Cohn, Macfarlane, Yanez, & Imai, 1995; Quadrel, Fischhoff, & Davis, 1993). The common public view that adolescents are less competent than adults in this area can encourage inappropriately protective and restrictive policies that limit choice (e.g., laws requiring parental consent for abortion) in addition to limiting the types of interventions that may be used with adolescents. The choices of adolescents are understandable if one comprehends their perceptions and values, including their evaluation of the costs and benefits of contraceptive use and their motivation (or lack of motivation) for protecting themselves against pregnancy and STDs.

Like the rest of us, adolescents are trying to steer the best course for themselves. We need to develop social policies and intervention strategies that will provide them with the best possible options and with information that will enable them to make wise choices. We need more research to give us better information on the considerations that influence adolescents' choices and on ways to assure that they accurately perceive both the immediate and long-term consequences of their choices. We also need better research on how the characteristics of the male partner, in combination with the characteristics of the female, influence contraceptive choice. Interventions designed for males and also for couples can then be added to the strategies now used to reduce adolescent pregnancy and STDs. Finally, we need research on the distal and proximal situational factors that encourage or impede contraceptive use so that societal-level interventions can also be used. Adolescent pregnancy and STDs are costly problems in the United States in terms of both individual and societal costs. Obtaining effective interventions to combat them will amply justify the necessary investment and effort at all of these levels.

References

Adler, N. E., Kegeles, S. M., Irwin, C. E., & Wibbelsman, C. (1990). Adolescent contraceptive behavior: An assessment of decision processes. *Journal of Pediatrics, 116,* 463-471.

Adler, N. E., Moore, P. J., & Tschann, J. M. (in press). Planning skills of adolescents: The case of contraceptive use and non-use. In S. L. Friedman & E. K. Scholnick (Eds.), *Why, how, and when do we plan? The developmental psychology of planning.* Hillsdale, NJ: Erlbaum.

Adler, N. E., & Tschann, J. M. (1993). Conscious and preconscious motivation for pregnancy among female adolescents. In A. Lawson & D. Rhode (Eds.), *The politics of pregnancy: Adolescent sexuality and public policy* (pp. 144-158). New Haven, CT: Yale University Press.

Alan Guttmacher Institute. (1994, August). Teenage reproductive health in the United States. *Facts in brief.* New York: Author.

Ajzen, I., & Fishbein, M. (1980). *Understanding attitudes and predicting social behavior.* Englewood Cliffs, NJ: Prentice Hall.

Barth, R. P., Leland, N., Kirby, D., & Fetro, J. V. (1992). Enhancing social and cognitive skills. In B. C. Miller, J. J. Card, R. L. Paikoff, & J. L. Peterson (Eds.), *Preventing adolescent pregnancy: Model programs and evaluations* (pp. 53-82). Newbury Park: Sage.

Brindis, C., Kapphahn, C., McCarter, V., & Wolfe, A. (1995). The impact of health insurance status on adolescents' utilization of school-based clinic services. *Journal of Adolescent Health, 16,* 18-25.

Brown, S., & Eisenberg, L. (Eds.). (1995). *The best intentions: Unintended pregnancy and the well-being of children and families.* Washington, DC: National Academy Press.

Centers for Disease Control. (1991). Current trends: Premarital sexual experience among adolescent women—United States, 1970-1988. *Morbidity and Mortality Weekly Report, 39,* 929-932.

Cohn, L., Macfarlane, S., Yanez, C., & Imai, W. (1995). Risk-perception: Differences between adolescents and adults. *Health Psychology, 14,* 217-222.

Danielson, R., Marcy, S., Plunkett, A., Wiest, W., & Greenlick, M. (1990). Reproductive health counseling for young men: What does it do? *Family Planning Perspectives, 22,* 115-121.

Darling, C. A., Davidson, J. K., & Passarello, L. C. (1992). The mystique of first intercourse among college youth: The role of partners, contraceptive practices, and psychological reactions. *Journal of Youth and Adolescence, 21,* 97-117.

Division of STD/HIV Prevention. (1993). *Sexually transmitted diseases.* Atlanta, GA: Centers for Disease Control and Prevention.

Eisen, M., Zellman, G., & McAlister, A. (1990). Evaluating the impact of a theory-based sexuality and contraceptive education program. *Family Planning Perspectives, 22,* 261-271.

Haffner, D. W. (1988). AIDS and adolescents: School health education must begin now. *Journal of School Health, 58,* 154-155.

Hayes, C. D. (Ed.). (1987). *Risking the future.* Washington, DC: National Academy Press.

Hingson, R. W., Strunin, L., Berlin, B. M., & Heeran, T. (1990). Beliefs about AIDS, use of alcohol and drugs, and unprotected sex among Massachusetts adolescents. *American Journal of Public Health, 80,* 259-299.

Howard, M., & McCabe, J. (1990). Helping teenagers postpone sexual involvement. *Family Planning Perspectives, 22,* 21-26.

Irwin, C. E., & Shafer, M. A. (1992). Adolescent sexuality: The problem of negative outcomes of a normative behavior. In D. E. Rogers & E. Ginzberg (Eds.), *Adolescents at risk: Medical and social perspectives* (pp. 35-79). Boulder, CO: Westview.

Jemmott, J. B., & Jemmott, L. S. (1993). Alcohol and drug use during sexual activity: Predicting the HIV-risk related behaviors of inner-city black male adolescents. *Journal of Adolescent Research, 8,* 41-57.

Jones, E. F., Forrest, J. D., Goldman, N., et al. (1987). *Teenage pregnancy in industrialized countries.* New Haven, CT: Yale University Press.

Jorgensen, S., Potts, V., & Camp, B. (1993). Six-month follow-up of a pregnancy prevention program for early adolescents. *Family Relations, 42,* 401-406.

Kegeles, S. M., Adler, N. E., & Irwin, C. E. (1989). Adolescents and condoms: Associations of beliefs with intentions to use. *American Journal of Diseases of Children, 143,* 911-915.

Kirby, D. (1985). The effects of selected sexuality education programs: Towards a more realistic view. *Journal of Sex Education & Therapy, 11,* 28-37.

Kirby, D., Waszak, C., & Ziegler, J. (1991). Six school-based health clinics: Their reproductive health services and impact on sexual behavior. *Family Planning Perspectives, 23,* 6-16.

Ku, L., Sonenstein, F. L., & Pleck, J. H. (1993). Young men's risk behaviors for HIV infection and sexually transmitted diseases, 1988 through 1991. *American Journal of Public Health, 83,* 1609-1615.

Leigh, B. C., Morrison, D. M., Trocki, K., & Temple, M. T. (1994). Sexual behavior of American adolescents: Results from a U.S. national survey. *Journal of Adolescent Health, 15,* 117-125.

Miller, H. G., Turner, C. F., & Moses, L. E. (Eds.). (1990). *AIDS: The second decade.* Washington, DC: National Academy Press.

Millstein, S. G. (1988). *The potential of school-linked centers to promote adolescent health and development.* Washington, DC: Carnegie Council on Adolescent Development.

Millstein, S. G. (1989). Adolescent health: Challenges for behavioral scientists. *American Psychologist, 44,* 837-842.

National Center for Health Statistics. (1991). Premarital sexual experience among adolescent women: U.S., 1970-1988. *Morbidity and Mortality Weekly Report, 39,* 932.

Pleck, J. H., Sonenstein, F. L., & Ku, L. C. (1993). Masculinity ideology: Its impact on adolescent males' heterosexual relationships. *Journal of Social Issues, 49*(3), 11-29.

Quadrel, M., Fischhoff, B., & Davis, W. (1993). Adolescent (in)vulnerability. *American Psychologist, 48,* 102-116.

Robertson, J. A., & Plant, M. A. (1988). Alcohol, sex and risks of HIV infection. *Drug and Alcohol Dependence, 22,* 75-78.

Robinson, R. B., & Frank, D. I. (1994). The relation between self-esteem, sexual activity, and pregnancy. *Adolescence, 29,* 27-35.

Stall, R., McKusick, L., Wiley, J., Coates, T. J., & Ostrow, D. J. (1986). Alcohol and drug use during sexual activity and compliance with safe sex guidelines for AIDS: The AIDS behavioral research project. *Health Education Quarterly, 13,* 359-371.

Terry, D. J., Gallois, C., & McCamish, M. (Eds.). (1993). *The theory of reasoned action: Its application to AIDS-preventive behaviors.* Oxford, England: Pergamon.

Tversky, A., & Kahneman, D. (1973). Availability: A heuristic for judging frequency and probability. *Cognitive Psychology, 5,* 207-232.

Visser, A. P., & van Bilsen, P. (1994). Effectiveness of sex education provided to adolescents. *Patient Education & Counselling, 23,* 147-160.

4

Denial and the AIDS Crisis: On Wishing Away the Threat of AIDS

KATHRYN A. MORRIS
WILLIAM B. SWANN, JR.

> Fear of disease forms the backbone of practically every preventive medi-
> cal educational campaign. It is primarily the fear of an enemy which jolts
> us into activity and drives us into a state of defense and active warfare
> against that enemy. The instinctive fear of death, destruction, or disease
> is the basis of self-preservation.
>
> —H. E. Kleinschmidt, 1936, p. 29

We Americans have always been rather skittish about sex and squeamish about sickness, so it should come as no surprise that when the two are combined, as in sexually transmitted diseases, considerable fear results. More surprising, however, may be that during the 1930s, the United States government fanned the flames of such fear into a roaring fire. In particular,

AUTHORS' NOTE: The authors thank Stephen Blumberg and the editors of this volume
for their comments on a previous draft of this chapter.

physicians, public health officials, and educators set their sights on creating an intense anxiety state called "syphilophobia" or fear of syphilis.

The creators of syphilophobia were not malicious people. To the contrary, they were well-intentioned public health officials who wanted to use funds available from the newly expanded federal government to combat rapidly growing rates of syphilis infection. They were convinced that syphilis was an epidemic of enormous proportions—some claimed that 10% of the population was infected (Parran, 1936), though in reality the true number was closer to .5% (Brandt, 1985). They also believed that syphilophobia was the only weapon in their arsenal that might be potent enough to curb people's powerful sexual urges. As noted by Dr. Abraham Wolbarst, "The sexual instinct is imperative and will only listen to fear. Ninety-nine out of one hundred persons could be frightened into being good by the fear of evil consequences" (quoted in Brandt, 1985, p. 27).

Public health officials' concerns about the syphilis epidemic began before U.S. involvement in World War I and by the 1930s it became a huge campaign designed to instill syphilophobia into the hearts of the American public. The country's soldiers were perceived to be at especially high risk for infection from foreign prostitutes. Military leaders worried that boatload upon boatload of infected men would return home after the war to infect their wives and girlfriends. As a result, before embarking to Europe and while abroad, soldiers were bombarded with messages designed to scare them into abstinence or condom use.

Such messages took varying forms, including exhibits, slides, pamphlets, posters, lectures, and films (Clarke, 1918). The messages were carefully crafted: to raise arousal through graphic display of victims, to elicit concern about infecting wives and girlfriends waiting at home, and to instill guilt that the United States might be defeated due to time lost because of infection. In World War II, foreign prostitutes were portrayed as worse than Hitler or Hirohito; infection with syphilis was equated with loss on the battlefields (see Brandt, 1985). The use of such scare tactics as sexual deterrents was seldom questioned. The New York State Health Commissioner argued that "although syphilophobia might create a few neurotics, it never killed anyone" (Parran, 1936, p. 410).

Were these public health efforts based on fear successful? When historian Allan Brandt (1985) reviewed the evidence, he concluded that as the use of fear tactics rose, so too did the rates of syphilis infection! The only strategies that were effective in reducing rates of syphilis infection seemed to be the increased availability of penicillin and condoms.

Of course, no one knows why the syphilophobia program seems to have had precisely the opposite effect from that intended. Brandt suggested that arousing fear of syphilis may have caused people to deny the fear and thus deny the possibility of becoming infected with syphilis. Such denial may have resulted in people's failure to protect themselves against infection and in higher rates of syphilis infection. In short, a process of psychological denial may have contributed to the paradoxical effects of the syphilophobia campaign.

Because this argument of Brandt's is based on indirect evidence, we will probably never know for sure whether his denial interpretation of the effects of the syphilophobia campaign is correct. Nevertheless, because attempts to curb rates of syphilis infection may provide a lesson about strategies for dealing with the AIDS epidemic, it is worth considering whether prevention programs based on fear of infection may backfire in the way that Brandt suggests. The key to his analysis is the construct of psychological denial.

Psychological Denial

Sigmund Freud (1961a, b; 1964, a, b) introduced the concept of denial into the psychoanalytic literature and it has remained popular there ever since (e.g., Moore & Rubinfine, 1969). Like many concepts introduced by Freud, denial elicits trepidation in the hearts of many psychologists. An immediate problem is an apparent logical paradox: How can people deny something without becoming aware of it and, if they do become aware, why do they engage in denial? There are several proposed solutions to this problem, but we find Greenwald's (1988) "junk mail" metaphor especially appealing. Greenwald argues that the process of denial (which he calls "knowledge avoidance") is analogous to what happens when people receive junk mail. After scanning the outside of the envelope, people often toss junk mail into the trash without opening it or examining its contents in detail. Similarly, when people realize that they are about to encounter frightening information or even think a scary thought, they try to "toss it in the trash" (prevent it from reaching consciousness) before it has the chance of scaring them deeply.

In recent years, constructs related to denial have begun to appear in the psychological research literature; one of the most conspicuous examples involves research on self-deception (e.g., Greenwald, 1988; Lockard, 1980; Lockard & Mateer, 1988; Sackeim & Gur, 1978; Shedler, Mayman, & Manis, 1993). One result of the sustained interest in the construct of denial is that it has acquired many meanings, only some of which we will be considering here (for thoughtful discussions, see Goldberger, 1983; Lazarus, 1983). We have chosen to use Breznitz's (1983) definition of denial as protection "from some painful or frightening information related to external reality" (p. 257). This definition refers explicitly to denial of external events and not to denial of emotion or intrapsychic conflict (for discussion, see McCrae, 1984; Rippetoe & Rogers, 1987), which is typically discussed under the rubric of repression (Clark, 1991; Eagle, 1988; Gladis, Michela, Walter, & Vaughan, 1992). The major consequence of denial, as defined in the preceding paragraphs, is the avoidance of anything that may be perceived as threatening. This may involve distancing oneself from any information that is relevant to the perceived threat or suppressing knowledge about the threat.

We should emphasize that denial processes are often adaptive, as when people can do nothing about a threatening situation (Janoff-Bulman, 1989; Janoff-Bulman & Timko, 1987). As noted by Goleman (1989, p. 194), denial and other illusions may help in "maintaining a sense of well-being, especially in the face of an overwhelming threat." Nevertheless, when people *can* do something to avert the threat, denial may be counterproductive (Lazarus, 1983). In the case of the AIDS crisis, denial reactions may diminish feelings of personal vulnerability among people who might otherwise take steps to avoid infection.

Denial and the AIDS Epidemic

The construct of denial is often raised in discussions of reactions to the AIDS epidemic. Denial has been cited as a coping mechanism to deal with HIV infection and AIDS (Buckingham & Rehm, 1987; Namir, Wolcott, Fawzy, & Alumbaugh, 1987) and to deal with the threat of HIV infection among uninfected people (Bauman & Siegel, 1987; Gladis, et al., 1992; Moore & Rosenthal, 1991; Woodcock, Stenner, & Ingham, 1992).

When will denial be used to cope with the threat of HIV? We assume that the greater the perceived relevance of the threat of HIV infection, the greater will be the denial in the form discussed in the preceding section (other types of denial will be covered later in the discussion section). We assume further that two classes of factors are likely to influence the perceived relevance of the threat of HIV infection: characteristics of the message and characteristics of the message recipient.

Characteristics of the Message

Not all persuasive messages should produce denial. For example, we suspect that relatively pallid persuasive communications (e.g., information pamphlets) that are merely designed to disseminate information will *not* be threatening enough to "get people's juices flowing" and therefore will not create denial reactions.

Unfortunately, although they may not trigger denial, pallid communications do not seem to change behavior either (Fisher & Fisher, 1992; Jemmott & Jones, 1993). Given that sheer knowledge about AIDS prevention does not appear to reduce risk behavior, the creators of some intervention programs have attempted to "turn up the volume" of AIDS-education programs by tailoring them to target populations (Cochran & Peplau, 1991; Fisher & Fisher, 1992; Freimuth, Hammond, Edgar, & Monahan, 1990; Jemmott & Jones, 1993). Others have created AIDS-prevention films that portray personal stories of people (similar to audience members) who are infected with HIV on the assumption that "personalizing" the crisis will make viewers take the AIDS crisis to heart and engage in preventive behaviors.

Conceivably, however, such personalized AIDS-prevention films may be ineffective or even counterproductive for some viewers. One potential difficulty with such films is that they may represent the first time many viewers have ever seen someone quite similar to themselves who is HIV infected. Therefore, as AIDS-prevention messages are tailored to become more and more personally relevant to the target audience, viewers' anxiety may soar to levels that threaten to overwhelm them. Viewers may attempt to control their anxiety level by engaging in one or more denial responses.

Characteristics of the Message Recipient

Of course, not everyone should display denial responses to AIDS-prevention messages. Because such responses are assumed to be triggered by the perception that one is at risk, people should experience denial only to the extent that they believe that they are in fact at risk. For example, because sexual activity is a known risk factor for HIV infection, people who are sexually active should be more inclined to display denial than virgins. The denial responses of sexually active people may come from two sources. First, AIDS-prevention messages may remind them of their own past risky behaviors. Second, AIDS-prevention messages may force them to consider that their future goals (e.g., continuing to have unprotected sexual intercourse with their relationship partners) involve putting themselves at risk for contracting HIV in the future.

For these reasons, sexually active participants may be likely to experience denial reactions to AIDS-prevention films. In contrast, because virgins have not engaged in sexual activity in the past and are less likely to be planning to put themselves at risk in the future, they should be less likely to display denial reactions. This, then, may explain why some researchers have found that some school-based intervention programs have supported the effectiveness of AIDS-education interventions for virgins but not for sexually active students (for a review, see Kirby et al., 1994).

Following from the arguments just outlined, sexually active people, but not virgins, should be likely to display denial reactions to AIDS-prevention films that personalize risk. How might such denial reactions be organized and measured? Breznitz (1983) has suggested that denial may take seven different forms. We will focus on two of his forms of denial because they may offer particularly convenient strategies for coping with the threat of AIDS.

One such strategy involves *denial of personal vulnerability* for contracting HIV. Several models of preventive behavior (for example, Rogers, 1983; Rosenstock, Strecher, & Becker, 1988) assume that without a sense of personal vulnerability, people are unlikely to alter their behavior in response to various appeals. The process of denial of personal vulnerability may be especially likely to occur among individuals who are at risk for the negative outcome in question (van der Pligt, Otten, Richard, & van der Velde, 1993). Such people may, for example, refuse to acknowledge that they could actually contract HIV, reasoning that they are not in a high-risk group or that because their previous sexual behaviors had no known negative outcomes, future negative outcomes are unlikely.

The use of a know-your-partner strategy of AIDS prevention (Swann & Gill, 1995; Swann, Silvera, & Proske, in press) may also encourage people to deny personal vulnerability for taking steps to avoid contracting HIV. This strategy involves assuming that, because one knows one's partner in a variety of AIDS-irrelevant domains (i.e., interests, career goals), one also knows one's partner in AIDS-relevant domains (i.e., their sexual history). General familiarity with one's partner can be translated into assumptions that the partner is not at high risk for HIV infection. Therefore, the use of this AIDS-prevention strategy may foster beliefs that one is not personally vulnerable to HIV infection.

The other denial strategy we will focus on here is *denial of threatening information* through systematic biases in information processing and behavioral information seeking. The information processing version of such denial has been dubbed *cognitive avoidance*. Krohne (1989, p. 235) discussed cognitive avoidance as a coping strategy for "changing the subjective representation of objective elements inherent in a threatening situation." Cognitive avoidance typically occurs by directing attention away from threatening information and directing attention toward less threatening information (Cloitre & Liebowitz, 1991; Lavy & van den Hout, 1994; Spence, 1983). Such attentional strategies may allow people to ignore information that is directly in opposition to their own attitudes and behaviors (Frey, 1986). Therefore, one reason people may fail to respond to AIDS-prevention films is that they may only focus on nonthreatening information in the film and they may suppress any information that is directly relevant to AIDS. Thus, in response to an AIDS-prevention message, it follows that cognitive avoidance will diminish memory for its content among certain viewers because of attentional biases that this content triggers.

In addition, people can deny threatening information through their behavior (*behavioral avoidance*). They may, for example, gravitate away from situations in which they can expect to encounter threatening information. In the case of AIDS, they may stay away from any activity that might make them think about the epidemic. This could express itself in failure to seek information about AIDS prevention or through disinterest in AIDS-prevention efforts.

Research Plan

The literature on denial suggests that some AIDS-prevention messages may be denied, especially if they employ methods that bring the AIDS epidemic "too close to home." AIDS-prevention messages that depict HIV-infected people who are similar to viewers are likely to cause higher levels of fear in sexually active participants but only minimal levels of fear in virgin participants. As a result, AIDS-prevention films may be more effective for virgins, who have not engaged in sexual activity in the past and who may only engage in safer sexual behavior when they do become sexually active. In contrast, sexually active participants may experience uncomfortably high levels of anxiety while viewing an AIDS-prevention film and engage in denial or fear-control processes, resulting in no behavior change. We conducted two investigations to test these hypotheses.

Study 1

In the first study, participants completed a sexual history questionnaire (based on the scale by Metzler, Noell, & Biglan, 1992) that allowed us to classify them as having engaged in sexual intercourse in the past (sexually active) or never having engaged in sexual intercourse in the past (virgin). Participants in the experimental condition then viewed a commercially available AIDS-prevention film (*Just Like Us: AIDS Prevention,* Sunburst, 1993). In this film, seven people who are HIV infected discuss their experiences both before and after contracting HIV. This is an emotionally powerful film that has been carefully crafted to foster feelings of vulnerability in viewers. The film also addresses various ways of dealing with the threat of HIV infection. Control participants did not view a film but spent 15 minutes reading various AIDS-prevention pamphlets.

All participants then moved to the task of completing dependent measures. The major dependent measures were perceptions of risk for HIV infection and information seeking. Participants rated their perceptions of risk for HIV infection (at some point in the next five years) using a scale modeled after Linville, Fischer, and Fischhoff (1993). This scale provided participants with percentages ranging from 0% to 100%, with heavy emphasis on very low percentages (examples of percentages from .01% to .09% and from .1% to .9% were provided and explained). Information seeking was measured by providing participants with their choice of nine information pamphlets at the conclusion of the experiment. After the participant left the laboratory, the experimenter recorded the number of pamphlets each participant took.

We expected virgin and sexually active participants to respond differently to the AIDS-prevention film. Specifically, we expected that the virgins who viewed the film would be more inclined to perceive that they were at risk for HIV infection and would seek more AIDS-prevention information. In contrast, we expected sexually active participants who viewed the film to display denial of personal vulnerability (lowered perceptions of risk) and behavioral avoidance (reduced information seeking).

Results.[1] The results generally supported these predictions. Although virgins who viewed the film reported similar perceptions of risk (mean = 1.9%) as virgin controls (mean = 1.2%), sexually active participants who viewed the film reported perceptions of risk approximately 17 times lower (mean = 0.6%) than sexually active controls (mean = 10.9%). A somewhat similar but only marginally significant interaction occurred for information seeking. Virgins who viewed the film took on average twice as many information pamphlets at the conclusion of the study (mean = 2.8) as virgin controls (mean = 1.4). Sexually active participants who viewed the film, however, took fewer information pamphlets (mean = 1.9) than sexually active controls (mean = 2.2).

To determine the longer-term implications of the film, participants were phoned one week after participation in the study and were asked to report their perceptions of risk again. At the one-week follow-up a similar but only marginally significant pattern of results occurred: Virgins who viewed the film reported perceptions of risk almost twice that of virgin controls, whereas sexually active participants who viewed the film reported perceptions of risk about 17 times lower than sexually active controls.

These results generally confirmed the prediction that sexually active participants who viewed the film would report lower perceptions of risk both immediately after viewing the film and one week later, and would seek less information after viewing the film. These results support the hypothesis that sexually active participants were denying personal vulnerability of the threat and were engaging in behavioral avoidance.

Although virgin participants who viewed the film sought more information about AIDS prevention than did their counterparts in the control condition, they did not report increased perceptions of risk for HIV infection immediately after viewing the film. Such an increase in perceptions of risk was reported at the one-week follow-up, however.

Gender Effects.[2] Recent reports indicate that the group experiencing the greatest increase in new AIDS cases is heterosexual women ("Update," 1995). To the extent that such statistics engender heightened perceptions of risk for HIV infection among heterosexual women, they should lead to stronger denial reactions among heterosexual women than among men. Our findings supported this prediction. For instance, sexually active females in the control condition reported marginally higher perceptions of risk (mean = 15.3%) and significantly more information seeking (mean = 3.0) than sexually active males in this condition (mean perception of risk = 3.3%; mean information seeking = 0.8). Furthermore, these behaviors seemed to be related to reduced perceptions of risk. Thus, for example, sexually active females who viewed the film reported perceptions of risk 51 times lower (mean = 0.3%) than sexually active females in the control condition (as stated previously, mean = 15.3%). In contrast, sexually active males who viewed the film reported perceptions of risk (mean = 1.0%) similar to sexually active males in the control condition (as stated previously, mean = 3.3%).

Study 2

The results of this first study left several questions unanswered. First, were the denial effects displayed by sexually active participants due to the nature of the specific film we used in the study? In addition, is it possible that these results were due to feelings of reassurance on the part of the sexually active participants? For example, sexually active participants who viewed the film could have decided that they were at less risk for HIV infection than they previously believed either because they decided that they were adequately protecting themselves (for instance, by "knowing their partners") or because they decided only to engage in safer sexual behavior in the future. Such an hypothesis would explain these participants' lowered perceptions of risk and reduced information seeking. To address these questions, we conducted a second study.

As in the first study, participants completed a sexual history questionnaire and were classified as either virgins or sexually active, and half the participants viewed a second commercially available AIDS-prevention film (*Not Me: Innocence in the Time of AIDS,* Evers, 1993). This film is similar to the one used in the first study in that it portrays six HIV-infected young people talking about their experiences. This film, like the film used in our first study, is emotionally powerful and specifies several ways of avoiding the threat of HIV infection. In addition, this film includes several students (presumably not infected with HIV) who discuss AIDS-related issues with the HIV-infected individuals.

Control participants did not view a film but instead moved directly to the task of completing the dependent measures. In this study, the dependent measures included perceptions of risk, desire to attend and participate (as a peer educator) in AIDS-education efforts, and memory for events in the film. In addition, participants were contacted one week following the experiment and again reported their perceptions of risk.

Results. Results of this study mirrored the results of our first study. On the perceived risk measure, there was a marginally significant interaction between sexual history and experimental condition. Virgins who viewed the film reported perceptions of risk many times higher (mean = 8.0%) than virgins in the control condition (mean = 0.007%). However, sexually active participants who viewed the film reported perceptions of risk approximately 18 times lower (mean = 0.3%) than sexually active participants in the control condition (mean = 5.6%). Corresponding (and statistically significant) interactions occurred regarding desire to attend and to participate in AIDS-prevention programs (both of which were measured using 7-point Likert scales). Virgins who viewed the film reported increased desire to attend AIDS-prevention programs (mean = 3.4) compared with virgin controls (mean = 1.7), whereas sexually active participants who viewed the film reported decreased desire to attend such programs (mean = 3.4) compared with sexually active controls (mean = 4.9). In addition, virgins who viewed the film reported increased desire to become a peer educator involved with AIDS-prevention programs (mean = 2.8) relative to virgin controls (mean = 1.5), whereas sexually active participants who viewed the film reported decreased desire to become a peer educator (mean = 3.2) relative to sexually active controls (mean = 4.9).

To assess memory for events in the film, a 24-item true-false scale was developed. Each item described an event that either occurred or did not occur in the film, and participants responded as to whether they believed the event actually occurred in the film. Half of these items were AIDS-relevant (e.g., David contracted HIV from his first sexual partner), and half were AIDS-irrelevant (e.g., Antigone started drinking alcohol when she was 15 years old). Analyses revealed that, of the participants who viewed the film, sexually active and virgin participants had equal ability to recognize AIDS-irrelevant information in the film (mean memory for both groups = 11.6). Sexually active participants, however, were marginally less able to recognize AIDS-relevant information in the film (mean = 10.4) than virgins (mean = 11.4).

As in the first study, to determine the longer-term implications of the film participants were phoned one week after participation in the study and were asked to report their perceptions of risk again. At the one-week follow-up, virgins who viewed the film reported nonsignificantly higher perceptions of risk than virgin controls and sexually active participants who viewed the film reported similar perceptions of risk as sexually active controls. Apparently, one week following the experimental session sexually active control participants experienced a reduction in their perceptions of risk for HIV infection. Possibly, participating in the experiment caused these participants to think about their own vulnerability to HIV infection and thus engage in denial reactions similar to the reactions that sexually active participants in the experimental group experienced one week earlier.

Discussion

Although not all of our findings were statistically significant, the same pattern of results prevailed across the dependent variables and across the two studies. Our findings suggest that sexually active participants who viewed the AIDS-prevention films displayed evidence of denial of personal vulnerability and denial of threatening information (behavioral avoidance and cognitive avoidance). Note that sexually active participants in the control condition reported higher perceptions of risk than virgins in the control condition. Presumably, these differences in the extent to which virgins and sexually active participants perceived themselves to be at risk prior to viewing the AIDS-prevention films were responsible for their differential reactions to the films. That is, the greater the initial perception of risk for HIV infection, the more likely it is that denial will be employed in response to viewing the AIDS-prevention films.

Aside from being interesting in its own right, our evidence of behavioral avoidance and cognitive avoidance is useful in ruling out an alternative interpretation of our results. One such interpretation might be that sexually active participants in the experimental conditions were reassured by viewing the films. However, even if sexually active participants who viewed the films somehow determined that they were at objectively less risk because of their current or future preventive behaviors, this reasoning could not explain the fact that these participants were less inclined to become peer educators and had reduced memory for AIDS-relevant information in the film.

The fact that two different AIDS-prevention films produced denial reactions suggests that such reactions are not simply due to idiosyncrasies of a specific film. Although we would not go so far as to argue that all AIDS-prevention films necessarily engender denial among sexually active viewers, we believe that films similar to the ones we used should also produce denial reactions.

Of course, we gathered no evidence that the AIDS-prevention films we studied influenced the behavioral intentions of our participants. Nevertheless, our results demonstrate that viewing an AIDS-prevention film diminished perceived vulnerability for HIV infection among sexually active participants for at least one week. Given that perceived vulnerability is often viewed as a necessary condition for preventive behavior (for example, Rogers, 1983; Rosenstock, Strecher, & Becker, 1988), the AIDS-prevention films used in our studies could have undercut preventive behavioral intentions to engage in safer sex.

Additional Forms of Denial That AIDS-Prevention Films May Trigger

Our findings suggest that sexually active people may experience several types of denial in response to AIDS-prevention films. One advantage of denial as a solution to the threat of HIV infection is its flexibility. Earlier, we mentioned two of Breznitz's (1983) forms of denial (denial of personal vulnerability and denial of threatening information). There are two additional forms of denial that may be relevant to the threat of AIDS: denial of personal relevance of the threat, and denial of personal responsibility for taking action.

First, people may *deny the personal relevance* of the threat of AIDS by convincing themselves that AIDS-prevention messages are relevant for others, but not for themselves.[3] To this end, people may engage in a variety of mental gymnastics, including psychologically distancing themselves from other people they know to be HIV infected or at risk for contracting HIV. The media may encourage this form of denial by portraying AIDS as a disease of "deviants" (e.g., homosexual men and intravenous drug users). For example, early in the epidemic, hemophiliacs and newborns were publicized by the media as innocent victims of AIDS (Brandt, 1985). By emphasizing the innocence of such victims, the media implied that guilty villains also existed and that these villains were "deviants."

Second, people may *deny personal responsibility for taking action.* For example, they may reason that using condoms or convincing their partners to do so is simply impossible for them, so there is no point in making the effort. In this case, denial processes allow people to accept their own failure to take steps to protect themselves. Together, these denial processes may represent formidable adversaries against the arsenals of researchers and public health officials who devise and disseminate AIDS-prevention messages.

At the very least, then, our findings suggest that as we "turn up the volume" on our persuasive communications, it may be possible to turn up the volume too high—that is, that overly powerful messages may produce denial and therefore have an effect opposite to that intended on the people who are most at risk. The creators of AIDS-prevention programs must learn to walk the whisker-thin line between too little and too much—between making targets of persuasive communications care enough to attend to the message but not dismiss the message through denial processes.

Of course, we have much more to learn about denial reactions to AIDS-prevention messages before we can confidently assess their implications. For example, although our research found that two different films triggered denial reactions, we need to know much more about exactly what in the films triggered such reactions. Also, we need to know more about who is most likely to show such reactions. In particular, do people in known high-risk groups display denial reactions in response to AIDS-prevention messages similar to those displayed by our sexually active college students? We do know that some gay men who are at high risk for contracting HIV are reluctant to get HIV tests until they actually develop AIDS symptoms (McCann & Wadsworth, 1991; Siegel, Levine, Brooks, & Kern, 1989). Quite conceivably, such reluctance is a reflection of psychological denial.

Relevance of These Findings
for Theory on Fear and Persuasion

Our evidence that sexually active people may experience several types of denial in response to AIDS-prevention films dovetails with work on fear appeals (see Hovland, Janis, & Kelley, 1953; Janis & Feshbach, 1953; Leventhal, 1970, 1971). These earlier theorists posited an inverted-U-shaped relation between level of fear and amount of persuasion. Several studies have demonstrated empirical support for this type of relationship between fear and persuasion (e.g., Janis & Feshbach, 1953; Kohn, Goodstadt, Cook, Sheppard, & Chan, 1982). These studies show that as fear levels rise from low to moderate, messages become more persuasive. As fear levels increase further, however, the fear becomes too intense and messages become less persuasive. Classic theories on fear appeals suggest that AIDS-prevention messages that arouse too much fear may be ineffective because viewers must concentrate on controlling their fear rather than thinking about behavior that would help them avoid the threat of AIDS (Witte, 1992). Petty, Gleicher, and Jarvis (1993) specifically warned that AIDS-prevention messages that induce moderately high levels of fear, especially if they are not combined with a clear message about how to avoid contracting HIV, may be ineffective because viewers may divert their attention to controlling their fear at the expense of processing information about AIDS-prevention.

Although several of the preceding studies have supported an inverted-U-shaped relationship between fear and persuasion, the evidence has been weak and inconsistent (see Eagly & Chaiken, 1993; Witte, 1992). Most important in this respect, messages that were designed to produce high levels of fear have not always led to denial.

Given the limited empirical evidence for denial in previous work on fear appeals, why were we able to find support for it? One possibility is that our participants had more to deny than participants in previous research because messages about the negative consequences of HIV infection are likely to produce much higher levels of fear than those that were engendered in the high-fear conditions of some of the classic studies on the topic (e.g., ones that focused on gum disease and other nonfatal diseases). AIDS-prevention messages have the potential for invoking far more fear both because AIDS seems almost certain to lead to death and because of the stigmatization associated with living with AIDS (Epstein, 1992; Gilmore & Somerville, 1994; Herek, 1990; Weitz, 1993).

A second possibility is that our studies tapped a subgroup of people who are particularly likely to experience high levels of fear. Specifically, sexually active participants (who are at objectively higher risk for HIV infection than virgins) may view preventive behaviors such as abstinence and condom use as impossible insofar as these measures may threaten viewers' ability to maintain or initiate the romantic (and sexual) relationships that are a critical part of their lives. As a result, these people may feel that there is little they can do to avoid the catastrophe of contracting AIDS. Caught between a rock and a hard place, sexually active people may simply make the issue of AIDS prevention vanish through psychological denial. Because virgins are less likely to perceive themselves to be at risk for HIV infection prior to viewing the film, they are less likely to find themselves between the rock and the hard place after viewing the film. Therefore, they have less need to engage in denial.

In sum, the results of our research lend further support to the inverted-U-shaped relationship between fear and persuasion. That is, people at low risk for HIV infection (virgin participants) showed the intended effects after viewing a fearful persuasive message about AIDS prevention, whereas people at higher risk for HIV infection (sexually active participants) showed the opposite of the intended effects. In addition, it is likely that individual difference factors (in this case, sexual history or prior risk) may play an important role in people's reactions to fearful persuasive messages. We suggest that individual differences may affect both the level of fear one experiences while listening to a persuasive message and feelings of self-efficacy regarding preventive behavior.

Conclusions

We would like to conclude by discussing two implications of this line of research, one theoretical and one practical. Our theoretical point concerns future work on developing interventions. Researchers are just beginning to gather systematic evidence on the efficacy of AIDS-prevention programs. For instance, Kirby et al. (1994) reviewed studies assessing the efficacy of 26 school-based AIDS-prevention programs and concluded that there is evidence that some interventions "work" insofar as they convince teenagers to begin having sex later and increase the incidence of safe sex among those who do have sex. On the other hand, Kirby et al. also noted that some interventions have *no* effect, particularly for those who are at greatest risk: people who are sexually active.

One limitation of this recent work on the efficacy of AIDS-prevention programs, however, is that most of the intervention programs that "work" are multifaceted: They incorporate a combination of educational lectures, role playing, and AIDS-prevention films such as the ones we have studied. Because these interventions are multifaceted, conclusions can be drawn only about each intervention as a whole. Conclusions cannot be drawn about the effects of each individual intervention component or about the interactions among these components. This raises the possibility that some successful AIDS-prevention programs may incorporate some components that are actually counterproductive. Our findings suggest that AIDS-prevention films may be one such ineffective component.

To be sure, there were good reasons to develop multifaceted interventions. Because mere knowledge about AIDS prevention does not appear to reduce instances of risky behavior (Fisher & Fisher, 1992; Jemmott & Jones, 1993), researchers have assumed that, by itself, any given persuasion technique would be too weak to produce a substantial change in sexual practices. Therefore, more comprehensive AIDS-education programs have been developed. This technique is based on what we call the *small effects* assumption. As an analogy, proper plant care requires plant food, water, sunlight, and pruning. Each of these activities is assumed to contribute in a small way to the overall health of the plant. In a similar way, researchers have combined several AIDS-prevention techniques into multifaceted programs.

Although the small effects assumption is intuitively appealing, two other possibilities deserve consideration. The *interactive assumption* holds that, in isolation, some components of multifaceted interventions may even have the *opposite* of the effects intended and that they produce the desired effect only when combined with other intervention components. Expanding on the preceding analogy, certain plant foods may be toxic to the plant unless they are combined with a specific type of soil. Only when the food is combined with the specific type of soil is the regimen of care effective. Our results suggest that, in isolation, AIDS-prevention films may produce the opposite of the desired effect. However, we do not know whether combining such films with other intervention components will interact to produce the desired effect.

A third possibility is the *swamping assumption,* that posits that some intervention components may have the *opposite* of the effects intended but that these deleterious effects are swamped by the effects of one or more truly efficacious intervention components. In this case, the influence of ineffective components might dampen the desirable effects of the effective intervention components. By analogy, a new type of plant food might be mildly toxic under any condition but the toxicity of the food might not be noticed by the gardener because soil and water conditions override the effects of the plant food. In this case, however, the plant would not thrive as much if the plant food were incorporated in the regimen of care as it would if the plant food were excluded. With regard to AIDS-prevention programs, the swamping assumption would suggest that AIDS-prevention films are ineffective regardless of whether they are combined with other components of a multifaceted intervention. In this case, omitting the films would improve the effectiveness of such interventions.

The practical implications of these three possibilities are very different. The small effects assumption suggests that the more weak intervention components that are combined, the better. In contrast, the interactive assumption suggests that some intervention components should be used *only* in conjunction with other components with which they interact in a desirable fashion. Finally, the swamping assumption suggests that some intervention components should be completely discarded.

Although there is currently no way of knowing which of the preceding assumptions is valid, there is reason to take the interactive and swamping assumptions seriously. We believe that research designed to determine the effects of *individual* intervention components both alone and in combination with one another should become an important priority among AIDS-prevention researchers. Until such research is completed, it will be impossible to compare the effectiveness of specific intervention components. More generally, without such an approach AIDS-prevention researchers will be unable to exploit the full richness and complexity of their theoretical and methodological tools, and thus they will handicap themselves in much the same way that a concert pianist would be handicapped if required to play a Mozart concerto while wearing mittens.

Our research also has a practical implication. We began this chapter with a quote by H. E. Kleinschmidt (1936), who argued that fear is the basis of most, if not all, preventive behavior. More generally, the early advocates of syphilophobia justified their position by arguing that syphilophobia might cause a few neurotics but never killed anyone (see Parran, 1936). Our findings suggest that, in the case of AIDS, "creating a few neurotics" should not be dismissed so cavalierly, for doing so actually *could* lead to death indirectly. To the extent that fear appeals trigger denial reactions, they may cause people to assume that unprotected sex is much safer than it really is. If such reactions lull people into engaging in risky sexual practices, then denial could indirectly raise their risk of infection and death. Therefore, we should be careful to avoid inspiring too much fear in people at risk for HIV infection because such fear could lead them to disaster. As one author put it, "denial of death may be a stabilizer of action for life's sake, but seduced by it, we may also be brought closer to the death we wish to evade" (Wangh, 1989, p. 14).

Notes

1. All reported results are statistically significant unless otherwise specified. All results noted as marginally significant have a p of .08 or lower.

2. Analyses of gender effects were only conducted for Study 1. Study 2 did not include enough male subjects to allow such analyses.

3. Denial of personal relevance of the threat is different from denial of personal vulnerability (which involves beliefs that one is not personally vulnerable to HIV infection) because one could acknowledge personal vulnerability but not personal relevance and vice versa.

References

Bauman, L. J., & Siegel, K. (1987). Misperception among gay men of the risk for AIDS associated with their sexual behavior. *Journal of Applied Social Psychology, 17,* 329-350.

Brandt, A. M. (1985). *No magic bullet: A social history of venereal disease in the United States since 1880.* New York: Oxford University Press.

Breznitz, S. (1983). The seven kinds of stress. In S. Breznitz (Ed.), *The denial of stress* (pp. 257-280). New York: International Universities Press.

Buckingham, S. L., & Rehm, S. J. (1987). AIDS and women at risk. *Health and Social Work, 12,* 5-11.

Clark, A. J. (1991). The identification and modification of defense mechanisms in counseling. *Journal of Counseling and Development, 69,* 231-236.

Clarke, W. (1918). Social hygiene and the war. *Social Hygiene, 4,* 259-306.

Cloitre, M., & Liebowitz, M. R. (1991). Memory bias in panic disorder: An investigation of the cognitive avoidance hypothesis. *Cognitive Therapy and Research, 15,* 371-386.

Cochran, S. D., & Peplau, L. A. (1991). Sexual risk-reduction behaviors among young heterosexual adults. *Social Science and Medicine, 33,* 25-36.

Eagle, M. (1988). Psychoanalysis and self-deception. In J. S. Lockard & D. L. Paulhus (Eds.), *Self-deception: An adaptive mechanism?* (pp. 112-131). Englewood Cliffs, NJ: Prentice Hall.

Eagly, A. H., & Chaiken, S. (1993). *The psychology of attitudes.* New York: Harcourt, Brace, Jovanovich.

Epstein, J. (1992). AIDS, stigma, and narratives of containment. *American Imago, 49,* 293-310.

Evers, S. (Producer & Director). (1993). *Not me: Innocence in the time of AIDS* [Film]. (Available from Pyramid Film and Video, 2801 Colorado Ave., Santa Monica, CA 90404)

Fisher, J. D., & Fisher, W. A. (1992). Changing AIDS-risk behavior. *Psychological Bulletin, 111,* 455-474.

Freimuth, V. S., Hammond, S. L., Edgar, T., & Monahan, J. (1990). Reaching those at risk: A content-analytic study of AIDS PSAs. *Communication Research, 17,* 775-791.

Freud, S. (1961a). Fetishism. *The standard edition of the complete psychological works of Sigmund Freud* (Vol. 21). London: Hogarth. (Original work published 1927).

Freud, S. (1961b). The loss of reality in neurosis and psychosis. *The standard edition of the complete psychological works of Sigmund Freud* (Vol. 21). London: Hogarth. (Original work published 1927).

Freud, S. (1964a). An outline of psycho-analysis. *The standard edition of the complete psychological works of Sigmund Freud* (Vol. 21). London: Hogarth. (Original work published 1927).

Freud, S. (1964b). Splitting of the ego in the process of defense. *The standard edition of the complete psychological works of Sigmund Freud* (Vol. 21). London: Hogarth. (Original work published 1927).

Frey, D. (1986). Recent research on selective exposure to information. In L. Berkowitz (Ed.), *Advances in experimental social psychology* (Vol. 19, pp. 41-80). New York: Academic Press.

Gilmore, N., & Somerville, M. A. (1994). Stigmatization, scapegoating and discrimination in sexually transmitted diseases: Overcoming "them" and "us." *Social Science and Medicine, 39,* 1339-1358.

Gladis, M. M., Michela, J. L., Walter, H. J., & Vaughan, R. D. (1992). High school students' perceptions of AIDS risk: Realistic appraisal or motivated denial? *Health Psychology, 11,* 307-316.

Goldberger, L. (1983). The concept and mechanisms of denial: A selective overview. In S. Breznitz (Ed.), *The denial of stress* (pp. 83-101). New York: International Universities Press.

Goleman, D. J. (1989). What is negative about positive illusions? When benefits for the individual harm the collective. *Journal of Social and Clinical Psychology, 8,* 190-197.

Greenwald, A. G. (1988). Self-knowledge and self-deception. In J. S. Lockard & D. L. Paulhus (Eds.), *Self-deception: An adaptive mechanism?* (pp. 112-131). Englewood Cliffs, NJ: Prentice Hall.

Herek, G. M. (1990). Illness, stigma, and AIDS. In P. T. Costa, & G. R. VandenBos (Eds.), *Psychological aspects of serious illness: Chronic conditions, fatal diseases, and clinical care* (pp. 107-149). Washington, DC: American Psychological Association.

Hovland, C., Janis, I., & Kelley, H. (1953). *Communication and persuasion.* New Haven, CT: Yale University Press.

Janis, I., & Feshbach, S. (1953). Effects of fear-arousing communications. *Journal of Abnormal and Social Psychology, 48,* 78-92.

Janoff-Bulman, R. (1989). The benefits of illusions, the threat of disillusionment, and the limitations of inaccuracy. *Journal of Social and Clinical Psychology, 8,* 158-175.

Janoff-Bulman, R., & Timko, C. (1987). Coping with traumatic life events: The role of denial in light of people's assumptive worlds. In R. C. Snyder & C. Ford (Eds.), *Coping with negative life events: Clinical and social psychological perspectives* (pp. 135-159). New York: Plenum.

Jemmott, J. B., & Jones, J. M. (1993). Social psychology and AIDS among ethnic minority individuals: Risk behaviors and strategies for changing them. In J. B. Pryor & G. Reeder (Eds.), *The social psychology of HIV infection* (pp. 183-224). Hillsdale, NJ: Erlbaum.

Kirby, D., Short, L., Collins, J., Rugg, D., Kolbe, L., Howard, M., Miller, B., Sonenstein, F., & Zabin, L. S. (1994). *School-based programs to reduce sexual risk behaviors: A review of effectiveness.* Unpublished manuscript, ETR Associates, Santa Cruz, CA.

Kleinschmidt, H. E. (1936). Educational prophylaxis of venereal diseases. *Social Hygiene, 5,* 27-39.

Kohn, P. M., Goodstadt, M. S., Cook, G. M., Sheppard, M., & Chan, G. (1982). Ineffectiveness of threat appeals about drinking and driving. *Accident Analysis and Prevention, 14,* 457-464.

Krohne, H. W. (1989). The concept of coping modes: Relating cognitive person variables to actual coping behavior. *Advances in Behaviour Research and Therapy, 11,* 235-248.

Lavy, E. H., & van den Hout, M. A. (1994). Cognitive avoidance and attentional bias: Causal relationships. *Cognitive Therapy and Research, 18,* 179-181.

Lazarus, R. S. (1983). The costs and benefits of denial. In S. Breznitz (Ed.), *The denial of stress* (pp. 83-101). New York: International Universities Press.

Leventhal, H. (1970). Findings and theory in the study of fear communication. In L. Berkowitz (Ed.), *Advances in experimental social psychology* (Vol. 5, pp. 119-186). New York: Academic Press.

Leventhal, H. (1971). Fear appeals and persuasion: The differentiation of a motivational construct. *American Journal of Public Health, 61,* 1208-1224.

Linville, P. W., Fischer, G. W., & Fischhoff, B. (1993). AIDS risk perceptions and decision biases. In J. B. Pryor & G. Reeder (Eds.), *The social psychology of HIV infection* (pp. 5-38). Hillsdale, NJ: Erlbaum.

Lockard, J. S. (1980). Speculations on the adaptive significance of self-deception. In J. S. Lockard (Ed.), *The evolution of human social behavior* (pp. 257-275). Englewood Cliffs, NJ: Prentice Hall.

Lockard, J. S., & Mateer, C. A. (1988). Neural bases of self-deception. In J. S. Lockard & D. L. Paulhus (Eds.), *Self-deception: An adaptive mechanism?* (pp. 23-39). Englewood Cliffs, NJ: Prentice Hall.

McCann, K., & Wadsworth, E. (1991). The experience of having a positive HIV antibody test. *AIDS Care, 3,* 43-53.

McCrae, R. R. (1984). Situational determinants of coping responses: Loss, threat, and challenge. *Journal of Personality and Social Psychology, 46,* 919-928.

Metzler, C. W., Noell, J., & Biglan, A. (1992). The validation of a construct of high-risk sexual behavior in heterosexual adolescents. *Journal of Adolescent Research, 7,* 233-249.

Moore, B. E., & Rubinfine, D. L. (1969). *The mechanism of denial.* New York: International Universities Press.

Moore, S. M., & Rosenthal, D. A. (1991). Adolescent invulnerability and perceptions of AIDS risk. *Journal of Adolescent Research, 6,* 164-180.

Namir, S., Wolcott, D. L., Fawzy, F. I., & Alumbaugh, M. J. (1987). Coping with AIDS: Psychological and health implications. *Journal of Applied Social Psychology, 17,* 309-328.

Parran, T. (1936). The next great plague to go. *Survey Graphic, 25.*

Petty, R. E., Gleicher, F. H., & Jarvis, B. (1993). Persuasion theory and AIDS prevention. In J. B. Pryor & G. Reeder (Eds.), *The social psychology of HIV infection* (pp. 155-182). Hillsdale, NJ: Erlbaum.

Rippetoe, P. A., & Rogers, R. W. (1987). Effects of components of protection-motivation theory on adaptive and maladaptive coping with a health threat. *Journal of Personality and Social Psychology, 52,* 596-604.

Rogers, R. W. (1983). A protection motivation theory of fear appeals and attitude change. *Journal of Psychology, 91,* 93-114.

Rosenstock, I. M., Strecher, V. J., & Becker, M. H. (1988). Social learning theory and the health belief model. *Health Education Quarterly, 15,* 175-183.

Sackeim, H. A., & Gur, R. C. (1978). Self-deception, self-confrontation, and consciousness. In G. E. Schwartz & D. Shapiro (Eds.), *Consciousness and self-regulation: Advances in research* (Vol. 2, pp. 139-197). New York: Plenum.

Shedler, J., Mayman, M., & Manis, M. (1993). The *illusion* of mental health. *American Psychologist, 48,* 1117-1131.

Siegel, K., Levine, M. P., Brooks, C., & Kern, R. (1989). The motives of gay men for taking or not taking the HIV antibody test. *Social Problems, 4,* 368-383.

Spence, D. P. (1983). The paradox of denial. In S. Breznitz (Ed.), *The denial of stress* (pp. 103-123). New York: International Universities Press.

Sunburst Communications (Producer), & Marks, D. J. (Director). (1993). *Just like us: Aids prevention* [Film]. (Available from AIDS Risk Reduction Project, University of Connecticut, 406 Babbidge Rd., Storrs, CT 06269-1020)

Swann, W. B., Jr., & Gill, M. J. (1995). *Sex, confidence and the widow's ademoski: Do we know what we think we know about our sexual partners?* Paper presented at Symposium on Social and Cognitive Aspects of Metacognition, Louvain-la-Neuve, Belgium.

Swann, W. B., Jr., Silvera, D. H., & Proske, C. U. (in press). On "knowing your partner": Dangerous illusions in the age of AIDS. *Personal Relationships.*

Update: Acquired immune deficiency syndrome, United States. (1995). *Morbidity and Mortality Weekly Report, 44*(4), 64-67.

van der Pligt, J., Otten, W., Richard, R., & van der Velde, F. (1993). Perceived risk of AIDS: Unrealistic optimism and self-protective action. In J. B. Pryor & G. Reeder (Eds.), *The social psychology of HIV infection* (pp. 39-58). Hillsdale, NJ: Erlbaum.

Wangh, M. (1989). The evolution of psychoanalytic thought on negation and denial. In E. L. Edelstein, D. L. Nathanson, & A. M. Stone (Eds.), *Denial: A clarification of concepts and research* (pp. 5-15). New York: Plenum.

Weitz, R. (1993). Living with the stigma of AIDS. In M. Nagler (Ed.), *Perspectives on disability* (pp. 137-147). Palo Alto, CA: Health Markets Research.

Witte, K. (1992). Putting the fear back into fear appeals: The extended parallel process model. *Communication Monographs, 59,* 329-349.

Woodcock, A. J., Stenner, K., & Ingham, R. (1992). Young people talking about HIV and AIDS: Interpretations of personal risk of infection. *Health Education Research, 7,* 229-247.

5

The Role of Attraction
in Partner Assessments
and Heterosexual Risk
for HIV

LESLIE F. CLARK
KIM S. MILLER
JANET S. HARRISON
KELLY L. KAY
JANET MOORE

Heterosexual activity as a category for HIV transmission has been steadily growing (Centers for Disease Control and Prevention [CDC], 1992). From 1991 to 1992, heterosexual contact was the category having the largest proportionate increase in AIDS cases diagnosed among males and females 13-24 years old. For women over age 24, heterosexual contact accounted for 35% of all AIDS cases reported through December 1992 (Lindegren, Hanson, Miller, Byers, & Onorato, 1994). Currently, the most effective modes of protection from HIV consist of abstinence or, for sexually active individuals, refraining from sexual intercourse with infected partners and proper and consistent use of latex condoms (CDC, 1992).

Although data indicate that condom use is increasing, research has shown that many individuals adopt a version of the second option—

refraining from sex with infected partners—to avoid HIV. Specifically, they report the use of partner-related strategies to avoid HIV such as sexual monogamy, limiting the number of partners, or selecting "safe" (uninfected) partners (Baldwin & Baldwin, 1988; Butcher, Manning, & O'Neal, 1991; Carroll, 1991; Strunin & Hingson, 1987).

Some individuals may engage in unprotected intercourse because they believe that their sexual partners are not putting them at risk for HIV infection (Gerard, Gibbons, Warner, & Smith, 1993; Maticka-Tyndale, 1991). What is the basis of judgments that a given partner is safe? Some individuals base their perceptions of safety on information obtained through the exchange of sexual histories. However, research indicates that potential partners may misrepresent or may not disclose the number of their past sexual partners, their history of high-risk sexual acts, or even whether or not they have had an HIV test (Cochran & Mays, 1990). Other individuals may rely on stereotypes or "implicit personality theories" about the characteristics of an HIV-infected person to assess the HIV risk of a sexual partner (Fisher & Fisher, this volume; Williams et al., 1992). These implicit personality theories consist of beliefs and stereotypes people use in "diagnosing" a potential partner's HIV status (e.g., the person appears promiscuous or looks unhealthy). Thus, partner assessments may play a large role in determining whether or not the individual is motivated to engage in a behavior such as condom use with a particular sexual partner.

Some public health messages have advocated "choosing safe partners" or "knowing your partner" as prevention strategies for reducing the risk of acquiring sexually transmitted diseases (STDs). Unfortunately, it is often difficult to rule out the possibility that a partner is HIV infected. However, for many people, the belief persists that individuals can protect themselves from HIV by selecting a "safe partner" and being sexually monogamous with that partner. Such supposed risk-reduction strategies may preempt the use of other, more effective, strategies such as consistent condom use.

Goals of the Chapter

In this chapter we suggest that the reasons individuals are drawn to potential partners—such as physical appearance, a common bond that increases a sense of familiarity, or the experience of passion and romance—may affect their judgment about a particular partner's HIV risk. Social psychological literature on attraction may provide insight into how some individuals come to believe that their partners are not putting them at risk for HIV. In particular, we will discuss the factors that make people feel safe with a sexual partner when, in fact, they may not be safe. Knowledge of these factors could be used to design interventions that help individuals to become aware of their own biases in partner assessments and that reinforce the need to use condoms in new or high-risk relationships.

Our goal is not to present an overarching theory of attraction and HIV risk but rather to begin a discussion of the role that attraction may play in individuals' HIV risk assessments and risk behaviors. Toward this end, we will present two unrelated studies, one involving African American and Puerto Rican adolescents and the other involving Puerto Rican women. These studies provide examples of the ways attraction to a partner may affect risk assessments and risk behaviors. In particular, these studies are presented to demonstrate the usefulness of attraction research in understanding the basis of judgments about partner safety and the associations between such judgments and HIV risk behaviors. The first study investigated adolescents' beliefs that a sense of knowing or familiarity (a known predictor of attraction) can be used to determine a person's HIV status. The second study examined the effects of strong romantic attraction on assessments of a partner's HIV risk in relationships that were not sexually monogamous.

Partner Safety Beliefs

In reviewing the sexual practices of teens and young adults, Maticka-Tyndale (1991) concluded that heterosexual adolescents believed that by selecting "safe" partners they decreased the risk of AIDS and therefore they did not need to use condoms. A question faced by public health workers is how to discourage the use of the partner assessment strategy and encourage consistent condom use. To do this, we must first understand how individuals decide that a particular partner is safe.

Work by Clark, Milner, and Holmes (1994) used items based on well-established predictors of attraction—familiarity, trust, and similarity to oneself (see Berscheid, 1985)—to develop a scale assessing beliefs about how to judge a partner's HIV safety. In this work, college students' assessments of partner safety were shown to be determined by a combination of risk information about the partner, similarity of the partner to the respondent, and an assessment of the partner as a credible source of information. Clark (1994a, b) used the information from this pilot study to develop a Partner Safety Beliefs Scale. This scale assesses one's beliefs that a partner's HIV status can be determined by (a) how familiar the partner seems, (b) how similar the partner is to oneself, (c) how trustworthy (credible) the partner is judged to be, and (d) one's beliefs about HIV-infected individuals. High scores on the scale indicate that an individual has confidence in the usefulness of the preceding information to determine a partner's HIV status, whereas low scores indicate low confidence (or skepticism) that such information can accurately "diagnose" a partner's HIV status.

Clark (1994a, b) concluded that for some people, familiarity, similarity, and trustworthiness not only foster attraction and intimacy but are also associated with the belief that the partner is a safe (HIV-uninfected) partner. In particular, for those who score high on the Partner Safety Beliefs Scale, the same pieces of information that increase their feelings of attraction and intimacy toward a partner also lower their judgment of that partner as a potential health threat. This finding could be due to a general halo effect or positivity bias (e.g., people who are generally considered attractive don't have STDs), or it could be a form of the self-serving attributional bias (e.g., anyone I am attracted to could not have a STD).

Study 1: Partner Safety Beliefs, HIV Risk Behavior, and Judging Partners' HIV Risk

Building on past work, the present study examined the relationships among Partner Safety Beliefs Scale scores and HIV risk perception and risk behaviors among minority youth. Focusing only on sexually active teens, this study proposed three hypotheses—that those teens who express confidence in the items of the Partner Safety Beliefs Scale as ways to determine partners' HIV status will: (1) estimate the HIV risk

Table 5.1
Demographics of Overall Adolescent Sample
and of Sexually Active Subgroup

Variable	Overall sample (N = 907)	Sexually active (N = 362)
Gender		
Male	43%	58%
Female	57%	42%
Ethnicity		
African American	44%	53%
Latino	52%	43%
Other	4%	4%
Study Site		
New York	43%	44%
Alabama	28%	35%
Puerto Rico	29%	20%

of their own past sexual partners as *lower,* (2) report having a greater number of lifetime sex partners, and (3) be *less* likely to consistently use condoms, than skeptical teens. The underlying reasoning here was that teens who place confidence in the ability of such information about a partner to diagnose the partner's HIV status will be less likely to have engaged in other preventive measures (e.g., restricting the number of sexual partners or using condoms).

Sample and Methods

Adolescents from age 14 to 16 were recruited through public high schools for a study of parental and teen values, communication, and sexual behavior. Two high schools were chosen in Montgomery, Alabama, one in San Juan, Puerto Rico, and two in the Bronx, New York. Table 5.1 presents the demographics for the total sample and for the subset of teens who reported being sexually active. The respondents in Montgomery were predominately African American, those in Puerto Rico were predominately Latino, and those from the Bronx were a mixture of African American and Latino youths.

Using an interviewer-administered format, the respondents completed the Partner Safety Beliefs Scale. They were asked to indicate how much they agreed or disagreed with scale statement, each of which began with "I would feel pretty sure that a person I was considering as a sex partner did not have the AIDS virus (HIV) if . . . ." An example of an item ending was, ". . . this person was a part of my circle of close friends." Response options ranged from 1 (strongly disagree) to 4 (strongly agree). In addition, they responded to a number of questions regarding their sexual activity, knowledge of HIV, risk perceptions, and communication with parents.

For the report in this chapter we analyzed data only for sexually active teens on the following dependent variables: (a) their ratings of the HIV risk of their sexual partners, (b) their number of lifetime sex partners, and (c) their reported condom use. Ratings of the likelihood that any of their sexual partners were HIV infected were made on a scale of 1 (no chance) to 4 (high chance). Condom use was measured in terms of lifetime condom use and use of condoms in the last six months, with response options ranging from 1 (never) to 5 (always).

Scale Construction

Preliminary analyses of the Partner Safety Beliefs Scale used the overall sample of adolescents (both sexually active and those not yet sexually active). This was done with the goal of making the scale an instrument that could be used with all teens, not just those who were already sexually active.

Principal component factor analysis indicated that the scale contained two significant factors with eigenvalues greater than 1.0. The first factor, labeled Personal Characteristics, contained ten items concerning respondents' confidence that specific attributes of another person such as perceived promiscuity, trustworthiness, familiarity, and similarity to the self, would allow them to determine that person's HIV status. This subscale showed high internal consistency, with Cronbach alpha coefficients of .84 for males and .92 for females.

The second factor, labeled Sexual Network, consisted of three items. These three items involved the dimension of familiarity and the idea that respondents could determine a person's HIV status from information about his or her past sexual partners. This subscale had Cronbach

Table 5.2
Items of Personal Characteristics and Social
Network Subscales of the Partner Safety Beliefs Scale

Stem: I would feel pretty sure that a person I was considering as a sex partner did not have the AIDS virus (HIV) if . . .

Personal Characteristics Subscale

This person looked very healthy.

This person seemed trustworthy and believable.

  I met this person at a party given by one of my close friends.

This person did not act like he or she had a lot of sexual experience.

This person was very physically attractive.

This person came from a background similar to mine.

This person had the same interests and values as me.

This person seemed like a "good" person.

This person did not flirt too much.

This person went to the same high school as me.

Sexual Network Subscale

This person was a part of my circle of close friends.

This person had already dated someone that I know well.

This person and I talked about our own personal sexual histories.

---

alpha coefficients of .60 for males and .83 for females. Table 5.2 displays the items for each subscale.

Results: HIV Risk of Sexual Partners
and HIV-Relevant Behaviors

Analyses of HIV risk perceptions and risk behaviors were conducted only with the subset of sexually active adolescents and were performed separately for males and females. Table 5.3 shows the descriptive statistics for sexually active males' and females' scores on the Partner Safety Beliefs subscales and for HIV risk perceptions and behaviors. There was less variability for females than for males on number of sexual partners; 73% of these sexually active females reported only one or two lifetime sexual partners, and 89% reported having three or less.

Table 5.3
Percentages of Responses on
HIV Risk Assessment and Behavior Variables
for Sexually Active Male and Female Adolescents

Variable	Males (N = 211)	Females (N = 151)
Likelihood of partner's being HIV infected		
No chance	63%	60%
Small chance	29	27
Some chance	5	10
Large chance	2	3
Number of lifetime sexual partners		
1	24	44
2	15	28
3-5	33	25
> 5	28	3
Condom use (6 months)		
Never	14	13
< 50% of the time	4	10
50% of the time	7	9
> 50% of the time	13	8
Always	62	60
Condom use (lifetime)		
Never	13	10
< 50% of the time	7	10
50% of the time	14	13
> 50% of the time	21	17
Always	45	50

Partner Safety Beliefs subscale scores did not significantly predict HIV risk outcomes for female teens; therefore only the results for males follows.

For these sexually active male teens, sexual network subscale scores predicted perceived HIV risk of partners. Males with greater confidence in the ability of sexual network information to determine a partner's HIV status reported a lower likelihood that any of their past sexual partners could have been HIV infected ($r = .15$, $p < .05$).

Both the sexual network subscale scores and the personal characteristics subscale scores were significantly correlated with male teens' reports of their number of lifetime sexual partners ($r = .15$, $p < .05$, and $r = .14$, $p < .05$, respectively). In addition, the personal characteristics subscale scores predicted their reports of condom use. Specifically, males with more confidence that they could determine a person's HIV status from their impression of that person's personal characteristics, in comparison with their more skeptical counterparts, reported less condom use across their lifetime ($r = -.15$, $p < .05$) and during the last 6 months ($r = -.20$, $p < .02$).

Conclusions, Limitations, and Needed Research

This study of adolescents' HIV risk perceptions and risk behaviors constitutes a first step in a research program that examines the usefulness of a tool for assessing perceptions of partner safety. However, there were several limitations to the study. Most notably, the three hypotheses were supported for male teens but not for females and the significant correlations were low ($<$ or $= .20$).

The fact that female teens' Partner Safety Beliefs scores were unrelated to risk behaviors may have been due to the females' limited range of sexual experience in this sample. Also possible is that the lack of correlation with reported condom use may be because condom behavior is more influenced by the male partner for these female teens than it is by the females' perceptions of partner safety. This study should be replicated with a more sexually experienced female sample to determine whether the females' null finding was due to their restricted ranges on outcome variables or whether there is a real gender difference in the relationships among perceived partner safety, perceived HIV risk of partners, and HIV risk behavior.

The relationship between males' overconfidence in partner information as a clue to partner safety and their reported sexual experience suggests that male teens may be using perceptions of partner safety to help determine their own sexual risk-taking behaviors. Possible alternative interpretations are that those with more sexual experience may be more confident in general or may just be reporting confident beliefs as a way of justifying their own risky sexual behaviors.

This study examined the relationships between teenagers' beliefs about their ability to "diagnose" a potential sexual partner's HIV status, the perceived HIV risk of their actual partners, and their reported past risky sexual behaviors. The study did not explicitly examine whether such beliefs are actually used as a strategy for partner selection. Research is needed to determine the extent to which individuals use partner perceptions as a strategy in making actual partner choices.

Beliefs that one's partner is "safe" may be relied on more heavily when individuals are using substances such as alcohol or drugs. Evidence indicates that teens engage in riskier behavior while under the influence of drugs or alcohol (Fullilove, Fullilove, Bowser, & Gross, 1990; Hingson, Strunin, Berlin, & Heeren, 1990; Keller et al., 1991). Reseachers have suggested that this is due in part to teens' reduced ability to gauge risk in such circumstances. More research is needed to understand the link between substance use and reliance on partner safety judgments.

Also important is to determine the source of teens' beliefs about making safe partner choices. There is some evidence that female teens may attain their confidence or skepticism about partner safety through sexual socialization by their mothers, possibly including discussions about sexual partners (Miller, Clark, Wendell, & Hennessy, 1995). Future research should examine the ways teens acquire partner safety beliefs and the best avenues for communicating to them that the use of such beliefs is not a totally effective strategy.

Implications for Interventions

These findings have implications for working with adolescents to reduce their sexual risk-taking behaviors. Due to the lack of significant findings for female teenagers, we will restrict this discussion to male adolescents. Beliefs about partner safety may be difficult to disconfirm because conclusions that a partner is safe are rarely verified with antibody testing and because HIV infection may be unnoticed for several years. Because of this, it may be difficult to convince a male teen that using such beliefs to protect oneself from HIV is a potentially fallible strategy. For these reasons, it may be important to intervene with male teens *before* they engage in sexual behaviors.

Behavioral inoculation theory suggests that health messages should be given to a target audience before they enact the risky behavior, to "inoculate" them against the social pressure to perform the risky behavior (Austin, 1995; Pfau, 1995). Inoculation theory has been used to guide successful interventions to prevent smoking in teens, in which preteens are exposed to smoking prevention messages to reduce the likelihood that they will later begin smoking. Similarly, behavioral inoculation could be used to guide early interventions concerning sexual behavior for male teens prior to their sexual initiation, which would have the potential of reducing their reliance on beliefs about partner safety *before* they are motivated to defend their current sexual practices.

For male adolescents who are already sexually active and who have contracted an STD, counseling them about overconfidence in partner assessments during STD clinic visits may be useful. Counselors could use this opportunity to point out that reliance on such beliefs did not keep the teen from contracting an STD from a sexual partner. Evidence that partner safety beliefs are fallible in the context of other STDs may weaken an individual's confidence in their value for avoiding HIV infection.

Exposing faulty beliefs about a person's ability to select safe partners may be one prerequisite for persuading them to practice safe sex behaviors. Adolescents may not even realize that they are putting themselves at risk by relying on their own judgments of a potential partner as a preventive measure. If this is true, interventions aimed at minimizing the social "costs" of condom use should be augmented by approaches that highlight the possible pitfalls of attempting to choose "safe" partners.

Study 2: Passionate Love, Infidelity, and Judging Partner HIV Risk

The remainder of this chapter focuses on a second example of attraction in relation to partner assessment: namely, women's perceptions of their partner's HIV risk in the context of ongoing relationships with a sexually risky partner. This is important because women report less safe-sex communication and less condom use with steady partners or close partners than with nonsteady partners (Morill, 1994; Ickovics, Morrill, Golubchikov, Beren, & Rodin, 1995).

Existing data also suggest that women may be at risk for HIV not because they themselves have multiple partners but primarily because their male partners do (Díaz et al., 1994; Seidman, Mosher, & Aral, 1992; Smith, 1991). In addition, qualitative data indicate that women's relatively low evaluation of HIV risk may be a form of denial concerning the unpleasant realities of a partner's behavior (Moore, Harrison, & Doll, 1994). The present study addressed the role that passionate love plays in partner risk assessment. Specifically, we examined the possibility that women who are experiencing a passionate involvement with a partner who is not monogamous are more likely to downplay partner risk than are women who are not experiencing passionate love for an unfaithful partner. In other words, feelings of passionate love may keep the woman from accurately perceiving her own HIV risk from the unfaithful partner.

Relationship researchers have noted for some time that individuals can feel strong positive emotions toward someone who may not have their best interests at heart (Berscheid, 1985). This intense emotion, labeled "passionate love," entails a romanticized view of one's partner and it may disrupt an individual's ability to draw appropriate inferences regarding the health risks of a sexual partner.

Passionate love may have implications for HIV risk assessment in the following way. Passionate love is characterized as having a swift onset and strong feelings of sexual desire. In addition, researchers have documented that it includes reliance on fantasy, idealization of the partner, and a focus on anticipated rewards through future association (Berscheid, 1985). Overall, these features of passionate love are inconsistent with an objective assessment of one's partner and his or her risk for HIV.

Passionate love is also associated with perceived dependence and a willingness to tolerate unpleasant aspects of the partner. These conditions may make it difficult for a person to negotiate safe-sex strategies with a partner. Finally, punishment in the form of suffering, fears, and frustration does not diminish passionate love and may even increase it (Berscheid, 1985). Based on this finding, to the extent that a partner's lack of commitment regarding sexual monogamy creates anguish for an individual, such suffering may even serve to increase the individual's passionate love for the uncommitted partner.

How might passionate love affect a woman's perception of HIV risk from a partner? One possibility is that women who are passionately in love with a partner may think of that person in terms of his unique characteristics—those that set him apart from other men. This phenomenon is called "individuating" a person from a social group. In such a case, women may believe that their partner is not like other men who have multiple sexual partners—that is, men who are placing themselves at risk for HIV.

Study 2 examined the effects of passionate love on womens' perceptions of partner safety and on their perceptions of the partner's similarity to men who are at heterosexual risk for HIV. These relationships were explored in a group of Puerto Rican women living in an area of high HIV prevalence. Several studies have suggested that Hispanic women may be at especially high risk for acquiring HIV heterosexually because Hispanic men may be more likely to have multiple sex partners than are men from other ethnic groups (Choi, Catania, & Dolcini, 1994; Marín, Gómez, & Hearst, 1993; Marín, Gómez, & Tschann, 1993; Sabogal, Faigeles, & Catania, 1993).

Sample and Methods

Puerto Rican women who were potentially at risk for HIV were interviewed for this study ($N = 129$). Women were eligible for the study if they were in a relationship for one year or more with a man who they knew or strongly suspected had other sexual partners outside the relationship. Participants were recruited for an interview study to examine relationships among interpersonal power, communication, and condom use.

Women in this study were considered to be at risk for HIV by virtue of living in a high prevalence area (the Bronx, New York) and their belief that their primary partner had other sex partners in the last year. The analyses reported here were confined to women who had Puerto Rican partners because a dependent variable of interest was the women's perceptions that their partner was similar to Puerto Rican men who were unfaithful (and therefore at risk for HIV). Most of the women in the sample were high-school educated, had dependent children, and lived with their male partner.

We proposed three hypotheses concerning passionate love: Women who report being passionately in love with their partners will be *less likely* than other women to (a) perceive their partners as putting them at risk for HIV, (b) request that their partners use condoms, and (c) perceive their partners as similar to a group of risky Puerto Rican males.

Women were defined as experiencing passionate love if they gave the highest possible rating on *both* of the following questions: (a) How much do you love your partner? and (b) How much do you feel swept away with love for your partner? The response scale ranged from 0 (not at all) to 3 (a lot), and everyone who answered "a lot" to question (b) answered "a lot" to question (a). Using this criterion, 39% of the sample were experiencing passionate love. The length of time that women had been in their relationship with the primary partner was not significantly different for women reporting passionate love ($M = 5.26$ years) than for all other women in the sample ($M = 4.64$ years), $t(1,116) = .87$, *ns.*

Perceptions of HIV risk were assessed through a series of questions. Community-level HIV risk was assessed through women's responses to the question: How big a problem is HIV/AIDS in your community? Response options ranged from 0 (not a problem at all) to 3 (a big problem). Perceived self-risk was assessed by summing responses to two questions: (a) How much do you worry about getting HIV? (from $0 = $ none at all, to $3 = $ quite a lot), and (b) What do you think your chances are of getting HIV? (from $0 = $ no chance, to $3 = $ good chance). Cronbach's alpha for the self-risk index was .88.

Perceived partner risk was measured by summing responses to three questions: (a) How much do you worry about getting HIV from your husband/boyfriend? (from $0 = $ not at all, to $3 = $ quite a lot), (b) What do you think the chances are that your boyfriend will get HIV?, and (c) What do you think your chances are of getting HIV from your husband/boyfriend? (options on the latter two questions were from $0 = $ no chance, to $3 = $ good chance). Cronbach's alpha for the index of partner risk was .87.

Results

Table 5.4 presents the means for the three assessments of HIV risk. Perceptions of community-level HIV risk and HIV self-risk were not influenced by a woman's passionate love. However, women experienc-

Table 5.4
Mean Assessments of HIV Risk by
Women Low and High in Passionate Love

	Passionate Love		
Risk Assessment	*Low*	*High*	*p of t*
HIV risk in community	2.58	2.41	*ns*
HIV self-risk	4.64	4.44	*ns*
HIV risk from primary partner	6.76	5.46	*.05*

ing passionate love reported lower perceived partner risk than did the other women. Perceiving the partner as less at risk for getting and transmitting HIV may be a part of the overall idealization of the partner experienced by women who are passionately in love.

Does passionate love also affect women's requests to their partner for safe sex behavior? The results showed that fewer women who reported being passionately in love requested that their partners use a condom when having sex with them (39%) compared to the other women respondents (66%) $X^2 = 8.28$, $p < .004$. One possible interpretation is that lower perceived partner risk may lead passionately involved women to feel less need to enact risk-reduction behaviors. Alternatively, passionately involved women may be more dependent on their partners, making it more difficult for them to enact condom negotiation behaviors (Fullilove, Fullilove, Haynes, & Gross, 1990; Nyamathti & Lewis, 1991; Wingood & DiClemente, 1992).

Does passionate love lead a woman to individuate her partner from the high-risk stereotype or category of unfaithful Puerto Rican men? That is, even if a woman admits her partner is unfaithful, does she downplay his HIV risk by maintaining that her partner doesn't fit the stereotype of Puerto Rican men who are at risk for HIV? When asked to rate how similar their partner was to the group of "unfaithful Puerto Rican men" (on a scale from 0 = not at all, to 3 = very similar), passionately involved women rated their partners as being less similar to that group ($M = 1.06$) than did women who were not passionately involved ($M = 1.70$), $t(1, 126) = 3.52$, $p < .001$.

A mediation model was tested using correlations and multiple regression to examine whether passionate love influenced perceived HIV risk

Table 5.5
Summary of Regression Analysis for
Variables Predicting Partner Risk Index (N = 127)

Variable	B	SE of B	β
Passionate love	–.06	.48	–.01
Perceived similarity	1.38	.22	.51***

NOTE: R^2 = .25; ***p<.0001

from the partner by causing passionately involved women to individuate their partner from the group of unfaithful (risky) Puerto Rican men.
Initially, perceived risk from the partner was marginally predicted by
passionate love (r = .16, p < .07). When perceived similarity of partner
to the group and passionate love were entered as predictors in a multiple
regression analysis, perceived risk from the partner was no longer
predicted by passionate love but was predicted by perceived similarity
to the risky group. The results of the multiple regression analysis are
presented in Table 5.5. These findings suggest that the effect of passionate love on perceived partner risk was mediated by individuation (i.e.,
low perceived similarity) of the partner from a sexually risky group
(Puerto Rican men who are unfaithful).

Conclusions and Limitations of the Study

This first study relating passionate love to assessment of partner risk
has several limitations. First, only two items were used to assess passionate love, so a replication is needed using standardized measures of
passionate love. In addition, there was no objective indicator of whether
or not women who were passionately in love with their male partners
were in fact at less HIV risk from these partners than the other women.
Conceivably, these male partners were actually less likely to transmit
HIV to their female partners because they used condoms with the
respondent or because they had fewer outside sexual relationships than
did the partners of the other women. However, this seems unlikely
because in this data set passionately involved women did not differ from
the rest of the sample in their reports of condom use or the perceived

number of their man's additional sexual partners. In addition, the effect of passionate love on assessments of partner risk does not seem to have been a result of "better" relationships in general because passionately involved women reported the same degree of physical abuse and verbal/emotional abuse from their male partners as did other women. Clearly it would be useful in future research on this issue to examine the male partners' perspectives in addition to the females'. Finally, it would be useful to know whether the effect of passionate love on partner assessments is similar among male partners and for other ethnic groups.

Implications for Interventions

What do these findings say about the use of interventions to change risky sexual behaviors for passionately-in-love women in risky relationships? First, we cannot assume that a woman's admission that her partner has other sexual partners necessarily means that she is confronting the HIV risk implications of such behaviors for her partner or for herself. The women in this study were recruited on the basis of their knowledge or strong suspicion that their male partners had additional sexual partners. Yet the women who reported being passionately involved were less likely to rate their partners as putting them at risk for HIV. These findings suggest the need for research on interventions that address the emotional barriers to self-protection.

New methodologies for protection against HIV have recently been developed, such as the female condom, that allow women more control over their use. Findings from this study suggest that women who are passionately in love may not be likely to use such female-controlled methods because they may see themselves as being at low risk from their male partners.

Interventions aimed at countering the specific ways in which women may bias assessments of partner risk should be tested against more general recommendations for caution. For example, prevention messages might specifically address the fact that some women may downplay risk and that emotions may affect one's ability to make realistic assessments. Role-model stories could be developed in which women who downplayed their partner's risk due to emotional attachment suffered the negative health consequences of having unprotected sex with a risky partner. Finally, women seeking treatment of a STD who themselves have only one sex partner (a situation that characterized all of our passionately-in-love women) could be counseled about the importance of accurate partner assessments and the serious health risks incurred from a partner who has additional sex partners.

This work also emphasizes the need to think of women in the context of a relationship with a particular partner. Though it is possible that women reporting passionate love may be dispositionally prone to such involvements, for the purpose of convincing them to enact prevention behaviors with a particular partner it seems wisest to focus on the existing relationship rather than on their personal patterns of affiliation.

Summary

This chapter has proposed using research findings from the social psychological study of attraction to examine partner risk assessments as they relate to HIV self-risk and sexual risk behaviors. Applying principles from attraction research to risk assessments is valuable because they: (a) are based on rich theoretical frameworks, (b) emphasize the dyadic nature of protective behaviors, (c) provide insights for the development of interventions, and (d) highlight potential barriers to the effectiveness of current behavior-change interventions. The partner perception approach suggests that one's perceived risk of HIV is a function of the way that one feels toward his or her partner.

Examining perceived HIV risk from the perspective of perceived partner safety can contribute to risk-reduction efforts by illuminating the complexities inherent in sexual situations. Individuals may not realize that they can put themselves at risk by relying solely on their own judgments of a partner as a strategy for avoiding HIV risk. Even for individuals who can acknowledge that their partners are engaging in sexually risky behavior, romantic involvement may keep them from acknowledging the partner as a health threat.

Exposing one's potentially faulty beliefs about ability to select safe partners and confronting one's denial of a partner's risk may be prerequisites to the enactment of safe sex behaviors. If this is true, current prevention efforts should be augmented by interventions that highlight the dangers of risk assessments guided by the heart.

References

Austin, E. W. (1995). Reaching young audiences: Developmental considerations in designing health messages. In E. Maibach & R. Parrot (Eds.), *Designing health messages: Approaches from communication theory and public health practice* (pp. 114-144). Thousand Oaks, CA: Sage.

Baldwin, J. D., & Baldwin, J. I. (1988). Factors affecting AIDS-related sexual behavior among college students. *Journal of Sex Research, 25,* 181-196.

Berscheid, E. (1985). Interpersonal attraction. In G. Lindzey & E. Aronson (Eds.), *Handbook of social psychology* (3rd edition, Vol. 2, pp. 413-484). New York: Random House.

Butcher, A. H., Manning, D. T., & O'Neal, E. (1991). HIV-related sexual behavior of college students. *Journal of American College Health, 40,* 5-12.

Carroll, L. (1991). Gender, knowledge about AIDS, reported behavioral change, and the sexual behavior of college students. *College Health, 40,* 5-12.

Centers for Disease Control and Prevention. (1992, January). *HIV/AIDS surveillance report.* Atlanta, GA: Author.

Choi, K. H., Catania, J. A., & Dolcini, M. M. (1994). Extramarital sex and HIV risk behavior among U.S. Adults: Results from the national AIDS behavioral survey. *American Journal of Public Health, 84,* 2003-2007.

Clark, L. F. (1994, October). *Partner perceptions, HIV risk behaviors, and risk-reduction behaviors.* Paper presented at Society of Experimental Social Psychology meeting, Lake Tahoe, CA.

Clark, L. F., Milner, F., & Holmes, S. (1994, August). *Perceived safety in partner choice.* Paper presented at American Psychological Association meeting, Los Angeles.

Cochran, S. D., & Mays, V. M. (1990). Sex, lies, and HIV. *New England Journal of Medicine, 322,* 774.

Díaz, T., Chu, S. Y., Conti, L., Sorvillo, F., Caeca, P. J., & Hermann, P. (1994). Risk behaviors for persons with heterosexually acquired HIV infection in the United States: Results of a multisite surveillance project. *Journal of Acquired Immune Deficiency Syndromes, 7,* 958-963.

Fullilove, M. T., Fullilove, R. E., Haynes, K. E., & Gross, S. A. (1990). Black women and AIDS prevention: A view towards understanding the gender uses. *Journal of Sex Research, 27,* 4-64.

Fullilove, R. E., Fullilove, M. T., Bowser, B. P., & Gross, S. (1990). Risk of sexually transmitted disease among black adolescent crack users in Oakland and San Francisco, California. *Journal of the American Medical Association, 263*(6), 851-855.

Gerard, M., Gibbons, F. X., Warner, T. D., & Smith, G. E. (1993). Perceived vulnerability to HIV infection and AIDS preventive behavior: A critical review of the evidence. In J. B. Pryor & G. D. Reeder (Eds.), *The social psychology of HIV infection* (pp. 59-84). Hillsdale, NJ: Erlbaum.

Hingson, R. W., Strunin, L., Berlin, B. M., & Heeren, T. (1990). Beliefs about AIDS, use of alcohol and drugs, and unprotected sex among Massachusetts adolescents. *American Journal of Public Health, 80,* 295-299.

Ickovics, J. R., Morrill, A. C., Golubchikov, V. V., Beren, S. E., & Rodin, J. (1995, February). *Safer sex: Social and psychological predictors of behavioral maintenance and change among heterosexual women.* Paper presented at the HIV Infection in Women Conference, Washington, DC.

Keller, S. E., Bartlett, J. A., Schleifer, S. J., Johnson, R. L., Pinner, E., & Delaney, B. (1991). HIV-relevant sexual behavior among a healthy inner-city heterosexual adolescent population in an endemic area of HIV. *Journal of Adolescent Health, 12,* 44-48.

Lindegren, M. L., Hanson, C., Miller, K., Byers, R. H., & Onorato, I. (1994). Epidemiology of infectious human immunodeficiency virus infection in adolescents, United States. *Pediatric Disease Journal, 13,* 525-535.

Marín, B. V., Gómez, C. A., & Hearst, N. (1993). Multiple heterosexual partners and condom use among Hispanics and non-Hispanic whites. *Family Planning Perspectives, 25*(4), 170-174.

Marín, B. V., Gómez, C. A., & Tschann, J. M. (1993). Condom use among Hispanic men with secondary female sex partners. *Public Health Reports, 108,* 742-750.

Maticka-Tyndale, E. (1991). Sexual scripts and AIDS prevention: Variations in adherence to safer sex guidelines by heterosexual adolescents. *Journal of Sex Research, 28,* 45-66.

Miller, K. S., Clark, L. F., Wendell, D., & Hennessy, M. (1995, February). *Like mother like daughter: The transmission of partner beliefs.* Paper presented at National Women's Conference on HIV/AIDS, Washington, DC.

Moore, J. S., Harrison, J. S., & Doll, L. S. (1994). Interventions for sexually active, heterosexual women in the United States. In R. J. DiClemente & J. L. Peterson (Eds.), *Preventing AIDS: Theories and methods of behavioral interventions* (pp. 243-266). New York: Plenum.

Morill, A. C. (1994, May). *An interpersonal model of HIV risk for heterosexual women.* Paper presented at American Psychological Association conference on Psychosocial Factors in Women's Health, Washington, DC.

Nyamathi, A. M., & Lewis, C. E. (1991). Coping of African-American women at risk for AIDS. *Women's Health Issues, 1,* 53-62.

Pfau, M. (1995). Designing messages for behavioral inoculation. In E. Maibach & R. Parrot (Eds.) *Designing health messages: Approaches from communication theory and public health practice* (pp. 99-113). Thousand Oaks, CA: Sage.

Sabogal, F., Faigeles, B., & Catania, J. A. (1993). Multiple sexual partners among Hispanics in high-risk cities. *Family Planning Perspectives, 25,* 257-262.

Seidman, S. N., Mosher, W. D., & Aral, S. O. (1992). Women with multiple sex partners: United States 1988. *American Journal of Public Health, 82,* 1388-1394.

Smith, T. W. (1991). Adult sexual behavior in 1989: Number of partners, frequency of intercourse, and risk of AIDS. *Family Planning Perspectives, 23,* 102-106.

Strunin, L., & Hingson, R. (1987). AIDS and adolescents: Knowledge, beliefs, attitudes and behavior. *Pediatrics, 79,* 825-828.

Williams, S. S., Kimble, D. L., Covell, N. H., Weiss, L. H., Newton, K. J., Fisher, W. A., & Fisher, J. D. (1992). College students use implicit personality theory instead of safer sex. *Journal of Applied Social Psychology, 22,* 921-933.

Wingood, G., & DiClemente, R. J. (1992). Cultural, gender, and psychosocial influences on HIV-related behavior of African-American female adolescents: Implications for the development of tailored prevention programs. *Ethnicity and Disease, 3,* 381-388.

6

The Information-Motivation-Behavioral Skills Model of AIDS Risk Behavior Change: Empirical Support and Application

JEFFREY D. FISHER
WILLIAM A. FISHER

Acquired Immune Deficiency Syndrome has rapidly become a major global public health threat. Worldwide, it is estimated that over 4.5 million people have been diagnosed with AIDS and 19.5 million persons are infected with Human Immunodeficiency Virus or HIV, the agent that causes AIDS (World Health

AUTHORS' NOTE: This research was supported by a grant from the National Institute of Health (MH 46224-05) to the first and second authors, and by a National Health Scientist (AIDS) award from Health and Welfare Canada and an Ortho-McNeil award to the second author. We wish to thank all the individuals who have helped us in every phase of our 5-year program of NIMH-supported research, particularly Patricia Fitzgerald, Jill Hammer-Goldman, Nancy Hertzog-Covell, Kelly Hooper, Diane Kimble, Andrea Leclerc, Tom Malloy, Stephen Misovich, Kim Newton, Jessica Offir, Laura Pittman, Laura Weiss, and Sunyna Williams, in addition to all of the undergraduate students who have assisted us in this research program.

Organization, 1995). By the year 2000, an estimated 110 million individuals worldwide may have contracted HIV and the rate of new infections may reach as many as 3,000 per day (Mann, Tarantola, & Netter, 1992). In the U.S., approximately 500,000 persons have been diagnosed with AIDS (Centers for Disease Control and Prevention [CDC], 1995), an estimated one million Americans are infected with HIV (Mann et al., 1992), and AIDS is now the leading cause of death of adults between the ages of 25 to 44 (National Center for Health Statistics, 1994). The speed with which the AIDS epidemic has accelerated is frightening as well. In the U.S., for example, it took ten years for the first 100,000 AIDS cases to be reported but only two additional years for the next 100,000 cases to occur (*Morbidity and Mortality Weekly Report,* 1992).

HIV is communicated by the exchange of infected blood and bodily fluids and affects those who practice behaviors that pose a risk of infection (Winkelstein & Johnson, 1990). For this reason, HIV has had devastating effects on U.S. gay men (e.g., CDC, 1995), minorities (e.g., Jemmott & Jemmott, 1994), hemophiliacs (e.g., Dublin, Rosenberg, & Goedert, 1992), and injection drug users (IDUs) (e.g., CDC, 1995). Evidence is converging to indicate that the general heterosexually active public is at considerable risk as well (e.g., Burke et al., 1990; CDC, 1995; Edlin, Keeling, Gayle, & Holmberg, 1994; Winslow, Franzini, & Hwang, 1992).

Because HIV is communicated behaviorally, it can be prevented by behavioral change, including the avoidance of risky behaviors such as unprotected intercourse and the practice of preventive behaviors such as condom use. Nevertheless, risky behaviors remain relatively common and preventive behaviors remain inconsistent among gay men (D'Augelli, 1992; Ekstrand 1992; Kelly, 1994; McCusker, Stoddard, McDonald, Zapka, & Mayer, 1992), minorities (Catania et al., 1992, 1993; Jemmott & Jemmott, 1994), hemophiliacs (CDC, 1987; Clemow et al., 1989; Dublin et al., 1992), and IDUs and their partners (Friedman, Des Jarlais, & Ward, 1994; Khalsa, Kowalewski, Anglin, & Wang, 1992; Vanichseni et al., 1993; Watkins, Metzger, Woody, & McLellan, 1993). Risky behaviors also remain exceedingly common and preventive behaviors uncommon among the heterosexually active general population (Caron, Davis, Wynn, & Roberts, 1992; Catania et al., 1992, 1993; J. Fisher, Misovich, & Fisher, 1992; Trocki, 1992).

The progression of the AIDS epidemic makes the identification of interventions that are effective at changing AIDS risk behavior extraordinarily important. Unfortunately, past interventions have typically been characterized by a number of limitations that curtail their effect (Coates, 1990; J. Fisher & Fisher, 1992a). First, although relevant conceptual frameworks have been proposed (e.g., the Health Belief Model, Rosenstock, Strecher, & Becker, 1994; the AIDS Risk Reduction Model, Catania, Gibson, Chitwood, & Coates, 1990; the Theory of Reasoned Action, Fishbein, Middlestadt, & Hitchcock, 1994; Social Cognitive Theory, Bandura, 1994; the Information-Motivation-Behavioral Skills Model of AIDS Risk Behavior Change, J. Fisher & Fisher, 1992a), most interventions to date have been intuitively and not conceptually based. Consequently they have failed to benefit from the substantial theoretical literature that is available to provide guidance for behavior change interventions (see Coates, 1990; J. Fisher & Fisher, 1992a; W. Fisher & Fisher, 1993, for discussion of this issue).

Second, relatively few interventions have systematically assessed target group members' *preintervention* information base, their AIDS risk reduction motivation, and their behavioral skills with regard to AIDS prevention to "tailor" the intervention to target groups' needs. Consequently, most interventions have involved untargeted "shooting in the dark" (see J. Fisher & Fisher, 1992a; W. Fisher & Fisher, 1993, for discussion of this issue). Third, interventions often focus on changing general patterns of behavior (e.g., encouraging persons to practice "safer sex") as opposed to focusing on increasing individuals' inclination to practice specific risk-reduction acts, even though a great deal of social psychological research suggests that it would be more effective to focus on specific acts than on general patterns of behavior (see Ajzen & Fishbein, 1980; Fishbein et al., 1994, for discussion of this issue).

Fourth, existing interventions often focus solely on providing information about HIV. Even within this narrow focus, the information that they provide is often irrelevant to preventive behavior (e.g., information about T-cells is not directly relevant to AIDS prevention). Fifth, interventions often fail to motivate individuals to change their risky behavior or to provide training to help individuals acquire, rehearse, and refine the behavioral skills necessary for AIDS risk behavior change (J. Fisher & Fisher, 1992a; W. Fisher & Fisher, 1993). Sixth, existing interventions have generally not been evaluated with sufficient rigor to determine whether intended changes in mediating factors (e.g., knowledge, behavioral skills) and in AIDS-preventive behavior have actually occurred in the short or long term and in relation to both direct and indirect indicators of intervention outcomes (see Johnson, Ostrow,

& Joseph, 1990; Kelly, Murphy, Sikkema, & Kalichman, 1993; Leviton & Valdiserri, 1990; O'Keeffe, Nesselhof-Kendall, & Baum, 1990, for discussion of this issue).

The Information-Motivation-
Behavioral Skills Model

The Information-Motivation-Behavioral skills (IMB) model of AIDS risk behavior change (J. Fisher & Fisher, 1992a; W. Fisher & Fisher, 1993) was designed to address many of these conceptual and empirical limitations. The assumptions of the model have been confirmed in model-testing research across several populations at risk for HIV (J. Fisher, Fisher, Williams, & Malloy, 1994; W. Fisher, Williams, Fisher, & Malloy, 1995) and the model has been used to design, implement, and evaluate a successful AIDS risk-reduction intervention targeted at young adults (J. Fisher, Fisher, Misovich, Kimble, & Malloy, in press). The IMB model can also be readily applied to the design, implementation, and evaluation of population-specific interventions targeted at any group at risk for HIV.

The IMB model holds that AIDS risk-reduction information, motivation, and behavioral skills are the fundamental determinants of AIDS-preventive behavior. According to the model, *information* that is directly relevant to AIDS transmission and prevention is an initial prerequisite of AIDS-preventive behavior. *Motivation* to engage in AIDS-preventive behavior, including personal motivation (attitudes toward AIDS-preventive acts), social motivation (perceived social support for performing these acts), and perceptions of personal vulnerability to AIDS, is a second critical prerequisite of AIDS-preventive behavior. Finally, *behavioral skills* for performing specific AIDS-preventive acts, including objective skills for performing such behaviors and a sense of self-efficacy for doing so, are a third critical prerequisite of AIDS-preventive behavior (Bandura, 1994; W. Fisher, 1990; Kelly & St. Lawrence, 1988). In terms of the IMB model, deficits in AIDS risk-reduction information, motivation, and behavioral skills result in deficits in AIDS-preventive behavior. To promote the initiation and maintenance of AIDS-preventive behavior, one should increase the levels of each of these factors.

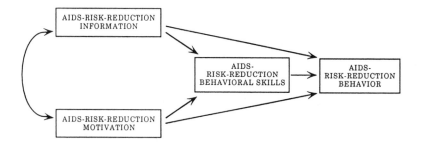

Figure 6.1.   The Information-Motivation-Behavioral skills model (J. Fisher & W. Fisher, 1992a).

The IMB model specifies that AIDS prevention information and AIDS prevention motivation work largely through AIDS prevention behavioral skills to affect preventive behavior. Usually, an individual's AIDS prevention information and motivation are expressed through the individual's AIDS prevention behavioral skills and will therefore work through this component of the model to affect the initiation and maintenance of AIDS-preventive behavior. AIDS prevention information and motivation may also have direct effects on preventive behavior when complicated or novel behavioral skills are unnecessary to effect prevention (see Figure 6.1). An example of information having a direct effect on behavior when complicated or novel behavioral skills are unnecessary would be an individual switching from using natural skin to latex condoms after learning that the former are less effective at preventing HIV. An example of motivation having a direct effect on behavior would be a highly motivated individual simply maintaining a sexually abstinent pattern—which may not require sophisticated behavioral skills—as opposed to being sexually active but *safe,* which may require skills such as discussing concerns about HIV with partners, negotiating condom use with partners, and refusing overtures to unsafe sex. Finally, AIDS prevention information and motivation are regarded as generally independent constructs within the model. Well-informed individuals may have either high or low motivation to practice AIDS-preventive behavior, and well-motivated individuals may or may not be well-informed (J. Fisher et al., 1994).[1]

The information, motivation, and behavioral skills constructs of the IMB model are regarded as highly generalizable determinants of AIDS-preventive behavior in diverse populations of interest (J. Fisher & Fisher, 1992a; W. Fisher & Fisher, 1993). At the same time, these constructs should have *content* that is specific to particular target populations (e.g., different racial, ethnic, and cultural groups, and individuals with differing sexual orientations), in addition to content that is specific to particular AIDS-preventive behaviors (e.g., the act of using condoms as opposed to the act of seeking HIV antibody testing). Within the model, specific types of information, specific motivational issues, and specific behavioral skills can be identified as important to a particular group's performance of a particular type of AIDS preventive behavior. For example, for heterosexual adults the information that is relevant to prevention, the motivational factors associated with prevention, and the behavioral skills required for prevention may differ for the acts of using condoms versus seeking HIV antibody testing. Moreover, these factors may differ from the information, motivation, and behavioral skills elements required for gay men's use of condoms or seeking of HIV antibody testing. The IMB model specifies a set of procedures for empirically identifying the AIDS prevention information, motivation, and behavioral skills content that is specific to particular target populations and particular preventive acts (J. Fisher & Fisher, 1992a; W. Fisher & Fisher, 1993). These procedures may serve as the basis for understanding and promoting AIDS-preventive behavior within specific target populations.

The IMB model also proposes that particular causal elements in the model and particular causal paths among them will prove to be more or less powerful determinants of AIDS-preventive behavior for specific populations and for specific AIDS preventive acts (J. Fisher et al., 1994). The model specifies a set of measurement and statistical procedures for identifying the particular causal elements and paths that will be especially powerful in determining the practice of a given AIDS-preventive behavior in a particular population (J. Fisher et al., 1994; W. Fisher et al., 1995). Identifying the most important causal elements and paths can provide significant information for understanding and modifying AIDS risk behavior through targeted interventions.

Finally, the IMB model proposes a highly generalizable set of operations to be used to construct, implement, and evaluate interventions to promote AIDS risk reduction within target populations of interest (J. Fisher & Fisher, 1992a; J. Fisher et al., in press; W. Fisher & Fisher, 1993). First, *elicitation research,* conducted within a subsample of the target population, is used to empirically identify the population-specific deficits in AIDS risk-reduction information, motivation, and behavioral skills that are associated with risky behavior and that must be remedied to accomplish prevention. Second, *population-specific interventions* are constructed on the basis of elicitation research findings and implemented to modify empirically identified, population-specific deficits in AIDS risk-reduction information, motivation, and behavioral skills, for the population's most significant AIDS risk behaviors. Finally, methodologically rigorous *evaluation research* is conducted to determine whether the intervention has produced short- and long-term changes in multiple indicators of AIDS risk-reduction information, motivation, behavioral skills, and AIDS risk behavior.

Tests of the IMB Model

The IMB model's theorized relationships (see Figure 6.1) have been empirically tested in a series of investigations with university students ($N = 174$), gay men ($N = 91$), and urban, sexually active high school students ($N = 146$). The university student sample consisted of undergraduate introductory psychology students at the University of Connecticut; the gay male sample consisted of members of gay male affinity groups in Connecticut and in Massachusetts; and the high school sample was recruited from high schools in Miami, Florida, an area hit hard by the HIV epidemic (Burke et al., 1990). To test the relationships among the constructs in the model, each sample's levels of AIDS risk-reduction information, motivation, behavioral skills, and behavior were measured using indicators that have been specifically developed and validated for assessing these constructs (J. Fisher et al., 1994; W. Fisher & Fisher, 1993; W. Fisher et al., 1995; Williams et al., 1993). In keeping with the IMB model, the particular information, motivation, and behavioral skills indicators that were used varied somewhat for each population to reflect the critical information, motivation, and behavioral skills elements that are necessary for producing AIDS-preventive behavior within that population, as determined by elicitation research. Across the three samples under study, each of the IMB model constructs was generally measured by two or more moderately correlated indicators

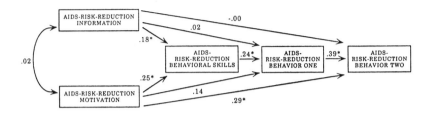

Figure 6.2. Structural equation test of the IMB model with university students (*$p < .05$).

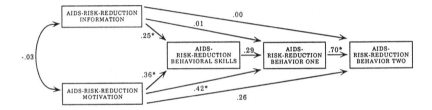

Figure 6.3. Structural equation test of the IMB model with gay men (*$p < .05$, +$p < .10$).

and the theorized relationships among the IMB model's constructs were examined using structural equation modeling procedures (Bollen & Long, 1993; Kenny, 1979).

As predicted by the IMB model and within each of the three samples under study, AIDS prevention information and AIDS prevention motivation were independent factors, each was reliably linked with AIDS prevention behavioral skills, and AIDS prevention behavioral skills were linked with AIDS-preventive behavior. (See Figures 6.2, 6.3, and 6.4, which indicate the significant causal paths that were observed for the hypothesized relations among IMB model constructs, in separate tests of the model with university students, gay men, and sexually active, urban high school students, respectively.) For each of the three samples and again as proposed by the model, an independent link between AIDS prevention motivation and preventive behavior was observed as well, because some of the preventive behavior criteria in question did not require the performance of novel or complicated

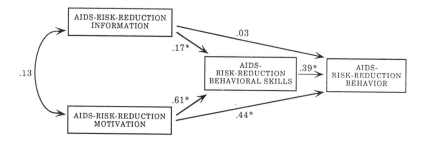

Figure 6.4. Structural equation test of the IMB model with sexually active, urban high school students (*p<.05).

behavioral skills. Overall, the constructs of the IMB model accounted for an average of 30% of the variance in AIDS-preventive behavior across the three samples under study (J. Fisher et al., 1994; W. Fisher et al., 1995). For the university student and gay male samples, for which two-month posttest measures of AIDS-preventive behavior were also available, the model proved to be highly stable in terms of the consistent prediction of preventive behavior across time (J. Fisher et al., 1994).

To our knowledge, these structural equation models provide the only complete tests of any of the more comprehensive AIDS risk-reduction models that have been proposed in the literature (i.e., the AIDS Risk Reduction Model, Catania et al., 1990; Bandura's self-efficacy theory articulated to HIV prevention, Bandura, 1994; and our IMB model). The tests were consistently supportive of the specific assumptions of the IMB model across three populations that have considerable public health significance, across time, and across somewhat different, population-specific measures of both IMB model constructs and AIDS risk-reduction criteria. These tests indicate that AIDS risk-reduction information, motivation, and behavioral skills are each important determinants of AIDS-preventive behavior; that these three constructs work together as hypothesized in the IMB model to affect AIDS-preventive behavior; and that they should constitute critical intervention foci. With these confirmatory tests of the IMB model's basic relationships, generality, stability, and predictive power accomplished, our research turned to application of the model to promote AIDS-preventive behavior.

Applying the IMB Model to Promote AIDS Preventive Behavior

Elicitation research has been carried out by our research team to empirically identify deficits in AIDS prevention information, motivation, behavioral skills, and behavior in samples of university students, HIV-negative and HIV-positive gay men, and minority high school students. As suggested by the IMB model, this research has used both closed-ended research strategies (e.g., questionnaire measures of IMB-model constructs) and open-ended techniques (e.g., focus group strategies to assess IMB model constructs and to better understand the *dynamics* of AIDS risk behavior) in efforts to gain the fullest possible understanding of the determinants and dynamics of AIDS risk behavior within populations at risk. Here we will briefly review representative findings from our elicitation research with heterosexual university students, which served as the basis for the design of a large-scale AIDS risk-reduction intervention with this population that is described later.

Elicitation Research:
Closed-Ended Research Findings

In initial elicitation studies (e.g., J. Fisher & Misovich, 1990a; J. Fisher, Hertzog-Covell, & Fisher, 1993), we used closed-ended questionnaire methods to assess levels of AIDS prevention information, motivation, behavioral skills, and behavior among undergraduate students at the University of Connecticut.

Concerning *information,* the students were generally well informed about the critical facts regarding AIDS transmission and prevention (J. Fisher et al., 1993) but had specific and potentially important deficits as well. For example, elicitation research found that most students did not know the relative riskiness of certain HIV risk behaviors (e.g., only 25% knew that oral sex is less risky than sexual intercourse), that only 33% knew that in some parts of the world HIV is found mostly among heterosexual men and women, and that only 40% knew that HIV can be transmitted from mother to child through breast milk. (For additional closed-ended elicitation findings concerning information deficits in the university student sample, see J. Fisher & Misovich, 1990a; J. Fisher et al., 1993). The observed information deficits may be incompatible with effective AIDS-preventive behavior, and they comprised foci for our later AIDS prevention intervention with university students.

Concerning *motivation,* heterosexual university students reported limited personal and social motivation to practice AIDS-preventive behaviors (J. Fisher et al., 1993). With regard to *personal motivation,* only 13% of the students surveyed had positive (favorable) attitudes toward abstinence; only about 50% had positive attitudes toward refusing to have unsafe sex or toward persuading a partner to practice safer sex; only 52% felt favorable toward purchasing condoms; only 65% felt favorable toward carrying or using condoms; only 54% had positive attitudes toward getting an HIV antibody test; and only 25% had positive attitudes toward asking a partner to do so. With regard to *social motivation,* only 23% of those sampled perceived that they had social support for being abstinent; only 44% felt they had social support for buying condoms; only 41% felt they had social support for carrying condoms; and only 61% felt they had social support for using condoms. Further, only 10% of those sampled perceived that they had social support for getting tested for HIV, and only 16% felt they had social support for asking a partner to be tested. With regard to *perceived vulnerability to HIV,* only 32% of the group of respondents who were sexually active, had not been tested for HIV, and used condoms inconsistently perceived that they had at least "some chance" of contracting HIV. In fact, these students' major motivation for using condoms was to avoid pregnancy, not HIV. Overall, these levels of personal motivation, social motivation, and perceived vulnerability to HIV are incompatible with AIDS-preventive behavior and they comprised empirically identified targets for our intervention with university students.

In addition to assessing university students' levels of motivation to practice AIDS-preventive behaviors, closed-ended elicitation studies based on the Theory of Reasoned Action (Ajzen & Fishbein, 1980; Fishbein et al., 1994) were conducted to determine whether the practice of nine critical AIDS-preventive behaviors in this population was governed primarily by personal motivation, by social motivation, or by both (W. Fisher et al., 1995). The nine behaviors were abstaining from sexual intercourse, discussing safer sex with a partner, buying, carrying, and using condoms, practicing only safer sex, refusing to have unsafe sex, getting an HIV antibody test, and asking a partner to get an HIV antibody test. Our findings indicated that these AIDS-preventive behaviors were generally governed by both personal *and* social motivation, with the exception of safer sex discussions and condom use for males, which were governed solely by personal motivation. These findings suggest that interventions to increase AIDS prevention motivation in university students should *generally* focus on increasing both personal and social motivation. However, interventions to increase safer sex discussions and condom use in males could be limited to increasing personal motivation, whereas interventions to increase these behaviors in females should focus on increasing both types of motivation. The findings played a significant role in the design of our intervention aimed at university students.

Concerning *behavioral skills,* heterosexual university students reported deficits in the AIDS prevention behavioral skills necessary for practicing AIDS-preventive behavior. For example, over one-third did not feel they had the ability to interrupt sex to go to get a condom, about 40% did not feel they had the ability to engage in nonpenetrative sexual activities if no condom was available, and only 21% reported that they could effectively ask a partner to be tested for HIV antibodies. Overall, reported levels of AIDS prevention behavioral skills, including those that are particularly relevant to individuals in relationships (e.g., negotiating HIV testing) fell short of those needed for effective preventive behavior. These skill deficits constituted empirically identified targets for our population-specific intervention to increase AIDS prevention in university students.

Finally, elicitation research revealed high levels of *AIDS risk behavior* and low levels of *AIDS preventive behavior* within the heterosexual university student sample. Among these university students, 72% had been sexually active during the preceding year and 44% of these individuals had had two or more sexual partners during that interval. Despite these levels of sexual activity and the fact that only 7% had been tested for HIV, relatively few university students practiced AIDS-preventive behavior consistently. Specifically, 75% of the sexually active university students did not always use condoms during sexual intercourse and 58% did not even discuss safer sex with each new partner.

Elicitation Research:
Open-Ended Focus Group Findings

Although elicitation research findings based on closed-ended measures such as those described in the preceding section provide important data on university students' levels of AIDS prevention information, motivation, behavioral skills, and behavior, open-ended focus group research was conducted to provide a fuller understanding of the dynamics of AIDS risk and preventive behavior within the university student population. Williams et al. (1992) conducted focus group research (cf. Basch, 1987; Krueger, 1988) with small same-sex and mixed-sex groups of students (overall $N = 146$ males and 168 females). Their focus group facilitators led two hours of discussion on safer and unsafe sex, on why students thought they had engaged in each type of behavior, and on the social contexts surrounding each type of behavior. Qualitative analyses revealed consistent themes with important implications for the design of an intervention for university students.

The focus group research revealed that university students rely on factors that are very poor indicators of their partner's actual HIV risk when judging the likelihood that their partner is HIV infected. Nevertheless, college students use these biased judgments of partner risk to determine whether or not to practice safer sex with their partners (Williams et al., 1992). Specifically, students relied on inaccurate *information heuristics* (e.g., that known partners are safe partners; that monogamous relationships are safe relationships) and on *implicit personality theories* of partner risk (e.g., that partners with generally positive characteristics are safe). Using these guidelines almost invariably resulted in their regarding partners they knew or liked or who had positive traits as being risk free, and thus precipitated the practice of unsafe sex with these individuals (see also Hammer-Goldman, Fisher, Fitzgerald, & Fisher, in press; Offir et al., 1993). We have found that such heuristics and implicit personality theories are very widely endorsed in the university student population and that to the extent that students endorse them, they are less likely to practice AIDS-preventive behavior (Misovich, Fisher, & Fisher, 1993).

In our focus group research we also observed that knowing, liking, or loving one's partner and viewing the partner as having positive traits were profoundly cognitively dissonant with regarding the partner as a source of potentially lethal risk (see Festinger, 1957). Such dissonance often resulted in cognitive distortion of any known, objective HIV risk factors in the partner's background (Hammer-Goldman et al., in press; Offir et al., 1993; Williams et al., 1992). On the other hand, students regarded new partners as potentially risky and tried to gauge their level of risk by scrutinizing their external characteristics in relation to an implicit personality theory of partner risk that was widely shared by focus group participants. Specifically, partners who were met in bars, who drank too much, who were dressed provocatively, and ones who appeared overly anxious for sex were regarded as risky and requiring condom use. However, condom use was generally abandoned once students got to know them better (Williams et al., 1992).

Our focus group research also corroborated the finding from our closed-end elicitation research that students regarded themselves as relatively invulnerable to HIV regardless of whether or not they engaged in unsafe sexual behaviors (Weinstein, 1989). They rationalized their low level of perceived AIDS risk by invoking a number of widely shared cognitions, such as that they "only have one partner," "are not homosexual," "are not a drug user," and that "AIDS is not a problem on college campuses." They buttressed these cognitions with the concrete "evidence" that they did not know anyone who had HIV, had never seen anyone who had HIV, and were unaware of anyone on their campus who had HIV. In addition, students often reported beliefs about condoms (e.g., about their physical unpleasantness or that using condoms communicated mistrust of one's relationship partner) that seemed strongly linked to the occurrence of unsafe sex (Williams et al., 1992).

Finally, analysis of focus group discussions made it clear that the "negotiation model" that is often taught in AIDS risk-reduction interventions—in which individuals are advised to bring up and to negotiate safer sexual practices with their partner prior to sexual contact —is often problematic. Sole reliance on presex negotiation as a means to insure safer sex may leave the many individuals who are too uncomfortable discussing sexual matters with no realistic alternative, thus promoting risky sex. Negotiation was also found to be a problem in the early stages of relationships when the desire for sexual activity itself had not been verbalized and in situations in which alcohol impairment or states of high sexual arousal were present. Negotiation also connotes the possibility of confrontation, which is aversive to many. For these reasons, our elicitation research suggested that brief, directive verbalizations (e.g., "Here, put this on"), "one liners" (e.g., "I'm really turned on—here's a condom") or unilateral behaviors (e.g., simply putting on a condom) may often be the most effective strategies for insuring the practice of safer sex and constitute necessary supplements to more complex presex negotiation techniques. Thus, we determined that our intervention for university students would stress brief directive verbalizations, "one liners," and unilateral safer sex behaviors in addition to training students in more complex presex negotiation scripts.

Population-Specific Intervention

According to the IMB model, the results of elicitation research may be used to design theoretically based, population-specific AIDS risk-reduction interventions. Our elicitation research revealed that heterosexual university students had high levels of AIDS risk behavior and displayed a coherent and potentially modifiable pattern of AIDS risk-reduction information, motivation, and behavioral skills deficits, and thus represented an ideal target group for the development and implementation of an initial IMB-model-based, population-specific AIDS risk-reduction intervention. Moreover, because there are 14.7 million college students in the United States (U.S. National Center for Educational Statistics, 1994) and because there is direct evidence that HIV is present in blood samples drawn on U.S. college campuses (Edlin et al., 1994; Gayle, Keeling, & Garcia-Tunon, 1990), university students represent a population of considerable public health significance for which no effective AIDS prevention intervention has been identified (Choi & Coates, 1994).

To test experimentally the efficacy of an IMB-model-based AIDS risk-reduction intervention targeting university students, entire female dormitory floors of University of Connecticut students were randomly assigned to receive the IMB-model-based intervention or to be in a no-treatment control condition. The study was performed in dormitories with alternating all-female and all-male floors, which is the most common type of dormitory at the university. Each female dormitory floor that was randomly assigned to receive the intervention was paired with the male floor above or below it with which its residents had the closest social ties. The male and female floors received the intervention together and each such group comprised an "experimental group unit." The pairing of female and male floors was done so that the intervention occurred in a mixed-sex context, combining men and women who had a significant amount of social interaction. This created the potential for change in intervention participants' perceptions of normative support for AIDS-preventive behavior within their social networks (e.g., J. Fisher, 1988) and used social networks to reinforce and to propagate proprevention intervention-induced changes. To create equivalent "control group units," the same procedure of linking female and male floors was followed in the no-treatment control condition. In this fashion, eight experimental group units and eight control group units were created. Experimental and control group subjects completed pretest measures of AIDS risk-reduction information, motivation, behavioral skills, and behavior one month before the experimental group received the intervention, and posttest measures of these constructs were made one month and two or more months after the experimental group received the intervention.

The IMB-model-based intervention (J. Fisher et al., in press) was constructed in accord with the elicitation research findings reviewed earlier. The intervention was delivered in three highly engaging and involving two-hour sessions held one week apart and facilitated by a health educator/peer educator team. The peer educators were included in an effort to emphasize the normativeness and acceptability of AIDS risk-reduction behavior change in the students' own peer group (Kelly et al., 1990a, 1990b; Kelly, 1994).

The *information* component of the intervention consisted principally of an "AIDS 101 Slide Show" that targeted information deficits that had been identified in elicitation research with the university student sample. The slide show included facts about HIV transmission and prevention, information about the relative risk of particular sexual behaviors, information about condom effectiveness, and information about HIV antibody testing and local sources of such testing. The slide show also targeted the use of implicit personality theories of HIV risk and the use of heuristics to evaluate a partner's HIV risk, which had been identified as problematic in elicitation research focus groups. The slide show's overall objective was to supply information that was lacking, in a form that was easy to translate into preventive behavior (e.g., information about relatively safer versus relatively risky sexual behaviors; information about the problems of relying on implicit personality theory-based or heuristic-based judgments of partner risk), and to correct misinformation that was widely shared by students and strongly implicated in their unsafe sexual practices.

The *motivation* component of the intervention was designed to influence students' sense of personal vulnerability to AIDS, their attitudes toward AIDS-preventive behaviors, and their perceptions of the normativeness of AIDS-preventive behaviors in their peer group, all of which had been identified as problematic in elicitation research. These issues were addressed first in the context of *People Like Us* (J. Fisher & Fisher, 1992b), a 39-minute broadcast-quality color video produced especially for this intervention. *People Like Us* consisted of actual documentary interviews with six young adults who were highly similar to the university students in the audience in terms of age, appearance, background, and sexual history, but who were all infected with HIV or had AIDS. *People Like Us* was designed to confront and to modify heterosexual university students' beliefs that people like them could never become infected with HIV, despite their unsafe sexual behaviors.

In addition to its motivational focus on personal vulnerability, *People Like Us* also emphasized the modification of personal motivation (attitudes toward AIDS-preventive behaviors) and social motivation (perceived social support for AIDS-preventive behaviors) through a process of social comparison. The similar others in the video affected viewers' attitudes by emphasizing the fact that the minimal discomforts of condom use were more than offset by the major real-life catastrophes associated with becoming HIV positive or contracting AIDS, and stressed that it was becoming more normative and even expected to practice safer sex. The motivational component of the intervention also included small-group discussions led by peer educators who were selected as attractive natural opinion leaders capable of changing both attitudes and perceptions of group norms (Kelly et al., 1990b; Kelly, 1994). These peer educators addressed specific negative attitudes and underlying beliefs about AIDS-preventive behavior that were identified in the elicitation research (e.g., that using condoms was tantamount to communicating mistrust of one's partner) and they attempted to modify them in a fashion more favorable to prevention. Peer educators also solicited proprevention sentiments from intervention participants and socially reinforced them, and sought to evoke and to reinforce statements concerning the normativeness of safer sexual behavior in students' peer groups, in part by providing themselves as peer examples.

The *behavioral skills* component of the intervention began with the presentation of *Sex, Condoms, and Videotape* (J. Fisher & Fisher, 1993), a humorous 24-minute broadcast-quality videotape produced especially for this intervention. This videotape featured peers who modeled AIDS prevention behavioral skills for anticipating intercourse, for buying condoms, for negotiating condom use, for avoiding, interrupting, and "exiting" unsafe situations, and for substituting safer sexual alternatives to intercourse when condoms were not available— all in an engaging, humorous, and effective fashion. Next, peer educators modeled safer sex behavioral skills for intervention participants, who discussed problems and solutions associated with their use. Subsequently, the group generated brief, directive verbalizations, effective "one liners," and nonverbal methods of communicating about condom use in sexual situations, the necessity of which had been indicated by our elicitation research. Finally, participants were shown how to use condoms correctly and each one practiced putting a condom on a wooden replica of a penis.

Evaluation Research

To evaluate the effect of our IMB-model-based intervention, measures of AIDS risk-reduction information, motivation, behavioral skills, and behavior were administered to the intervention group and the control group samples one month prior to the intervention, one month following the intervention, and two or more months following the intervention (J. Fisher et al., in press). Evaluation measures were administered by personnel ostensibly unrelated to the intervention and for an ostensibly unrelated purpose to lessen demand characteristics. Analysis of the one-month posttest data, comparing intervention groups with control groups, showed a significant effect of the intervention on participants' levels of AIDS risk-reduction information, motivation, and behavioral skills. Each of the two measures of AIDS risk-reduction information showed significant effects (both $p < .0001$), indicating that the intervention produced strong increases in participants' levels of HIV transmission and prevention information, and that it *decreased* the extent to which participants endorsed inaccurate AIDS prevention heuristics and implicit personality theories.

Two of the three motivation indicators showed significant effects as well (both $p < .0001$), indicating that the intervention resulted in more favorable attitudes toward performing AIDS-preventive behaviors and stronger intentions to do so; however, no intervention effect was observed on our measure of social motivation. We feel this may be because the intervention attempted to influence participants' perceptions of social norms regarding AIDS prevention on their dormitory floor, whereas the outcome measure tapped perceived social norms among "those who are important to me," which may have included sex partners, parents, physicians, and others, in addition to residents of the dormitory floor. Finally, both measures of behavioral skills showed significant effects (both $p < .0001$), indicating that the intervention produced increases in participants' perceived levels of the skills necessary to practice AIDS-preventive behavior and in their perceptions of self-efficacy regarding AIDS-preventive behavior practices.

More importantly, there were significant intervention effects on important indicators of AIDS risk behavior change. At the one-month posttest interval, these included increased discussion of safer sex with partners ($p < .001$), increased purchasing and carrying of condoms ($p < .001$), and increased use of condoms during sexual intercourse ($p < .05$). Findings at the two-or-more-month follow-up testing showed a significant, sustained intervention effect on critical AIDS-preventive behaviors, including increases in condom purchasing and carrying ($p < .001$), increases in condom use during intercourse ($p < .01$), and increases in obtaining HIV testing ($p < .05$), although the latter effect should be interpreted with considerable caution because an intraclass correlation suggesting nonindependence within treatment groups was present for this outcome.

Summary of IMB-Model-Based
AIDS Prevention Research

Overall, the preceding sequence of elicitation, intervention, and evaluation studies with a university student population demonstrates the effective use of the IMB model to design, implement, and evaluate an AIDS prevention intervention. Our IMB-model-based intervention to change AIDS risk behavior in university students comprises one of relatively few examples in the research literature of a successful, conceptually based, empirically targeted, and systematically evaluated AIDS risk reduction intervention in any population at risk for HIV (J. Fisher & Fisher, 1992a; J. Fisher et al., in press; W. Fisher & Fisher, 1993; Kelly et al., 1993), and it is the only instance to date of an effective intervention targeting college students (Choi & Coates, 1994). We believe the IMB model and its elicitation, intervention, and evaluation procedures could be used quite readily and effectively to change AIDS risk behavior in other populations at risk for HIV as well.

Future Use of the IMB Model in AIDS Prevention Research

Our initial use of the IMB model to change AIDS risk behavior has been with a university student population and we are planning future applications of the model to change AIDS risk behavior among individuals in relationships (gay men, heterosexual college students, and unmarried individuals between the ages of 30 and 40 who are in relationships). A recent review of the literature by our research team (Misovich, Fisher, & Fisher, 1995) indicates that across populations at risk for HIV (gay males, heterosexuals, IDUs, commercial sex workers), sexually active people within relationships engage in *more* risky behavior than do sexually active people who are *not* in relationships or people in relationships who are having extrarelational sex. This pattern of effects is extremely consistent and robust across populations, has been documented in nearly 50 separate studies, and appears to occur, in part, because people feel that they are very unlikely to contract HIV from someone they know, like, love, or trust (e.g., their relationship partner). Although individuals believe their relationship partner is very *unlikely* to be HIV infected, they believe it is very *likely* that an attempt to introduce condom use or HIV testing into their relationship would threaten the relationship and lead to temporary or permanent damage. Such "relationship maintenance concerns," we believe, are responsible for a great deal of risky behavior among those in relationships (Misovich et al., 1995a).

To increase safer behaviors among people in relationships, we have proposed and pilot-tested a couples-based intervention in which both relationship members are present (J. Fisher & Fisher, 1994). This intervention is structured so that people can attribute the need to use condoms or to be tested for HIV to a source *outside* the relationship (i.e., the intervention), rather than making more typical "relationship-threatening" attributions (e.g., that condom use or HIV testing are necessary because a member of the dyad has cheated, mistrusts the other, or has practiced stigmatized behaviors in the past; Hammer-

Goldman et al., in press). We believe that couples-based interventions with both members of a relationship present could be much more effective than interventions targeting individual members of relationships. In the latter type of situation, the unilateral introduction of change into the relationship by one of its members is likely to threaten the other and therefore is unlikely to be effective (Nadler & Fisher, 1992). Research in other areas (e.g., conjoint sex therapy) also suggests that threatening couples-based issues are best addressed at the couple level (Masters & Johnson, 1970; Spence, 1991; Whitehead, Mathews, & Ramage, 1987).

In addition to couples-based interventions focusing on the unique couple-level issues that elicit AIDS risk behavior in relationships, other types of IMB-model-based interventions are planned (e.g., interventions with high school students attending multiracial high schools—J. Fisher & Fisher, 1995). In these interventions, both classroom health teachers and popular students who are "natural opinion leaders" (cf. Kelly, 1994) will deliver an intervention targeting population-specific information, motivation, and behavioral skills deficits identified in elicitation research. Many elements from our successful university student intervention will be retained but they will be adapted to a multiracial high school audience. IMB-model-based interventions are also being created to assist HIV-positive gay men and IDUs in their attempts to practice safer behaviors (J. Fisher, 1995). In these projects, again, elicitation research is being conducted to understand the *dynamics* of risk behavior among HIV-positive individuals, and population-specific interventions are being designed on the basis of elicitation findings. Surprisingly, almost all formal behavior change interventions to date have targeted populations of HIV-negative people in an attempt to keep them from becoming HIV positive, and wholly inadequate attempts have been made to assist HIV-positive individuals with behavior change.

Other Applications of the IMB Model

Although the IMB model was originally proposed as an AIDS risk behavior change model, we are increasingly coming to view it more as a general health behavior change model. We feel that risk behavior-specific information, motivation, and behavioral skills are critical to change many unhealthy behaviors and that the elicitation research, intervention research, and evaluation research sequence proposed by the IMB model can be employed effectively to design and evaluate interventions aimed at changing a broad array of such behaviors. Moreover, we believe that a careful review of interventions across health domains would reveal that when health behavior change requires any significant effort or skills, which is the case in most health behavior change contexts, increases in information alone will be insufficient to effect behavior change (e.g., Berberian, Gross, Lovejoy, & Paparella, 1976; Botvin, Dusenbury, Baker, James-Ortiz, & Kerner, 1989; Caldas, 1993; J. Fisher & Fisher, 1992a; Malibach & Flora, 1993; Rothman, Salovey, & Turvey, 1993; Strube, Yost, & Haire-Joshu, 1993). In most such cases, increases in motivation and behavioral skills will prove necessary.

Support for this viewpoint is provided by successful interventions that have involved information, motivation, and behavioral skills components in the areas of preventing adolescents from smoking (e.g., Botvin et al., 1989), preventing substance abuse (Botvin, Baker, Filazzola, & Botvin, 1990), reducing problem drinking (Miller & Sanchez, 1994), reducing drug abuse (Pentz et al., 1989), enhancing the use of oral rehydration in Third World countries (Foote et al., 1985), reducing cardiovascular risk (Farquhar et al., 1990), and increasing contraceptive behavior in adolescents (W. Fisher, 1990a; Gilchrist & Schinke, 1983). In each of these domains, behavior has proved to be difficult to change, interventions that have involved "information only" have failed, and interventions that have included information, motivation, and behavioral skills elements have been quite successful.

Within our own program of research, we have recently tested the IMB model as applied to the desirable practice of breast self-examination among women over the age of 40 (Misovich, Martinez, & J. Fisher, 1995b). In this area, similar to our studies in the area of safer sexual behavior, we created multiple, moderately correlated indicators of each model component with regard to breast self-examination. In structural equation modeling tests of the IMB model in this area, it was found that the information, motivation, and behavioral skills components of the model accounted for approximately 80% of the variance in breast self-examination behavior. This research suggests the usefulness of the IMB model as a highly general conceptualization of preventive health behaviors.

Summary

This chapter has described the IMB model in some detail and presented correlational and experimental tests of the model in the context of AIDS risk behavior change. The chapter also summarized an IMB-model-based intervention that was effective in changing university students' AIDS risk behavior and discussed applications of the IMB model in other AIDS risk behavior change contexts. Finally, we suggested that the IMB model may be viewed as a general health behavior change model that can be applied in diverse health behavior change contexts.

Note

1. Although a number of other investigators also address AIDS prevention information, motivation, and behavioral skills as important factors in AIDS prevention (Coates, 1990; Miller et al., 1990; Winett et al., 1990), the IMB model is the first to specify (J. Fisher & Fisher, 1989, 1992a) and to empirically test (J. Fisher et al., 1994; W. Fisher et al., 1995) the specific linkages among these constructs.

References

Ajzen, I., & Fishbein, M. (1980). *Understanding attitudes and predicting social behavior.* Englewood Cliffs, NJ: Prentice Hall.

Bandura, A. (1989). Perceived self-efficacy in the exercise of control over HIV infection. In V. M. Mays, G. W. Albee, & S. F. Schneider (Eds.), *Primary prevention of AIDS* (pp. 128-140). Newbury Park, CA: Sage.

Bandura, A. (1994). Social cognitive theory and exercise of control over HIV infection. In R. J. DiClemente & J. L. Peterson (Eds.), *Preventing AIDS: Theories and methods of behavioral interventions* (pp. 25-59). New York: Plenum.

Basch, C. E. (1987). Focus group interview: An underutilized research technique for improving theory and practice in health education. *Health Education Quarterly, 14,* 411-448.

Berberian, R. M., Gross, C., Lovejoy, J., & Paparella, S. (1976). The effectiveness of drug education programs: A critical review. *Health Education Monograph, 4,* 377-398.

Bollen, K. A., & Long, J. S. (1993). *Testing structural equation models.* Newbury Park, CA: Sage.

Botvin, G. J., Baker, E., Filazzola, A. D., & Botvin, E. M. (1990). A cognitive behavioral approach to substance abuse prevention: A one-year follow-up. *Addictive Behaviors, 15,* 47-63.

Botvin, G. J., Dusenbury, L., Baker, E., James-Ortiz, S., & Kerner, J. (1989). A skills training approach to smoking prevention among Hispanic youth. *Journal of Behavioral Medicine, 12,* 279-296.

Burke, D. S., Brundage, J. F., Goldenbaum, M., Gardner, L. I., Peterson, M., Visintine, R., Redfield, R. R., & Walter Reed Retrovirus Research Group. (1990). Human immunodeficiency virus infections in teenagers: Seroprevalence among applicants for U.S. military service. *Journal of the American Medical Association, 263,* 2074-2077.

Caldas, S. J. (1993). Current theoretical perspectives on adolescent pregnancy and childbearing in the United States. *Journal of Adolescent Research, 8,* 4-20.

Caron, S. L., Davis, C. M., Wynn, R. L., & Roberts, L. W. (1992). "America responds to AIDS," but did college students? Differences between March, 1987, and September, 1988. *AIDS Education and Prevention, 4,* 18-28.

Catania, J. A., Coates, T. J., Kegeles, S., Fullilove, M. T., Peterson, J., Marín, B., Siegel, D., & Hulley, S. (1992). Condom use in multi-ethnic neighborhoods of San Francisco: The population-based AMEN (AIDS in Multi-Ethnic Neighborhoods) study. *American Journal of Public Health, 82,* 284-287.

Catania, J. A., Coates, T. J., Peterson, J., Dolcini, M. M., Kegeles, S., Siegel, D., Golden, E., & Fullilove, M. T. (1993). Changes in condom use among Black, Hispanic, and White heterosexuals in San Francisco: The AMEN cohort study. *Journal of Sex Research, 30,* 121-128.

Catania, J. A., Gibson, D. R., Chitwood, D. D., & Coates, T. J. (1990). Methodological problems in AIDS behavioral research: Influences on measurement error and participation bias in studies of sexual behavior. *Psychological Bulletin, 108,* 339-362.

Centers for Disease Control. (1987). HIV infection and pregnancies in sexual partners of HIV-seropositive hemophiliac men—United States. *Morbidity and Mortality Weekly Report, 36,* 593-595.

Centers for Disease Control. (1995, May). *HIV/AIDS Surveillance Report.* Atlanta, GA: Author.

Choi, K., & Coates, T. J. (1994). Prevention of HIV infection. *AIDS, 8,* 1371-1389.

Clemow, L. P., Saidi, P., Lerner, A., Kim, H. C., Matts, L., & Eisele, J. (1989, August). *Hemophiliacs, AIDS and safer sex: Psychosocial issues and one-year follow-up.* Paper presented at American Psychological Association meeting, New Orleans.

Coates, T. J. (1990). Strategies for modifying sexual behavior for primary and secondary prevention of HIV disease. *Journal of Consulting and Clinical Psychology, 58,* 57-69.

D'Augelli, A. R. (1992). Sexual behavior patterns of gay university men: Implications for preventing HIV infection. *Journal of American College Health, 41,* 25-29.

Dublin, S., Rosenberg, P. S., & Goedert, J. J. (1992). Patterns and predictors of high-risk sexual behavior in female partners of HIV-infected men with hemophilia. *AIDS, 6,* 475-482.

Edlin, B. R., Keeling, R. P., Gayle, H. D., & Holmberg, S. D. (1994). *Prevalence of human immunodeficiency virus infection among U.S. college students.* Unpublished manuscript, Division of HIV/AIDS, Centers for Disease Control and Prevention.

Ekstrand, M. L. (1992). Safer sex maintenance among gay men: Are we making any progress? *AIDS, 6,* 875-877.

Farquhar, J. W., Fortmann, S. P., Flora, J. A., Taylor, C. B., Haskell, W. L., Williams, P. T., Maccoby, N., & Wood, P. D. (1990). Effects of communitywide education on cardiovascular disease risk factors: The Stanford five-city project. *Journal of the American Medical Association, 264,* 359-365.

Festinger, L. (1957). *A theory of cognitive dissonance.* Palo Alto, CA: Stanford University Press.

Fishbein, M., Middlestadt, S. E., & Hitchcock, P. J. (1994). Using information to change sexually transmitted disease-related behaviors. In R. J. DiClemente & J. L. Peterson (Eds.), *Preventing AIDS: Theories and methods of behavioral interventions* (pp. 61-78). New York: Plenum.

Fisher, J. D. (1988). Possible effects of reference group-based social influence on AIDS-risk behavior and AIDS prevention. *American Psychologist, 43,* 914-920.

Fisher, J. D. (1995). *Understanding the dynamics of AIDS risk behavior in HIV+ men who have sex with men.* Unpublished manuscript, State of Connecticut Department of Public Health and Addiction Services.

Fisher, J. D., & Fisher, W. A. (1989). A general technology for AIDS risk behavior change. Unpublished manuscript, University of Connecticut, Storrs.

Fisher, J. D., & Fisher, W. A. (1992a). Changing AIDS risk behavior. *Psychological Bulletin, 111,* 455-474.

Fisher, J. D. & Fisher, W. A. (Producers), & Fisher, J. D. (Director). (1992b). *People like us* [Videotape]. (Available from AIDS Risk Reduction Project, University of Connecticut, 406 Babbidge Road U-20, Storrs, CT 06269-1020)

Fisher, J. D. & Fisher, W. A. (Producers), & Fisher, J. D. (Director). (1993). *Sex, condoms, and videotape* [Videotape]. (Available from AIDS Risk Reduction Project, University of Connecticut, 406 Babbidge Road U-20, Storrs, CT 06269-1020)

Fisher, J. D., & Fisher, W. A. (1994). *Changing AIDS risk behavior in relationships* (Grant application to NIMH). University of Connecticut, Storrs.

Fisher, J. D., & Fisher, W. A. (1995). *Changing AIDS risk behavior in high school students* (Grant application to NIMH). University of Connecticut, Storrs.

Fisher, J. D., Fisher, W. A., Misovich, S. J., Kimble, D. L., & Malloy, T. (in press). Changing AIDS risk behavior: Effects of an intervention emphasizing AIDS risk reduction information, motivation, and behavioral skills in a university student population. *Health Psychology.*

Fisher, J. D., Fisher, W. A., Williams, S. S., & Malloy, T. E. (1994). Empirical tests of an information-motivation-behavioral skills model of AIDS preventive behavior. *Health Psychology, 13,* 238-250.

Fisher, J. D., Hertzog-Covell, N., & Fisher, W. A. (1993). *AIDS-prevention knowledge, motivation, behavioral skills, and behavior in samples of gay men, high school students, and university students.* Unpublished manuscript, University of Connecticut, Storrs.

Fisher, J. D., & Misovich, S. (1990a). Evolution of college students' AIDS-related behavioral responses, attitudes, knowledge, and fear. *AIDS Education and Prevention: An Interdisciplinary Journal, 2,* 322-337.

Fisher, J. D., & Misovich, S. (1990b). Social influence and AIDS-preventive behavior. In J. Edwards et al. (Eds.), *Social influence processes and prevention* (pp. 39-70). New York: Plenum.

Fisher, J. D., Misovich, S. J., & Fisher, W. A. (1992). The impact of perceived social norms on adolescents' AIDS-risk behavior and prevention. In R. J. DiClemente (Ed.), *Adolescents and AIDS: A generation in jeopardy* (pp. 117-136). Beverly Hills, CA: Sage.

Fisher, W. A. (1990). Understanding adolescent pregnancy and sexually transmissible disease/AIDS. In J. Edwards, R. S. Tindale, C. Heath, & E. J. Posavac (Eds.), *Social influence processes and prevention* (pp. 71-101). New York: Plenum.

Fisher, W. A., & Fisher, J. D. (1993). A general social psychological model for changing AIDS risk behavior. In J. Pryor & G. Reeder (Eds.), *The social psychology of HIV infection* (pp. 127-153). Hillsdale, NJ: Erlbaum.

Fisher, W. A., Williams, S. S., Fisher, J. D., & Malloy, T. E. (1995). *Predicting AIDS risk behavior among urban adolescents: An empirical test of the information-motivation-behavioral skills model.* Manuscript submitted for publication.

Foote, D., Martorell, R., McDivitt, J. A., Snyder, L., Spain, P. L., Stone, S., & Storey, J. D. (1985). *Mass media and health practices evaluation in the Gambia: A report of the major findings.* Menlo Park, CA: Applied Communication Technologies.

Friedman, S. R., Des Jarlais, D. C., & Ward, T. P. (1994). Social models for changing health-relevant behavior. In R. J. DiClemente & J. L. Peterson (Eds.), *Preventing AIDS: Theories and methods of behavioral interventions* (pp. 95-116). New York: Plenum.

Gayle, H. D., Keeling, R. P., & Garcia-Tunon, M. (1990). Prevalence of the human immunodeficiency virus among university students. *New England Journal of Medicine, 323,* 1538-1541.

Gilchrist, L. D., & Schinke, S. P. (1983). Coping with contraception: Cognitive and behavioral methods with adolescents. *Cognitive Theory and Research, 7,* 379-388.

Hammer-Goldman, J. C., Fisher, J. D., Fitzgerald, P., & Fisher, W. A. (in press). When two heads aren't better than one: AIDS risk behavior in college-aged couples. *Journal of Applied Social Psychology.*

Jemmott, J. B., & Jemmott, L. S. (1994). Interventions for adolescents in community settings. In R. J. DiClemente & J. L. Peterson (Eds.), *Preventing AIDS: Theories and methods of behavioral interventions* (pp. 141-174). New York: Plenum.

Johnson, R. W., Ostrow, D. G., & Joseph, J. (1990). Educational strategies for prevention of sexual transmission of HIV. In D. G. Ostrow (Ed.), *Behavioral aspects of AIDS* (pp. 43-73). New York: Plenum.

Kelly, J. A. (1994). HIV prevention among gay and bisexual men in small cities. In R. J. DiClemente & J. L. Peterson (Eds.), *Preventing AIDS: Theories and methods of behavioral interventions* (pp. 297-317). New York: Plenum.

Kelly, J. A., Murphy, D. A., Sikkema, K. J., & Kalichman, S. C. (1993). Psychological interventions to prevent HIV infection are urgently needed: New priorities for behavioral research in the second decade of AIDS. *American Psychologist, 48,* 1023-1034.

Kelly, J. A., & St. Lawrence, J. S. (1988). *The AIDS health crisis: Psychological and social interventions.* New York: Plenum.

Kelly, J. A., St. Lawrence, J. S., Brasfield, T. L., Stevenson, L. Y., Díaz, Y. Y., & Hauth, A. C. (1990a). AIDS risk behavior patterns among gay men in small southern cities. *American Journal of Public Health, 80,* 416-418.

Kelly, J. A., St. Lawrence, J., Stevenson, Y., Díaz, Y., Hauth, A. C., Brasfield, T. L., Smith, J. E., Bradley, B. G., & Bahr, G. R. (1990b, June). *Population-wide risk behavior reduction through diffusion of innovation following intervention with natural opinion leaders.* Paper presented at the 6th International Conference on AIDS, San Francisco.

Kenny, D. A. (1979). *Correlation and causality.* New York: Wiley.

Khalsa, H. K., Kowalewski, M. R., Anglin, M. D., & Wang, J. (1992). HIV-related risk behaviors among cocaine users. *AIDS Education and Prevention, 4,* 71-83.

Krueger, R. A. (1988). *Focus groups: A practical guide for applied research.* Newbury Park, CA: Sage.

Leviton, L. C., & Valdiserri, R. O. (1990). Evaluating AIDS prevention: Outcome, implementation, and mediating variables. *Evaluation and Program Planning, 13,* 55-66.

Malibach, E., & Flora, J. A. (1993). Symbolic modeling and cognitive rehearsal: Using video to promote AIDS prevention self-efficacy. *Communication Research, 20,* 517-545.

Mann, J. M., Tarantola, D. J. M., & Netter, T. W. (1992). *AIDS in the world: A global report.* Cambridge, MA: Harvard University Press.

Masters, W. H., & Johnson, V. E. (1970). *Human sexual inadequacy.* Boston: Little, Brown.

McCusker, J., Stoddard, A. M., McDonald, M., Zapka, J. G., & Mayer, K. H. (1992). Maintenance of behavioral change in a cohort of homosexually active men. *AIDS, 6,* 861-868.

Miller, W. R., & Sanchez, V. C. (1994). Motivating young adults for treatment and lifestyle change. In G. Howard & P. E. Nathan (Eds.), *Alcohol use and misuse by young adults* (pp. 55-81). Notre Dame, IN: University of Notre Dame Press.

Misovich, S. J., Fisher, J. D., & Fisher, W. A. (1993). *The perceived AIDS-preventive utility of knowing one's partner well: A public health dictum and individuals' risky sexual behavior.* Unpublished manuscript, University of Connecticut, Storrs.

Misovich, S., Fisher, J. D., & Fisher, W. A. (1995a). *What's love got to do with it? Psychological processes underlying increased AIDS risk behavior in close relationships.* Unpublished manuscript, University of Connecticut, Storrs.

Misovich S. J., Martinez, T., & Fisher, J. D. (1995b). *Predicting breast self-examination among women: An empirical test of the information-motivation-behavioral skills model.* Unpublished manuscript, University of Connecticut, Storrs.

Morbidity and Mortality Weekly Report. (1992, January 17). The second 100,000 cases of acquired immunodeficiency syndrome—United States, June 1981-December 1991. Washington, DC: U.S. Public Health Service.

Nadler, A., & Fisher, J. D. (1992). Volitional personal change in an interpersonal perspective. In Y. Klar, J. Fisher, J. Chinsky, & A. Nadler (Eds.), *Initiating self change: Social psychological and clinical perspectives* (pp. 213-230). New York: Springer-Verlag.

National Center for Health Statistics. (1994). *Annual summary of births, marriages, divorces, and deaths: United States, 1993.* Hyattsville, MD: U.S. Public Health Service.

Offir, J. T., Williams, S. S., Fisher, J. D., & Fisher, W. A. (1993). Reasons for inconsistent AIDS prevention among gay men. *Journal of Sex Research, 30,* 62-69.

O'Keeffe, M. K., Nesselhof-Kendall, S., & Baum, A. (1990). Behavior and prevention of AIDS: Bases of research and intervention. *Personality and Social Psychology Bulletin, 16,* 166-180.

Pentz, M. A., Dwyer, J. H., MacKinnon, D. P., Flay, B. R., Hansen, W. B., Wang, E. Y., & Anderson-Johnson, C. (1989). A multicommunity trial for primary prevention of adolescent drug abuse: Effects of drug use prevalence. *Journal of the American Medical Association, 261,* 3256-3266.

Rosenstock, I. M., Strecher, V. J., & Becker, M. H. (1994). The health belief model and HIV risk behavior change. In R. J. DiClemente & J. L. Peterson (Eds.), *Preventing AIDS: Theories and methods of behavioral interventions* (pp. 5-24). New York: Plenum.

Rothman, A. J., Salovey, P., & Turvey, C. (1993). Attributions of responsibility and persuasion: Increasing mammography utilization among women over 40 with an internally oriented message. *Health Psychology, 12,* 39-47.

Spence, S. (1991). *Psychosexual therapy: A cognitive-behavioural approach.* London, England: Chapman & Hall.

Strube, M. J., Yost, J. H., & Haire-Joshu, D. (1993). Diabetes knowledge as a moderator of reactions to illness by patients with insulin-dependent diabetes mellitus. *Journal of Applied Social Psychology, 23,* 944-958.

Trocki, K. F. (1992). Patterns of sexuality and risky sexuality in the general population of a California county. *Journal of Sex Research, 29,* 85-94.

U.S. National Center for Education Statistics. (1994). *Digest of education statistics, 1994.* Washington, DC: Author.

Vanichseni, S., Des Jarlais, D. C., Choopanya, K., Friedman, P., Wenston, J., Sonchai, W., Sotheran, J. L., Raktham, S., Carballo, M., & Friedman, S. R. (1993). Condom use with primary partners among injecting drug users in Bangkok, Thailand and New York City, United States. *AIDS, 7,* 887-891.

Watkins, K. E., Metzger, D., Woody, G., & McLellan, A. T. (1993). Determinants of condom use among intravenous drug users. *AIDS, 7,* 719-723.

Weinstein, N. D. (1989). Perceptions of personal susceptibility to harm. In V. M. Mays, G. W. Albee, & S. F. Schneider (Eds.), *Primary prevention of AIDS: Psychological approaches* (pp. 142-167). London, England: Sage.

Whitehead, A., Mathews, A., & Ramage, M. (1987). The treatment of sexually unresponsive women: A comparative evaluation. *Behaviour Research and Therapy, 25,* 195-205.

Williams, S. S., Doyle, T., Pittman, L. D., Covell, N. H., Weiss, L. H., Fisher, J. D., & Fisher, W. A. (1993). *AIDS-preventive skills among college students: An investigation using roleplaying techniques.* Unpublished manuscript, State University of New York College at Buffalo.

Williams, S. S., Kimble, D. L., Covell, N. H., Weiss, L. H., Newton, K. J., Fisher, W. A., & Fisher, J. D. (1992). College students use implicit personality theory instead of safer sex. *Journal of Applied Social Psychology, 22,* 921-933.

Winkelstein, W., & Johnson, A. (1990). Epidemiology overview. *AIDS, 4*(Suppl. 1), S95-S97.

Winslow, R. W., Franzini, L. R., & Hwang, J. (1992). Perceived peer norms, casual sex, and AIDS risk prevention. *Journal of Applied Social Psychology, 22,* 1809-1827.

World Health Organization. (1995). The current global situation of the HIV/AIDS pandemic. *Global programme on AIDS.* Geneva, Switzerland: Author.

PART II

SPECIAL POPULATIONS

7

Social Psychological Influences on HIV Risk Behavior Among African American Youth

JOHN B. JEMMOTT, III

Despite tremendous advances in public health, biomedical and social sciences, the Human Immunodeficiency Virus, which causes Acquired Immune Deficiency Syndrome, continues to spread, eluding both a cure and a preventive vaccine. This chapter presents an overview of a program of research that seeks to understand the social psychological factors that contribute to HIV risk-associated sexual behavior among inner-city adolescents. The ultimate goal of this research is to identify theory-based, culturally sensitive, developmentally appropriate strategies to reduce those risk-associated behaviors.

HIV infection is spread by exposure to infected blood, semen, or vaginal secretions, usually through the sharing of contaminated hypodermic needles and other drug paraphernalia by injection drug users or as a result of sexual activities (Centers for Disease Control and Preven-

AUTHOR'S NOTE: Preparation of this manuscript was supported in part by grants R01-MH45668 and R01-MH52035 from the National Institute of Mental Health and R01-HD24921 and U01-HD30145 from the National Institute of Child Health and Human Development.

tion (CDC), 1995). Although HIV can also be transmitted from infected mothers to their newborns (Jemmott & Miller, in press), it is primarily the behavior of individuals that heightens their risk of HIV infection. One can argue that behavior-change interventions are the only effective means for preventing AIDS, until a vaccine or treatment is developed. However, we believe that behavior-change interventions will be essential for primary prevention of HIV infection well beyond the time when vaccines and treatments for AIDS have been developed. Medical science alone cannot control disease. For example, despite effective, inexpensive, and easily delivered technologies for treating many sexually transmitted diseases (STDs), epidemics of gonorrhea, chlamydia, and primary syphilis have raged in recent years.

For the most part, our research has focused on inner-city African American adolescents. Evidence from several sources suggests that they are an important group to study in relation to AIDS. For example, AIDS surveillance reports document the disproportionate toll that AIDS has levied on African Americans. African Americans comprise only 12% of the United States population (U.S. Bureau of the Census, 1989), but account for 34% of the reported AIDS cases in the United States (CDC, 1995). Although adolescents represent fewer than 1% of the cumulative total reported AIDS cases, the long latency period between infection with HIV and the diagnosis of AIDS may mask the magnitude of the problem. About 18% of AIDS cases have been among young adults in their twenties, many of whom were probably infected during adolescence. Reports of newly diagnosed cases of HIV infection coming from the 27 states with mandatory testing also help to clarify adolescents' risk of HIV infection. Youth 13 to 24 years of age comprised 21.7% of new cases of HIV infection reported in 1993 and 19.3% of the cumulative HIV infections reported as of June 1994. A higher HIV seroprevalence has been observed among African American and Latino civilian applicants for military service than among their American Indian, Alaskan Native, White, or Asian and Pacific Islander counterparts (CDC, 1990). Higher HIV seroprevalence rates have also been observed among African Americans than among Whites (CDC, 1990) in data on entrants to the Job Corps, a residential job-training program for urban and rural disadvantaged youth aged 16 to 21 years.

Rates of unintended pregnancy and sexually transmitted disease also suggest an elevated risk of HIV infection among adolescents, particularly inner-city African American youth. The adolescent pregnancy rate is more than twice as high among African American adolescents as among White adolescents (Hatcher et al., 1994; Jones et al., 1986; Pratt, Mosher, Bachrach, & Horn, 1984). The rates of syphilis, gonorrhea, and hospitalization for pelvic inflammatory disease are highest among adolescents, but low-income African American adolescents are particularly at risk (Bell & Holmes, 1984; Cates, 1987; Hatcher et al., 1994). The prevalence of injection drug use in the inner city also greatly heightens the risk of HIV infection for African American adolescent residents. Although the youths themselves may not inject drugs, they may have sexual relationships with injection drug users or with individuals who have had sex with such potentially infected persons.

Efforts to dissuade adolescents from engaging in HIV risk-associated behavior may be most effective if they have a solid theoretical foundation. Theory can be used in the development of intervention procedures and theory can also drive the selection of variables to be assessed. By measuring the theoretical mediators of intervention-induced behavior change, a better conceptual understanding of risk behavior should emerge. While maintaining an emphasis on a theory-based approach to HIV risk-reduction, this chapter also focuses on practical questions regarding the most effective way to intervene to reduce the risk of HIV infection. We will return to this point later.

Applying the Theory of Planned Behavior to HIV Risk-Associated Behavior

As an organizing conceptual framework, our research has drawn on the Theory of Planned Behavior (Ajzen, 1991; Madden, Ellen, & Ajzen, 1992), which is an extension of the more widely known Theory of Reasoned Action (Ajzen & Fishbein, 1980; Fishbein & Ajzen, 1975; Fishbein, Middlestadt, & Hitchcock, 1994). The Theory of Reasoned Action has been used successfully to predict and explain a broad range of health-related behaviors, including breast self-examination (Temko, 1987), smoking cessation (Fishbein, 1982), weight control (Schifter & Ajzen, 1985), infant feeding (Manstead, Profitt, & Smart, 1983), and contraceptive use (Fisher, 1984; Davidson & Jaccard, 1979). According to the theory, behavior is the result of a specific intention to perform that behavior. A behavioral intention is seen as determined by (a) one's attitude toward the specific behavior—that is, overall positive or negative feeling toward performing the behavior—and (b) one's subjective norm regarding the behavior—that is, perception of whether significant others would approve or disapprove of one performing the behavior. Thus, people intend to perform a behavior when they evaluate that behavior positively and when they believe significant others think they should perform it. An additional feature of the theory is that it directs attention to why people hold certain attitudes and subjective norms. One's attitude toward a behavior is seen as reflecting behavioral beliefs—that is, salient beliefs about the consequences of performing the act—and one's negative or positive evaluation of those consequences. Subjective norms are seen as the product of one's salient beliefs about what specific reference persons or groups think should be done regarding the behavior and one's motivation to comply with these referents.

According to the Theory of Reasoned Action, attitudes and subjective norms are the sole direct determinants of intentions. Other variables may affect intentions but only indirectly, mediated by the effects of such variables on the attitudinal component, the normative component, or both. In this way, the theory can accommodate variables that are external to it (Fishbein & Middlestadt, 1989). A fundamental assumption of the Theory of Reasoned Action is that its predictive power is greatest for behaviors that are fully under the volitional control of individuals. Ajzen (1985, 1991; Ajzen & Madden, 1986; Madden, Ellen, & Ajzen, 1992; Schifter & Ajzen, 1985) later proposed the Theory of Planned Behavior to account for behaviors that are subject to forces that are beyond individuals' control. For instance, perfor-mance of the behavior might depend on another person's actions or the behavior might be performed in the context of strong emotions. Under such circumstances, Ajzen reasoned, prediction of intentions might be enhanced by considering not only attitudes and subjective norms but also perceived behavioral control.

Perceived behavioral control, defined as the perceived ease versus difficulty of performing the behavior, reflects past experience in addition to anticipated impediments, obstacles, resources, and opportunities. Perceived behavioral control has affinity with the construct of perceived self-efficacy in social cognitive theory—that is, individuals' conviction that they can perform a specific behavior (Bandura, 1986, 1989, 1994; O'Leary, 1985). In fact, much of what is known about perceived behavioral control comes from research on perceived self-efficacy by Bandura and his associates. What the Theory of Planned Behavior does is to place the construct of perceived self-efficacy or perceived behavioral control within a more general framework of the relations among beliefs, attitudes, intentions, and behaviors (Ajzen, 1991). Perceived behavioral control is determined by control beliefs —beliefs about factors that facilitate or inhibit performance of the behavior.

We hypothesized that the Theory of Reasoned Action and its extension, the Theory of Planned Behavior, would be valuable to an understanding of HIV risk-associated sexual behavior. Sexual behaviors are performed in the context of strong emotions, and safer sex practices are not always under the individual's direct control because they may require a sexual partner's cooperation. Based on this theoretical view, to implement safer sex practices it might be useful to increase perceived behavioral control in addition to inducing positive attitudes and supportive subjective norms.

Application to Condom Use

We have applied the Theory of Planned Behavior to HIV risk-associated sexual behavior, specifically the behavior of condom use. As shown in Figure 7.1, the behavior is a function of the intention to use condoms. Condom use intention is determined by attitudes toward condoms, subjective norms regarding condoms, and perceived behavioral control over condom use. This reflects our hypothesis that people intend to use condoms when they evaluate condom use positively, when they believe significant others think they should use condoms, and when they feel confident in their ability to implement condom use.

Several behavioral beliefs may affect attitudes toward condoms. Elicitation surveys conducted with inner-city African American adolescents suggest the importance of three behavioral beliefs in particular. Perhaps the most obvious are prevention beliefs—beliefs about whether the use of condoms will prevent pregnancy, sexually transmitted disease, and HIV infection in particular. Hedonistic beliefs—beliefs about the effects of condoms on sexual enjoyment—are also likely to be important to condom use attitude because if adolescents believe that using a condom ruins sexual enjoyment, their attitude toward using a condom should be negative. The third type of behavioral belief is

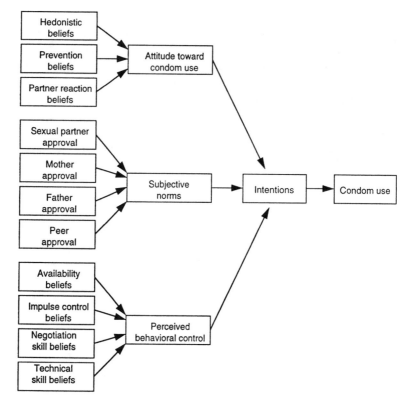

Figure 7.1. The theory of planned behavior as applied to condom use.

partner reaction beliefs—beliefs about how sexual partners will react to condom use.

Subjective norms are determined by normative beliefs, which are beliefs about whether salient reference persons or groups would approve or disapprove of the person's engaging in the behavior. The key referents that emerged in elicitation surveys included one's sexual partner, mother, father, other family members, and peers or friends. Thus, for example, to the extent that people believe that their sexual partners approve of using a condom, those people's subjective norms should be more supportive of condom use.

We have distinguished among four types of control beliefs that are hypothesized to influence perceived behavioral control. Availability beliefs concern adolescents' confidence that they can have condoms available for use when they need them. This includes their beliefs about the financial cost of condoms and beliefs about the appropriateness of carrying condoms. Impulse control or self-control beliefs concern adolescents' confidence that they can control themselves and use condoms in the midst of a sexual encounter. Negotiation skill beliefs concern adolescents' confidence that they can convince a sexual partner to use condoms. Technical skill beliefs concern adolescents' confidence that they can use condoms with facility, for example, without fumbling or ruining the mood. The focus here is on adolescents' confidence about their abilities, not on their actual abilities. Confidence and actual skill are likely to be correlated, but we focus on the belief. To the extent that people believe that they have the requisite skills and resources to use condoms, they should perceive greater control over performance of that behavior.

Intervening With Inner-City African American Adolescents

In this section, we will discuss several studies that illustrate our approach to HIV behavioral intervention research.

Research With African American Males

The first study (Jemmott, Jemmott, & Fong, 1992) focused on inner-city African American male adolescents for several reasons. These young males are important to study because they are considered difficult to reach and difficult to maintain in intervention trials. No previous HIV risk-reduction intervention studies had been focused on them. In addition, as mentioned earlier, they are at high risk of contracting and spreading STDs, including HIV. For the most part, research on adolescents' sexual behavior has focused on female adolescents. Male adolescents, especially African American male adolescents, typically have been left out of the picture. What makes the absence of intervention data on male adolescents especially troublesome is the fact that, aside from abstinence, the most often advocated means of protecting against sexually transmitted HIV infection is the male's use of a condom.

The study was designed to test the effectiveness of an intervention on HIV risk-associated sexual behavior and theory-based putative mediators of such behavior among inner-city African American male adolescents. We were also interested in a practical question—namely, whether the gender of the educational facilitator or health educator would moderate effectiveness of the intervention. A common assumption is that it is important to match the race and gender of participants and facilitators to maximize the effectiveness of an intervention with ethnic minority individuals. A facilitator of a similar race and gender might have greater credibility, might be able to establish rapport more rapidly, and might have a deeper understanding of pertinent aspects of the participants' lives. According to this line of reasoning, African American male adolescents may be more receptive to behavior change recommendations if they come from African American male facilitators rather than African American female facilitators. We tested that hypothesis.

The participants were 157 inner-city African American male adolescents from Philadelphia who were recruited from a local medical center, community-based organizations, and a local high school. They volunteered for a Risk Reduction Project, designed "to understand African American male youths' behaviors that may create risks such as unemployment, truancy, teenage pregnancy, and sexually transmitted diseases, especially AIDS, and to find ways to teach African American male youth how to reduce these risks." The overwhelming majority of the participants (97%) were currently enrolled in school and their median level in school was between 9th and 10th grade. Their chief risk was from heterosexual activities, particularly failure to use condoms. Although the mean age of the sample was only 14.6 years, about 83% of the participants reporting having had coitus at least once. About 21% of respondents who had coitus in the past 3 months reported that they never used condoms during those experiences and only 30% reported always using condoms. Few participants (less than 5%) reported ever engaging in same-gender sexual behavior or injection drug use.

The participants were assigned randomly to an HIV risk-reduction condition or a control condition on career opportunities. Both conditions featured a small group of about six boys led by a specially trained male or female African American facilitator. All the facilitators had a 4-year college degree and their average age was 36 years. The facilitators received 6 hours of training that emphasized strict adherence to the intervention protocol.

The adolescents in the HIV risk-reduction condition received an intensive 5-hour intervention. The intervention included videotapes, games, and exercises designed to influence AIDS-related knowledge, behavioral beliefs, attitudes, and perceived behavioral control supportive of safer sex practices. The intervention materials and activities were selected not only to influence the putative theoretical mediators but also to be interactive and enjoyable. For example, participants played AIDS basketball, a game in which the adolescents were divided into two teams that earned points by correctly answering factual questions about AIDS. In this game, which adolescents find especially entertaining, there are two-point questions, three-point bonus questions, and one-point foul shot questions. One video, *The Subject Is AIDS,* presented factual information about AIDS, was narrated by a African American woman, and had a multiethnic cast. Another video, *Condom Sense,* addressed negative attitudes toward the use of condoms and unfavorable hedonistic beliefs. The video attacked the idea that sex is substantially less pleasurable when a condom is used. A major character in it is an African American man who tries to convince a basketball buddy that his girlfriend's request that they use condoms during sex is reasonable. The intervention also addressed perceived behavioral control by including a condom exercise focused on familiarity with condoms and the steps involved in using them correctly. Participants also engaged in role-playing situations depicting potential problems in trying to implement safer-sex practices, including abstinence.

To control for Hawthorne effects—that is, to reduce the likelihood that effects of the HIV risk-reduction intervention could be attributed to nonspecific features including group interaction and special attention—adolescents randomly assigned to the control condition also received a 5-hour intervention. Structurally similar to the HIV risk-reduction intervention, the control condition involved culturally and developmentally appropriate videotapes, exercises, and games regarding career opportunities. For example, the participants played the Career Basketball Game in which teams earned points for correctly answering questions about careers and job hunting. This control intervention was designed to be both enjoyable and valuable. Although career-opportunity subjects did not learn about AIDS, given the high unemployment among inner-city African American male adolescents, the goal was to provide information that would be valuable to them as they planned their future.

Adolescents in both conditions completed questionnaires before the intervention, immediately afterward, and three months after the intervention. These questionnaires were administered not by the facilitators who implemented the interventions, but by project assistants. The project assistants, who were trained African American community residents, emphasized the importance of being honest. The participants also signed an "agreement" pledging to answer the questions as honestly as possible, a procedure that has been shown to yield more valid responses on sensitive issues. The project assistants told the participants that their responses would be used to create programs for other African American adolescents such as themselves and that the programs would be effective only if they answered the questions honestly. In this way, we sought to pit the social responsibility motive against the social desirability motive. In addition, the Marlowe-Crowne Social Desirability Scale (Crowne & Marlowe, 1964) was used to measure the tendency of participants to describe themselves in favorable, socially desirable terms.

Immediate Results. Analyses of covariance, controlling for preintervention measures, revealed that adolescents who received the HIV risk-reduction intervention subsequently had greater AIDS knowledge, less favorable attitudes toward HIV risk-associated sexual behaviors, and reduced intentions for such behaviors, compared with adolescents in the control condition. In addition, they expressed more favorable hedonistic beliefs and stronger perceived behavioral control regarding condom use than did their counterparts in the control condition. In sum, these analyses on postintervention data make clear that we achieved changes on theoretically relevant variables thought to mediate behavior change immediately after the intervention.

Follow-Up Methods and Findings. The next question was whether the intervention resulted in less risky behavior. The 3-month follow-up assessment was designed to address this question.

An important threat to the validity of studies such as ours involving several data collection points is the possibility of participant attrition, particularly differential attrition from conditions. Attrition reduces generalizability and differential attrition from conditions clouds causal interpretation of treatment effects. We allocated participant reimbursement to increase the likelihood that participants would return for the follow-up. The participants could receive a total of $40. They received $15 at the end of the intervention session, which involved an 8-hour time commitment, and they received $25 at the 3-month follow-up, which involved a 2-hour commitment.

Questions are sometimes raised about paying participants in HIV intervention studies. However, we believe that an important advantage

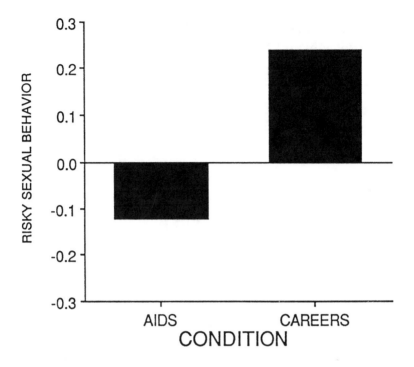

Figure 7.2.   Mean adjusted risky sexual behavior scores at the 3-month follow-up for African American male adolescents in two conditions.

of paying the participants is that it increases the diversity of the sample. If participants are not paid, then only those highly interested in risk reduction are likely to volunteer. By reimbursing participants, we recruited not only the highly interested but also those who were volunteering just for the money—hence, a broader population.

Of the original participants, 150 completed follow-up questionnaires three months after the intervention, a return rate of 95.5%. The return rate did not differ between conditions. Analysis of covariance, controlling for preintervention sexual behavior, indicated that adolescents in the HIV risk-reduction condition reported less HIV risk-associated sexual behavior in the 3 months after the intervention than did those in the control condition. This analysis was done on a composite score of risky sexual behavior, which combined responses to several sexual

Table 7.1
Adjusted Means for Specific Sexual Behaviors
During Last Three Months, by Experimental Condition

Sexual behavior	HIV risk-reduction condition	Career-opportunities condition	p
Coitus (0 = N, 1 = Y)	0.5	0.6	ns
Days had coitus (range = 0-50)	2.2	5.5	.008
Coital partners (range = 0-9)	0.9	1.8	.003
Rated condom-use frequency (1 = Never, 5 = Always)	4.4	3.5	.02
Days did not use condom during coitus (range = 0-19)	0.6	2.4	.003
Heterosexual anal sex (0 = N, 1 = Y)	0.1	0.3	.02

NOTE: For each variable, the preintervention measure is partialled out of the 3-month follow-up measure.

behavior questions. Because the behaviors had different means and standard deviations, the responses were standardized to z-scores, and the composite score was the mean z-score. The adjusted means are shown in Figure 7.2.

Additional analyses were performed on the specific behaviors that comprised the composite risky sexual behavior score. As shown in Table 7.1, the participants in the HIV risk-reduction condition, compared with those in the control condition, reported having coitus less frequently and with fewer women, reported using condoms more consistently during coitus, and fewer of them reported engaging in heterosexual anal intercourse. In addition, the HIV risk-reduction intervention participants still had greater AIDS knowledge and weaker intentions for risky behavior in the next three months than did the other participants. The Marlowe-Crowne Social Desirability Scale scores were unrelated to self-reports of risky sexual behavior at preintervention and at the 3-month follow-up, and also to the amount of change in these reports. In addition, the social desirability scores were unrelated to pre, post, or follow-up intentions and attitudes or to changes in these variables.

Interactions With Gender of Facilitator. We had expected Condition x Gender of Facilitator interactions such that the effects of the HIV risk-reduction intervention would be enhanced with facilitators who

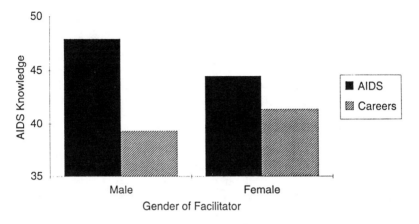

Figure 7.3.   Mean adjusted postintervention AIDS knowledge among African American male adolescents by condition and gender of facilitator.

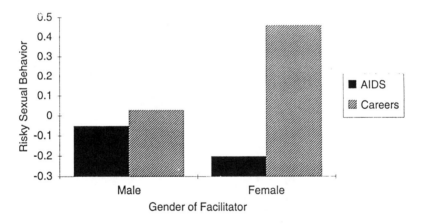

Figure 7.4.   Mean adjusted risky sexual behavior scores at the 3-month follow-up for African American male adolescents, by condition and gender of facilitator.

were African American males. Surprisingly, we did not find consistent support for this hypothesis. Consonant with the hypothesis, analyses on the postintervention questionnaire revealed a Condition x Gender of

Facilitator interaction such that the HIV risk-reduction intervention caused a greater increase in AIDS knowledge among participants who had a male facilitator than among those who had a female facilitator (see Figure 7.3). On the other hand, this interaction was not evident on postintervention measures of hedonistic beliefs, attitudes, perceived behavioral control, or intentions, or 3-month follow-up AIDS knowledge. In addition, the effects of the HIV risk-reduction intervention on attitudes and sexual behavior measured at the 3-month follow-up were significantly *stronger* with female facilitators than with male facilitators, which was opposite to the predicted result (see Figure 7.4).

Implications. This initial study indicated that a relatively brief intervention can have an effect on theory-based mediators of behavior change and self-reported HIV risk-associated sexual behaviors among African American adolescents. Since this study, our research has proceeded in two directions. The study raised the question of whether particular conceptual variables are especially important to achieving behavior change. Thus, one line of work sought to identify the particular conceptual variables that are most important to achieving intervention-induced sexual behavior change. In addition, the lack of consistent effects of facilitator gender and the fact that the study included only male adolescents left unanswered some practical questions about the best way to intervene with inner-city African American adolescents to reduce their risk of HIV infection. Thus, a second line of research sought to elucidate whether the effectiveness of HIV interventions is moderated by characteristics of facilitators such as gender and race.

Studies on Conceptual
Variables in Intervention

Research With African American Females. Jemmott, Jemmott, Spears, Hewitt, and Cruz-Collins (1992) conducted a study that focused on the conceptual variables that mediate African American female adolescents' intentions to use condoms. These authors compared the effects on condom-use intentions of three interventions: (a) a social-cognitive intervention designed to increase hedonistic beliefs and perceived behavioral control regarding condoms, (b) an information-alone intervention designed to increase general AIDS knowledge and specific prevention beliefs, and (c) a general health-promotion intervention designed to provide information about health problems other than AIDS. The subjects were 19 sexually active African American adolescent women from an inner-city family planning clinic. As in the Jemmott, Jemmott, and Fong (1992) study, all interventions lasted the same amount of time and involved the use of videos and small group exercises and games.

Analysis of covariance revealed that, although participants in both the social-cognitive condition and the information-alone condition scored significantly higher in AIDS knowledge and prevention beliefs than did those in the health-promotion condition, participants in the social-cognitive condition registered significantly greater intentions to use condoms than did those in the other two conditions. In addition, participants in the social-cognitive condition, as compared with the other conditions, reported significantly greater perceived self-efficacy/ behavioral control and more favorable hedonistic beliefs, the two hypothesized mediators of the effects of the intervention on condom-use intentions. The findings indicated that intervention-induced increases in AIDS knowledge and prevention beliefs do not portend changes in plans for risky behavior. In addition, it highlighted the importance of self-efficacy and hedonistic expectancies. Because the sample size of the study was small, it might be argued that the implications are limited. However, significance tests take sample size into account, and therefore the fact that the intervention had significant effects on intentions and other theoretically relevant variables is impressive.

In another study bearing on conceptual variables, Jemmott and Jemmott (1992) evaluated an HIV risk-reduction prevention program for inner-city adolescent women implemented by a community-based organization, the Urban League of Metropolitan Trenton. The 3-session, 5-hour HIV risk-reduction program drew on the two studies previously described and used many of the same activities. The intervention, implemented by an African American female facilitator, addressed perceived behavioral control, hedonistic beliefs, and prevention beliefs. After the program, as compared with before it, the 109 adolescent women who participated in the program scored higher in AIDS knowledge, registered more favorable prevention beliefs and hedonistic beliefs, expressed greater self-efficacy/perceived behavioral control, and scored higher in intention to use condoms. Additional analyses indicated that increases in perceived self-efficacy/behavioral control and hedonistic beliefs predicted increases in intentions to use condoms, whereas increases in general AIDS knowledge and specific prevention beliefs did not.

One weakness of this study was that the changes in intentions might reflect external (group) history effects rather than intervention effects. However, Jemmott and Jemmott (1992) reasoned that history was an unlikely explanation because the women participated in intervention groups that were run sequentially over a 6-month period. In this view, it is unlikely that events beyond the intervention activities could have occurred consistently between preintervention and postintervention for these multiple intervention groups so as to increase their scores. Also, history could not easily account for the differential predictive power of perceived self-efficacy and hedonistic beliefs as compared with AIDS knowledge and prevention beliefs. However, the fact that the study did not include a control group that did not receive HIV risk-reduction interventions limits the ability to draw causal inferences about intervention effects.

Jemmott, Jemmott, and Hacker (1992) tested the theory of planned behavior as a model of intention to use condoms among 179 inner-city adolescents (72% African American and 19% Latino) who attended a minority youth health conference organized by the Urban League of Metropolitan Trenton. Participants completed a confidential preconference questionnaire. Hierarchical multiple regression analysis was used to test the theory of planned behavior. In the first step, condom-use intentions were regressed on attitudes and subjective norms. The squared multiple correlation ($R^2 = .31$) was statistically significant, as were the regression coefficients for attitudes and subjective norms. According to the theory of reasoned action, only attitudes and subjective norms have direct effects on intentions. Thus, perceived behavioral control should not be significantly related to intentions if attitudes and subjective norms are in the regression equation. However, consistent with the theory of planned behavior, in step 2 of the hierarchical regression analysis, perceived behavioral control contributed a significant increment (.19) to the squared multiple correlation. Behavioral beliefs about the effects of condoms on sexual enjoyment, normative beliefs regarding sexual partners' and mothers' approval, and control beliefs regarding technical skill at using condoms were significantly associated with condom-use intentions. These results suggest the usefulness of the theory of planned behavior for understanding condom-use decisions among inner-city African American adolescents.

Research on Characteristics of Facilitators

A second line of our research focused on practical questions about the best way to intervene with inner-city African American adolescents. One issue of interest was further study of the effects of the facilitator's gender. This variable did not have consistent effects in the Jemmott, Jemmott, and Fong (1992) study, but that may have been because the study only included male adolescents. Perhaps gender of facilitator might be more important if the intervention participants were female adolescents. The literature on disclosure of personal information suggests that men and women prefer to discuss personal or embarrassing information with a woman rather than a man, and that this preference for female confidants is particularly strong among women (Bennett & Dickinson, 1980; Noller & Callan, 1990).

A second issue of interest was the race of the facilitator. We tested the hypothesis that an intervention with African American adolescents would be more effective if the facilitator were African American rather than White. A third issue the study addressed was the gender composition of the group. Interventions dealing with sexual behavior of adolescents may be more effective if implemented in single-sex groups. Further, the advantage of single-sex groups may be particularly great for female adolescents. We tested whether the effectiveness of the intervention would vary depending on whether the group contained participants of only one gender or both male and female adolescents (Jemmott, Jemmott, & Fong, 1995).

The participants in this study were 506 7th- and 8th-grade African American adolescents recruited from the public junior high schools and elementary schools of Trenton, New Jersey. They volunteered for a "Health Promotion Project" designed to reduce the chances that teenagers will develop devastating health problems, including cardiovascular disease, cancer, and AIDS. Although the mean age of the participants was only 13.1 years, about 55% reported having experienced coitus at least once, and about 31% of all respondents reported having coitus in the past 3 months. About 25% of those reporting coitus in the past 3 months indicated that they never used condoms during those experiences, whereas 30% indicated they had always used condoms during that period.

The participants were assigned randomly to either an HIV risk-reduction condition or the control condition; within these conditions they were randomly assigned to a small group that was either homogeneous or heterogeneous in gender and that was led by either a male or female facilitator who was either African American or White. All facilitators were specially trained as in our previous research. Adolescents in the HIV risk-reduction condition received a 5-hour intervention designed to influence variables theoretically important to behavior change and to be meaningful and culturally and developmentally appropriate for young inner-city African American adolescents. From a theoretical perspective, the intervention was designed (a) to increase perceived self-efficacy/behavioral control regarding the ability to implement condom use, including confidence that they could get their partner to use one; (b) to address hedonistic beliefs to allay participants' fears regarding adverse consequences of condoms on sexual enjoyment; and (c) to increase general knowledge of AIDS and STDs and specific beliefs regarding the use of condoms to prevent sexually transmitted HIV infection. As in our previous intervention studies, video-tapes, games, and exercises were used to facilitate learning and active participation.

Participants in the control condition received an intervention targeting behaviors (e.g., dietary and exercise habits and cigarette smoking) that affect the risk of certain health problems other than AIDS. These health problems, including cardiovascular disease, hypertension, and certain cancers, are leading causes of morbidity and mortality among African Americans (Gillum, 1982; Ibrahim, Chobanian, Horan, & Roccella, 1985; Page & Asire, 1985). Structurally similar to the HIV risk-reduction intervention, the general health-promotion intervention also lasted 5 hours and used culturally and developmentally appropriate videotapes, exercises, and games to reinforce learning and to encourage active participation.

Measurements were obtained from participants in both intervention conditions before, immediately after, 3 months after, and 6 months after the intervention. These questionnaires covered their intentions, hedonistic beliefs, prevention beliefs, perceived self-efficacy to use condoms, and AIDS knowledge. Also, the Marlowe-Crowne Social Desirability Scale, included in the preintervention questionnaire, was used to measure the tendency of participants to describe themselves in favorable, socially desirable terms.

Immediate Results. Scores on the postintervention measures were controlled for the preintervention measures of the particular dependent variable. These analyses found that adolescents in the HIV risk-reduction condition subsequently expressed stronger intentions to use condoms; had more favorable beliefs about the effects of condoms on sexual enjoyment and about the ability of condoms to prevent pregnancy, STD, and AIDS; had greater perceived self-efficacy to use condoms; and had greater knowledge about AIDS than did those in the control condition.

Follow-Up Results. Of the original participants, 489 (97%) took part in the 3-month follow-up and 469 (93%) took part in the 6-month follow-up. The effects of the HIV risk-reduction intervention on the conceptual variables were sustained over the 6-month time interval. At both follow-ups, participants in the HIV risk-reduction intervention scored higher on intentions to use condoms, AIDS knowledge, hedonistic beliefs, and perceived self-efficacy to use condoms than did the participants in the health-promotion condition. Although there were no significant effects of the HIV risk-reduction intervention on self-reports of unprotected coitus at the 3-month follow-up, there was a significant effect at the 6-month follow-up: Adolescents who had received the HIV risk-reduction intervention reported fewer days on which they had coitus without using a condom in the past 3 months than did those who had received the health-promotion intervention, again controlling for preintervention self-reports.

Pearson product-moment correlations and multiple regression analyses revealed that scores on the Marlowe-Crowne Social Desirability Scale were unrelated to self-reports of condom use at the preintervention phase, at the 3-month follow-up, or at the 6-month follow-up, or to changes in self-reports of condom use from preintervention to the 3-month or 6-month follow-up. Marlowe-Crowne Social Desirability scores were also unrelated to pre, post, 3-month follow-up, and 6-month follow-up intentions to use condoms, or to changes in intentions. Moreover, hierarchical multiple regression analyses showed that the social desirability scores did not interact with the experimental condition to affect self-reported condom use or intentions at the post-intervention, 3-month follow-up, or 6-month follow-up. The social desirability scores were also unrelated to self-reported condom use, intentions, or changes in these variables within the subsample of adolescents in the HIV risk-reduction condition.

Interactions With Race and Gender. Analyses also examined whether effects of the intervention varied as a function of race of the facilitator, gender of the facilitator, gender of the participants, and gender composition of the intervention groups. There were a large number of interactions that could be tested in this study. However, we limited our tests to eight specific interaction hypotheses that are of theoretical and practical importance, asking if each of these interactions was significant: First, the Condition x Facilitator Gender interaction: for example, are the effects of the HIV risk-reduction intervention enhanced if the facilitator is a woman as compared with a man? Second, the Condition x Facilitator Race interaction: Are the effects of the HIV risk-reduction intervention enhanced if the facilitator is African American as compared to White? Third, the Condition x Gender Composition interaction: Are the effects of the HIV risk-reduction intervention enhanced in single-gender as compared to mixed-gender groups? Fourth, the Condition x Gender Composition x Participant Gender interaction: Are the effects of the HIV risk-reduction intervention stronger in single-gender as compared to mixed-gender groups, particularly among female adolescents? Fifth, the Condition x Facilitator Gender x Participant Gender interaction: Are the effects of the HIV risk-reduction intervention enhanced if the gender of the participant and the facilitator is matched? Sixth, the Condition x Facilitator Gender x Participant Gender x Facilitator Race interaction: Are the effects of the HIV risk-reduction intervention stronger when the gender of the participant and the facilitator is matched and the facilitator is African American? Seventh, the Condition x Facilitator Gender x Participant Gender x Gender Composition interaction: Are the effects of the HIV risk-reduction intervention stronger when the gender of the participant and facilitator is matched and the group is single-gender? Eighth, the Condition x Facilitator Gender x Participant Gender x Gender Composition x Facilitator Race interaction: Are the effects of the HIV risk-reduction intervention stronger when the gender of the participant and the facilitator is matched and the group is single-gender and the facilitator is African American?

We tested these specific interaction hypotheses on four classes of variables: (a) the participants' perceptions of the intervention—how much they liked it, how much they talked, and how much they felt they learned; (b) the facilitators' perceptions of how much the subjects liked it, talked, and learned from the intervention; (c) the AIDS knowledge test, prevention beliefs, hedonistic beliefs, intentions, and perceived behavioral control; and (d) self-reported unprotected sexual intercourse. Despite the relatively large number of interactions tested—which would have increased the likelihood of a Type I error—none of the interactions were statistically significant. Thus, these factors did not moderate facilitators' reports of how the participants reacted to the intervention, nor participants' own reports of their reactions to the interventions, nor participants' AIDS knowledge, prevention beliefs, hedonistic beliefs, perceived self-efficacy, intentions, or self-reports of unprotected coitus. The effects of the HIV risk-reduction intervention were about the same irrespective of the race of the facilitator, the gender of the facilitator, the gender of the participants, and the gender composition of the intervention group.

Implications

The preceding studies suggest that intensive one-day interventions can influence theory-based motivational determinants of HIV risk-associated behavior among inner-city African American adolescents, including African American male adolescents. Second, the studies suggest that it is possible to influence self-reports of unprotected coitus among inner-city African American adolescents, including African American male adolescents. Third, the results suggest that the influence of the race and gender of facilitators or health educators may be more complex than previously assumed. Fourth, additional research is needed on other practical aspects of HIV prevention interventions: For example, are abstinence-based interventions more effective than safer-sex interventions? Are peer educators more effective than adult educators? Fifth, the results highlight the importance of culturally sensitive interventions.

The lack of effects of the facilitator's race is particularly surprising. In theory, African American facilitators should have a better grasp of the language, values, and experiences of African American adolescents, they should be better able to adapt prevention strategies to suit the adolescents, they should be less likely to offend the adolescents by using inaccurate and pernicious group stereotypes, and they should be able to establish rapport more readily and rapidly. All this should presumably translate into better intervention outcomes yet we found that race matching did not enhance intervention effects. One possible explanation for this is that race matching is less important than previously assumed.

However, a number of additional explanations should also be considered. Perhaps the race matching did not matter because the intervention itself was culturally sensitive. All of the intervention materials had been selected to be culturally appropriate. Second, the activities were highly structured and engaging, which would have minimized the importance of individual facilitators. Third, all facilitators trained together, which may have served to calibrate their behavior. The training of the facilitators emphasized the importance of implementing the interventions according to the protocol, which might have further minimized any differences between facilitators from different racial groups. Thus, the culturally sensitive nature of the intervention and the strict nature of the facilitator training protocol may have attenuated any effects of facilitator race. In the absence of such training, or if culturally inappropriate materials had been used, or if the intervention had been less highly structured, differences in facilitator behavior by race might have occurred. Under such circumstances, results might have been different from those observed in the present study. Of course, this is an empirical question that can only be answered by further research.

The significant effects of the interventions studied cannot be explained as a simple result of special attention received by the adolescents in the HIV risk-reduction intervention conditions. Participants in the control conditions (whether focusing on career opportunities or general health-promotion) received the same amount of attention, went through similar activities, and spent the same amount of time as those in the HIV risk-reduction condition.

By its very nature, HIV risk-associated sexual behavior is private behavior and consequently must be assessed with indirect measures. Hence, in our studies, self-reports of HIV risk-associated sexual behaviors, not the behaviors themselves, were examined. Thus, interpretations of findings should include consideration of the possibility that the participants' reports of their sexual practices might have been to some degree unintentionally or intentionally inaccurate. On several grounds, however, confidence about the accuracy of the responses in these experiments seems warranted. The fact that participants were asked to recall HIV risk-associated sexual behavior over a relatively brief period of time (i.e., 3 months) would facilitate their ability to recall their behavior. In addition, we employed a number of techniques to make it less likely that participants in these studies would minimize or exaggerate reports of their sexual experiences: (a) code numbers rather than names were used on the questionnaires, (b) facilitators were not involved in any way in the administration of questionnaires, (c) the importance of responding honestly was emphasized, (d) participants were assured that their responses would be kept confidential, and (e) they signed an agreement to respond honestly. In addition, if concern about how they would be viewed by others had influenced respondents' reports of their sexual behavior, the adolescents who were higher in the need for social approval might have differed from the other participants in self-reported HIV risk-associated sexual behavior or in the amount of change in their reports after the HIV risk-reduction intervention. However, analyses in two studies revealed that preintervention and follow-up self-reports of HIV risk-associated sexual behavior and the amount of change in these reports were unrelated to social desirability response bias (Jemmott, Jemmott, & Fong, 1992, 1995). Nevertheless, interpretations of our findings should include consideration of the possibility that the participants' self-reports might have been inaccurate.

In future research it would be valuable to include other measures of sexual behavior. Another approach to assessing sexual behavior would be to measure physiological proxy variables that are indicative of unprotected sexual intercourse. For example, clinically documented data regarding STDs (e.g., chlamydia, gonorrhea, syphilis) would provide valuable information. Still, it should be noted, even STD testing is not a perfect measure of unprotected sexual intercourse because it *underestimates* the actual frequency of unprotected sexual intercourse. Although a positive STD test establishes that unprotected sexual intercourse has occurred, a negative test result does not rule out that possibility. The test could be negative not because of the practice of safer sex or abstinence but because of unprotected sex with a partner who was not infected, or unprotected sex without catching the partner's infection.

One common argument against HIV risk-reduction education programs for adolescents and children has been that exposing them to information about sex will encourage them to engage in sexual activity. Our data, however, provide some evidence that the *opposite* may be true. Adolescents who received the HIV risk-reduction intervention were *less* likely to engage in sexual activity and those who did were more likely to engage in safe sexual activity. Thus, the fear that providing adolescents with information about AIDS will result in greater sexual activity may be unwarranted. In a future study, we plan to include interventions both for parents (because mothers are an important normative influence) and for adolescents.

Given the widely recognized potential risk of sexually transmitted HIV among inner-city African American adolescents, the results of these studies are encouraging. The findings of the experiments suggest that relatively brief but intensive interventions can have a significant effect on HIV risk behavior and on theory-based mediators of such behavior among African American inner-city adolescents. We are optimistic that continued work along these line will increase understanding of the social psychology of HIV risk-associated behavior and will help to curtail the spread of AIDS.

References

Ajzen, I. (1985). From intentions to actions: A theory of planned behavior. In J. Kuhl & J. Beckmann (Eds.), *Action-control: From cognition to behavior* (pp. 11-39). Heidelberg: Springer.

Ajzen, I. (1991). The theory of planned behavior. *Organizational Behavior and Human Decision Processes, 50,* 179-211.

Ajzen, I., & Fishbein, M. (1980). *Understanding attitudes and predicting social behavior.* Englewood Cliffs, NJ: Prentice-Hall.

Ajzen, I., & Madden, T. (1986). Prediction of goal-directed behavior: Attitudes, intentions, and perceived behavioral control. *Journal of Experimental Social Psychology, 22,* 453-74.

Bandura, A. (1986). *Social foundations of thought and action: A social cognitive theory.* Englewood Cliffs, NJ: Prentice-Hall.

Bandura, A. (1989). Perceived self-efficacy. In V. M. Mays, G. W. Albee, & S. F. Schneider (Eds.), *Primary prevention of AIDS: Psychological approaches* (pp. 128-141). Newbury Park, CA: Sage.

Bandura, A. (1994). Social cognitive theory and exercise of control over HIV infection. In R. DiClemente & J. Peterson (Eds.), *Preventing AIDS: Theory and practice of behavioral interventions* (pp. 25-60). New York: Plenum.

Bell, T. A., & Holmes, K. K. (1984). Age-specific risks of syphilis, gonorrhea, and hospitalized pelvic inflammatory disease in sexually experienced U.S. women. *Sexually Transmitted Diseases, 7,* 291.

Bennett, S. M., & Dickinson, W. B. (1980). Student-parent rapport and parent involvement in sex, birth control, and venereal disease education. *Journal of Sex Research, 16,* 114-130.

Cates, W., Jr. (1987). Epidemiology and control of sexually transmitted diseases: Strategic evolution. *Infectious Disease Clinics of North America, 1,* 1-23.

Centers for Disease Control. (1990). *National HIV seroprevalence surveys: Summary of results: Data from serosurveillance activities through 1989.* Atlanta: Center for Infectious Disease, Author.

Centers for Disease Control and Prevention (CDC). (1995). *HIV/AIDS Surveillance Report, 7*(1), 1-34.

Chu, S., Buehler, J., & Berkelman, R. (1990). Impact of the human immunodeficiency virus epidemic on mortality in women of reproductive age. *Journal of the American Medical Association, 264,* 225-229.

Crowne, D., & Marlowe, D. (1964). *The approval motive.* New York: Wiley.

Davidson, A. R. & Jaccard, J. J. (1979). Variables that moderate the attitude-behavior relation: Results of a longitudinal survey. *Journal of Personality and Social Psychology, 37,* 1364-1376.

Fishbein, M. (1982). Social psychological analysis of smoking behavior. In J. R. Eiser (Ed.), *Social psychology and behavioral medicine* (pp. 179-197). New York: Wiley.

Fishbein, M., & Ajzen, I. (1975). *Belief, attitude, intention, and behavior: An introduction to theory and research.* Boston: Addison-Wesley.

Fishbein, M., & Middlestadt, S. (1989). Using the theory of reasoned action as a framework for understanding and changing AIDS-related behaviors. In V. Mays, G. Albee, & S. Schneider (Eds.), *Primary prevention of AIDS: Psychological approaches* (pp. 93-110). Newbury Park, CA: Sage.

Fishbein, M., Middlestadt, S., & Hitchcock, P. J. (1994). Using information to change sexually transmitted disease-related behaviors: An analysis based on the theory of reasoned action. In R. DiClemente & J. Peterson (Eds.), *Preventing AIDS: Theory and practice of behavioral interventions* (pp. 61-78). New York: Plenum.

Fisher, W. A. (1984). Predicting contraceptive behavior among university men: The roles of emotions and behavioral intentions. *Journal of Applied Social Psychology, 14,* 104-123.

Gillum, R. F. (1982). Coronary heart disease in Black populations: I. Mortality and morbidity. *American Heart Journal, 104,* 839-843.

Hatcher, R. A., Trussell, J., Stewart, F., Stewart, G. K., Kowal, D., Guest, F., Cates, W., Jr., & Policar, M. S. (1994). *Contraceptive technology* (16th rev. ed.). New York: Irvington.

Ibrahim, M., Chobanian, A. V., Horan, M., & Roccella, E. J. (1985). Hypertension prevalence and the status of awareness, treatment, and control in the United States: Final report of the Subcommittee on Definition and Prevalence of the 1984 Joint National Committee on Detection, Evaluation, and Treatment of High Blood Pressure. *Hypertension, 7,* 453-468.

Jemmott, J. B., III, & Jemmott, L. S. (1994). Interventions for adolescents in community settings. In R. DiClemente & J. Peterson (Eds.), *Preventing AIDS: Theory and practice of behavioral interventions* (pp. 141-174). New York: Plenum.

Jemmott, J. B., III, Jemmott, L. S., & Fong, G. T. (1992). Reductions in HIV risk-associated sexual behaviors among Black male adolescents: Effects of an AIDS prevention intervention. *American Journal of Public Health, 82,* 372-377.

Jemmott, J. B., III, Jemmott, L. S., & Fong, G. T. (1995). *Reducing the risk of AIDS in Black adolescents: Evidence for the generality of intervention effects.* Unpublished manuscript, Princeton University.

Jemmott, J. B., III, Jemmott, L. S., & Hacker, C. I. (1992). Predicting intentions to use condoms among African American adolescents: The theory of planned behavior as a model of HIV risk associated behavior. *Journal of Ethnicity and Disease, 2,* 371-380.

Jemmott, J. B., III, Jemmott, L. S., Spears, H., Hewitt, N., & Cruz-Collins, M. (1992). Self-efficacy, hedonistic expectancies, and condom-use intentions among inner-city Black adolescent women: A social cognitive approach to AIDS risk behavior. *Journal of Adolescent Health, 13,* 512-519.

Jemmott, J. B., III, & Jones, J. M. (1993). Social psychology and AIDS among ethnic minority individuals: Risk behaviors and strategies for changing them. In J. B. Pryor & G. D. Reeder (Eds.), *The social psychology of HIV infection.* Hillsdale, NJ: Erlbaum.

Jemmott, J. B., III, & Miller, S. M. (in press). Women's reproductive decisions in the context of HIV infection. In A. O'Leary & L. S. Jemmott (Eds.), *Women and AIDS: Issues in coping and caring.* New York: Plenum.

Jemmott, J. B., III, Sanderson, C., & Miller, S. M. (1995). Changes in psychological distress and HIV risk-associated behavior: Consequences of HIV antibody testing? In R. T. Croyle (Ed.), *Psychosocial effects of screening for disease prevention and detection* (pp. 82-125). New York: Plenum.

Jemmott, L. S., & Jemmott, J. B., III. (1992). Increasing condom-use intentions among sexually active inner-city Black adolescent women: Effects of an AIDS prevention program. *Nursing Research, 41,* 273-279.

Jones, E. F., Forrest, J. D., Goldman, N., Henshaw, S., Lincoln, R., Rosoff, J. I., Westoff, C. F., & Wulf, D. (1986). *Teenage pregnancy in industrialized countries.* New Haven, CT: Yale University Press.

Madden, T. J., Ellen, P. S., & Ajzen, I. (1992). A comparison of the theory of planned behavior and the theory of reasoned action. *Personality and Social Psychology Bulletin, 18,* 3-9.

Manstead, A. S. R., Profitt, C., & Smart, J. L. (1983). Predicting and understanding mothers' infant-feeding intentions and behaviors. *Journal of Applied Social Psychology, 14,* 104-123.

National Center for Health Statistics. (1993). *Annual summary of births, marriages, divorces, and deaths: United States, 1992* (monthly vital statistics report, Vol. 42, No. 2, suppl.). Hyattsville, MD: U.S. Department of Health and Human Services, Public Health Service.

Noller, P., & Callan, V. J. (1990). Adolescents' perceptions of the nature of their communication with parents. *Journal of Youth and Adolescence, 19,* 349-362.

O'Leary, A. (1985). Self-efficacy and health. *Behavioral Research and Therapy, 23,* 437-451.

Page, H. S., & Asire, A. J. (1985). *Cancer rates and risks* (3rd ed.) (NIH Publication No. 85-691). Bethesda, MD: National Institutes of Health.

Pratt, W., Mosher, W., Bachrach, C., & Horn, M. (1984). Understanding U.S. fertility: Findings from the National Survey of Family Growth, cycle III. *Population Bulletin, 39,* 1-42.

Rogers, R. (1983). Cognitive and physiological processes in fear appeals and attitude change: A revised theory of protection motivation. In J. Cacioppo & R. Petty (Eds.), *Social psychophysiology: A sourcebook* (pp. 153-176). New York: Guilford.

Rosenstock, I. M. (1990). The health belief model: Explaining health behavior through expectancies. In K. Glanz, F. M. Lewis, & B. K. Rimer (Eds.), *Health behavior and health education: Theory, research, and practice* (pp. 39-62). San Francisco: Jossey-Bass.

Schifter, D. E. & Ajzen, I. (1985). Intention, perceived control, and weight loss: An application of the theory of planned behavior. *Journal of Personality and Social Psychology, 49,* 843-851.

The subject is AIDS [film]. (Available from Select Media, 60 Warren Street, New York, NY 10007.)

Temko, C. (1987). Seeking medical care for a breast cancer symptom: Determinants of intentions to engage in prompt or delay behavior. *Health Psychology, 6,* 305-328.

U.S. Bureau of the Census. (1989). Projections of the population of the United States, by age, sex, and race: 1988-2080. *Current Population Reports* (Series P-25, No. 1018). Washington, DC: U.S. Government Printing Office.

8

Cultural Issues in HIV Prevention for Latinos: Should We Try To Change Gender Roles?

BARBARA VANOSS MARÍN

Human behavior, including sexual behavior, has many meanings that help explain why a person may not behave "logically" at all times. In concentration camps, when hungry prisoners give their last ration of food to a sick or dying stranger, one must look beyond logic to the meaning for them of that act (Frankl, 1992). A commercial sex worker who consistently uses condoms with "tricks" but refuses to use them with a drug-using "primary" partner illustrates some of the meanings of sex: as a job or monetary transaction as opposed to an act of love, caring, or intimacy. So, the meanings that someone assigns to a particular sex act can tell us much about their motivations and can help us to understand seemingly "irrational" behavior.

Culture is a particularly important source of meanings both because it is pervasive and because the power of those meanings is often unrecognized. *Culture* can be defined as a shared set of meanings that are held by a group. The meanings are so commonly held that they are generally unquestioned within the group, even though outsiders may

AUTHOR'S NOTE: This chapter was supported in part by grants from the National Institute of Mental Health, No. MH46789 and MH51515.

find them puzzling. They are so unquestioned, in fact, that members of the group may be unable to understand others who do not share those meanings. A simple example would be a behavior that has very different meanings in different cultural contexts. Joining the tips of the thumb and forefinger to form an "o" means "OK" in one culture and is a sexual symbol with a "dirty" meaning in another. Thus, a person from one culture may use the sign without realizing the difference in meaning and be confused by the shock it evokes. More important, cultures transmit values that powerfully influence how their members behave and how they perceive others' behavior.

Given this, it is surprising how little attention has been paid to the issues of culture and meaning in research on condom use. Since the early and mid-1980s, scientists and activists have been struggling to help an ever-widening number of people change their sexual behavior to include a small piece of latex. Initially, many interventions naively assumed that providing information to people about a deadly virus would be sufficient to change behavior. Soon it was recognized that certain skills would also be needed, including not only how to put on a condom, but also negotiation skills. This emphasis on skills has been derived from cognitive models of behavior change (Bandura, 1986; Catania, Kegeles, & Coates, 1990; Fishbein & Ajzen, 1975; Fisher & Fisher, 1992).

Although skill-based approaches have shown some important successes (e.g., Kelly et al., 1994), sexual behavior—being emotional, physical, and dyadic, much more than cognitive—has been only partially understood using these models. Amaro (1995) has suggested that there are four issues that must be included in future theoretical models attempting to explain women's risk behaviors: (1) women's social status as a central feature of women's risk, (2) the importance of connection for women, (3) male partners' key role in women's risk, and (4) women's experience of fear and abuse. She strongly points to the importance of gender-role socialization of both men and women as a determinant of women's risk. This chapter explores data we have obtained that also suggest the importance of traditional gender-role ideas in the sexual risk behavior of Latinos, both men and women.

I will begin by identifying the sources of data used in this chapter and then review the evidence that the cultural meanings of gender roles among Latinos may have an important effect on sexual behavior. Gender roles dictate how men and women are expected to behave in relation to sexuality and many other aspects of their lives, and they have important relationships to sexual comfort and sexual coercion. Finally, I will discuss important implications of these findings for HIV-prevention interventions.

Data Sources

Dr. Cynthia Gómez and I have been engaged in a program of research on Latino sexuality relevant to HIV prevention over the past 5 years. During that time we have conducted both qualitative and quantitative research, which provide the data for this chapter. As part of the qualitative research, and to develop culturally sensitive survey instruments for the following two surveys, focus groups were conducted separately with Latino men or women during the fall of 1990 and the fall of 1992. Focus groups (8 with men and 8 with women) conducted in both San Francisco and Boston encouraged participants to discuss how sex was treated during their childhood, issues in sexual communication, reasons for not using condoms, likely consequences of using or not using condoms, gender-role beliefs, and other topics. Focus groups were conducted in both English and Spanish.

An additional 10 focus groups were conducted in the spring of 1995 to assist us in developing an HIV-prevention intervention for middle school students in heavily Latino schools. Six of these groups involved exclusively Latino students whereas the other groups were of mixed ethnicity; four were conducted with adolescent girls and six with boys.

Spring 1991 Telephone Survey

In the spring of 1991 we conducted a telephone survey with a stratified random sample of Latino households in nine states with concentrations of Latinos ranging from 5% to 38%. The sampled states (New York, New Jersey, Massachusetts, and Connecticut in the Northeast, and California, Arizona, Colorado, New Mexico, and Texas in the Southwest) contain 77% of all U.S. Latinos. Latinos in the Northeast were oversampled because they have been disproportionately affected by the AIDS epidemic. A random subset of non-Latino white respondents also was interviewed. These individuals were not necessarily representative of non-Latino whites in these nine states, but rather of non-Latino whites living in areas where Latinos were found. A total of 1,592 Latinos and 692 non-Latino whites between 18 and 49 years of age were interviewed for the survey.[1]

The screening procedure involved identifying the ethnicity, gender, and age of household members. Potential respondents were asked "Do you or any of the members of your household consider yourselves to be Latinos or Hispanics?" An eligible Latino respondent in the household was selected using a random procedure known as the Kish method. Interviewers were bilingual males and females. Due to prior experience of the survey research organization (Communication Technologies, San Francisco) with Latino women who had difficulty answering questions on sexuality asked by a male interviewer, only female interviewers conducted interviews with female respondents. The interviewers were experienced and received specific training on how to ask the highly personal questions used in this research. Respondents were interviewed in the language of their choice. Interviews were conducted between March and July 1991. The final instrument was completed in an average of 24 minutes per interview and included a number of psychosocial predictors of condom use with four- or five-level response scales.

Fall 1993 Survey

In the fall of 1993 we again conducted a telephone survey, this time with unmarried Latino adults only. This survey included a representative sample of 1600 Latinos, aged 18-49, from 10 states in the Northeast and Southwest (adding Illinois and Florida and deleting Connecticut) representing 87% of Latinos in the U.S. Half-hour telephone interviews elicited detailed data not only on the sexual behavior of these respondents but also on their beliefs and attitudes about condoms and sex, their gender-role beliefs, sexual comfort, and homophobia. This survey was designed to provide more in-depth information about unmarried Latinos, the segment of the Latino population with a greater likelihood of reporting multiple sexual partners in the recent past (Marín, Gómez, & Hearst, 1993) and therefore with a greater potential for HIV risk. There were some changes in the sampling procedure and stratification that allowed sampling to occur more efficiently. The percentages reported here for individual items from this survey are based on the heterosexually active respondents only.

The Cultural Meanings of Sexual Behavior Among Latinos

"Culture is to society what memory is to individuals" (Triandis, 1994, p. 1). Culture tells us what has worked in the past and contains unstated assumptions about the way the world works, how people should act, and what actions mean. Cultural meanings of sexual behavior are learned in constant but subtle ways throughout a person's life. Many cultures may share certain meanings and individuals within a culture may differ in the extent to which they subscribe to the overriding cultural beliefs (e.g., although U.S. culture and many ethnic subgroups within the U.S. are generally homophobic, individuals vary greatly in their levels of homophobia). The ways that men and women are expected to interact with each other are strongly dictated by culture, including the ways they interact in sexual contexts.

Traditional Gender Roles

Traditional gender roles—the prescribed ways in which men and women are supposed to interact—continue to have an important effect on the meanings of sex for Latinos. Anthropological literature is surprisingly consistent in describing "machismo" and "marianismo" among Puerto Ricans (Burgos & Díaz-Perez, 1986) and Mexicans (Carrier, 1985; Goldwert, 1985; Pavich, 1986). *Machismo* refers to the cultural prescriptions for men's behavior—such expectations as being strong, having sexual prowess, and providing well for the family. *Marianismo* refers to the expectations about women's behavior—that a good woman is a virgin until marriage, passively suffers "like the Virgin," is not well-informed about sex, and is interested primarily in home and children; whereas a bad woman is sexually available but not suitable wife material. A number of authors have been uncomfortable with the simplistic generalizations of this anthropological work and have challenged the existence and prevalence of these traditional ideas (Cromwell & Ruiz, 1979; Soto, 1983; Vazquez-Nuttal, Romero-García, & DeLeon, 1987). In general, these challenges have pointed out that gender roles among Latinos are sometimes subtle and varied, and that as individuals acculturate to U.S. mainstream culture they become more egalitarian.

Our own work in focus group discussions, in addition to data from the 1993 survey of unmarried adults, confirmed the continued existence of many gender-role stereotypes, especially in sexual contexts. The distinction between "good" women and "bad" women was clear in the minds of focus group participants. Good or decent women are virgins, mothers, and essentially nonsexual, whereas bad women are sexually available and aggressive. This distinction has important implications for sexual behavior. Women who wish to conform to the cultural mandates are not supposed to know about sex, are very restricted in their sexual activity, and view sex as something dangerous and hidden. In our survey, 43% of unmarried sexually active adults (almost as many women as men) agreed that "it is important for women to be virgins at marriage," and 50% agreed that "a decent woman refuses to take part in certain sexual activities."

Sexual ambivalence, which may be a natural part of sexual encounters because of the powerful nature of sex, becomes more complicated when culture dictates that women not be sexual if they are to be good. This sexual ambivalence may also manifest itself in feelings of discomfort about sex, which are commonly reported by women. This discomfort has implications for risky behavior. For example, men in focus groups reported that if they stopped to look for a condom, the woman might change her mind.

Among Latinos, the messages that men receive about sex differ strongly from those given women. Men are expected to be passionate and to have a sexual desire that, once ignited, is beyond their control. In the 1993 survey, only 40% of the respondents agreed that "men can control their sexual desires as easily as women," whereas 36% felt that "it is harmful for men to be sexually excited without ejaculating." Men are also supposed to be dominant and knowledgeable in sexual relationships with women, so women who know as much or more than a man about sex are viewed with suspicion.

In our work with focus groups it was clear that both men and women expected men to be more passionate, which included having extramarital affairs. In actuality, our 1991 survey found that Latino married men were significantly more likely than non-Latino white married men to report multiple sexual partners in the 12 months prior to the interview (18% of Latino men vs. 9% of non-Latino white men) (Marín, Gómez, & Hearst, 1993). In the 1993 survey of unmarried adults, 42% of the sample agreed that it is more important for a man than a woman to have sexual experiences before marriage.

These findings suggest that men are expected to be sexual and women are expected to be restraining men's sex drives. If this were not enough conflict for women, an additional complication is that men generally have more power and status than women in Latino culture. This power differential puts women at a disadvantage in terms of obtaining what they desire and coping with coercion. As one example, Cunningham and her colleagues (1994), in a very large survey of Puerto Rican college students, reported that most college women they surveyed who engaged in anal intercourse did it to please their partner rather than for their own pleasure.

One must note that women often find means to get what they want and need from men and women have significant power within the family, but that power tends to be indirect and covert. There are some areas of home life in which women are considered the experts (e.g., housekeeping, child rearing, health care) and men may defer to them on decisions in those areas. However, a common scenario is for a woman to decide on something, such as changing a child's school, and then suggest it to her partner in such a way that he feels like he made the decision. Women reported in focus groups that they did this so as not to threaten the partner's need for power. Cromwell and Ruiz (1979) noted that decision making was done jointly in a majority of couples in the four studies of Latino decision making they reviewed, but that wives made fewer unilateral decisions than husbands.

Latino women are in a double bind. On one hand, they are taught to please and serve men (including their brothers) and acknowledge their dominance from early childhood, whereas at the same time, if they are sexually pleasing to men, they risk losing their virginity and status as a "good" woman. Men do not generally have this sexual ambivalence. They have been taught instead that for a man sex is an important way to prove masculinity. Díaz (in press) indicates that it is a great privilege to be a man in Latino culture but that one is not really considered a man until he proves it. Proving masculinity is commonly done through sexual conquest. To complicate matters further, 48% of men and 33% of women in the 1993 study believed that "women like dominant men."

Moving to the topic of HIV, gender-role beliefs in the sexual domain have a powerful effect on the ability of men and women to effectively prevent HIV. Women are less able to prevent exposure to HIV if they are uninformed and uncomfortable about seeking information, if they feel men make the decisions, and if they feel obliged to please men. Men may also be less able to use condoms and more likely to be coercive if they believe that they are not able to control their sexual urges.

The following sections discuss how traditional gender roles influence two important topics: comfort with sexuality and sexual coercion.

Comfort With Sexuality

The level of comfort that people feel regarding their own and others' sexual behaviors is probably determined both by gender-role beliefs and by culture more generally. Sexual comfort is the opposite of the concept of erotophobia, which has been studied by William Fisher. He found that individuals who were more erotophobic (i.e., uncomfortable with various aspects of sex) avoided sexual self-care activities such as breast self-exam, and were less likely to use condoms or birth control methods that required insertion of objects into the vagina (Fisher, 1984; Fisher, Byrne, White, & Kelley, 1988).

In our 1993 study of Latino unmarried adults, 27% of the unmarried men and 48% of the unmarried women reported that they would be uncomfortable having sex with the lights on. In the dark, it is very difficult to put condoms on or use a dental dam (latex protection for a woman who is receiving oral sex), and this fact makes sexual comfort an important prerequisite for safer sex. Several studies have now shown that Latino individuals who are more uncomfortable about sex are also less likely to buy and carry condoms (Marín & Marín, 1992; Marín, Gómez, & Tschann, 1993). For example, 14% of the Latino women in San Francisco who said they were embarrassed to buy condoms reported carrying them, compared with 29% of those who said they were not embarrassed to buy them (Marín & Marín, 1992). Among Latino heterosexual men in the 1991 survey, sexual comfort was associated with a more positive attitude toward condoms and greater self-efficacy to use condoms (Marín, Gómez, & Tschann, 1993). In Latino unmarried women in the 1993 survey, comfort with sexuality correlated .28 with self-efficacy to use condoms.

There are a number of ways that discomfort with sexuality contributes to sex being something that is "in the dark." Sexual activity that is literally in the dark can interfere with putting on a condom. But sex is also "in the dark" because it is not talked about or may be talked about constantly (particularly among men) but always in a joking fashion that is not really informative (Carrier, 1985; Carrillo, 1995). In our 1993 data set, 50% of the unmarried Latino adults who were interviewed indicated that neither of their parents had ever talked to them about sex. This lack of communication about sex probably contributes to the low levels of basic information about anatomy and other sex-related facts among Latinos reported by many investigators (Dawson, Cynamon, & Fitti, 1987; Forrest, Austin, Valdes, Fuentes, & Wilson, 1993; Marín & Marín, 1990; Padilla & Baird, 1991; Padilla & O'Grady, 1987; Scrimshaw, Carballo, Ramos, & Blair, 1991; Villas, Bouvet, & Bernal, 1992). Similarly, only 52% of Latino parents reported talking to their children about AIDS, whereas 63% of non-Latino parents had done so (CDC, 1991).

But the problem goes beyond information to meaning. For women, the silence around sex suggests that sex is something you should not know about. In our 1993 survey, 23% of these Latino adults agreed that "a man shows less respect for a woman if he talks to her about sex," and 17% believed "it is dangerous for a woman to know as much or more about sex as a man." If a woman talks about sex and condoms, appears to know how to protect herself, or is well-informed, there may be many meanings attached, such as that she is "bad," or "easy," or that she is looking for sex.

For men, the situation may not be much better. Men are even less likely than women to have received information about sex from a parent and are likely to receive much of their information from friends in the form of jokes or innuendo; yet they are expected to be experts about sex.

In our 1993 survey, we found that traditional gender role beliefs, such as "it is dangerous for a woman to know as much or more about sex as a man" were correlated with discomfort with sexuality ($r = .33$ for women and .25 for men). So, cultural messages about gender roles contribute to sexual discomfort, which in turn is associated with less efficacy to use condoms and less carrying of condoms (Marín, Gómez, & Tschann, 1993).

In sum, sexual discomfort is relatively common among Latinos and manifests itself in a number of ways including embarrassment in buying or using condoms and avoidance of talking to children about sex. Sexual discomfort has clear cultural origins in beliefs about sex as dangerous and sexual knowledge as inappropriate for women. Culture clearly influences attitudes and behaviors relevant to HIV prevention.

Sexual Coercion

One definition of sexual coercion is "the use of contingent threats or bodily force to compel a person to engage in sexual activity" (Tedeschi & Felson, 1994, p. 307). However, coercive sexual behavior is often more subtle than this description, for it may include lying or misrepresentation of affection, continually asking for sex, and verbal abuse. Situations become coercive in nature when one party is intrinsically less powerful than the other. In the case of heterosexual relationships, men are usually more powerful than women due to greater age, greater physical strength, and greater status. When men in more powerful positions insist on sex, women may acquiesce in a desire to appear "normal," to avoid being raped, or to avoid losing the partner (Gavey, 1993; Linton & Muehlenhard, 1985).

Much of the recent literature on sexual coercion has focused on mainstream college samples. These data indicate that the problem of sexual coercion is pervasive (Baier, Rosenzweig, & Whipple, 1991; Koss & Oros, 1982; Lane & Gwartney-Gibbs, 1985; Stets & Pirog-Good, 1989). Reports show that women more frequently admit having been physically forced to have sex when they did not wish it, than they admit being raped (e.g., "I've been forced into having intercourse, but I've never really felt as though I was raped"—Gavey, 1993, p. 104). In another study, men's most frequent strategies for obtaining sex when women were uninterested were verbal coercion and simply ignoring women's protests (Rapaport & Burkhard, 1984).

Traditional gender roles play an important part in sexual coercion. In a study of college males, those men who had engaged in sexual assault reported more traditional gender-role beliefs than those who had not (Muehlenhard & Linton, 1987). Several studies indicate that men who have more traditional gender-role beliefs are more accepting of forcible rape (Burt, 1980; Fischer, 1987). The power differential between Latino men and women, pressure to prove manhood through penetration, and the belief that passion is uncontrollable may lead Latino men to forcefully insist on sex when their female partner is unwilling. In our 1993 study of unmarried Latinos, 73% of sexually active women reported that during the past year a male partner had insisted on having sex when the women were not interested, and 68% of the men indicated that they had insisted on sex when their partner was not interested during the same period. In that survey, we also asked women whether they had ever been raped or sexually abused. Over 20% of the sample said yes, a figure that suggests that sexual assault is not uncommon among Latinos. Of course, even these reports are likely to be an underestimate.

Many investigators have studied race, ethnicity, social class, and family makeup factors as predictors of sexual abuse or assault. In a review of high-quality community surveys of childhood sexual abuse, Finkelhor (1993) concluded that sexual abuse was not more common among persons of lower socioeconomic status and that mixed findings concerning ethnic groups suggested that no firm conclusions could be drawn about ethnic group as a risk factor for sexual abuse. Recent studies suggest that Latinos are less likely to report sexual assault (Choi, Binson, Adelson, & Catania, 1995; Sorenson & Siegel, 1992); however, Latinos may also experience more fear of victim-blaming from the community, which would tend to discourage reporting (Lefley, Scott, Llabre, & Hicks, 1993), in addition to more fear of going to the police, especially in the current anti-immigrant climate. Thus, if reports of sexual abuse are less common among Latinos, it may be because of underreporting rather than lower levels of abuse.

As might be expected, our data show that Latino men with more traditional gender-role beliefs more frequently insisted on sex when their partner was not interested and more frequently lied to obtain sex than did men with less traditional beliefs (Gómez, Marín, & Grinstead, 1994). In fact, in factor analyses of the items regarding traditional gender-role beliefs and those measuring coercive behavior (perpetrated by the men or experienced by the women), we found that these two very different kinds of items formed a single factor. This result held true in separate analyses for the men and the women and suggests that in the minds of the respondents coercive sexual behavior was intimately linked to traditional gender roles. Thus, men who believed that men have an uncontrollable sex drive and who felt women should not know as much as men do about sex reported more coercive sexual behavior than those who subscribed to more egalitarian beliefs. In parallel, women with more traditional beliefs reported experiencing more coercive behavior from their partner than women with less traditional beliefs.

Sexual gender norms contribute to high-risk sexual activity in important ways. The ideas that discussing sex is disrespectful, that sex is uncontrollable, and that all men are highly sexual but only bad women are, can lead to greater sexual coercion on the part of Latino men and greater acceptance of that coercion on the part of women. In addition, sexual coercion may be indirectly related to less condom use. Latino women who fear that their partner will be angry if condom use is requested report using condoms less (Gómez & Marín, in press).

Implications for Intervention

Cultural meanings of sex are transmitted during the socialization process. A boy whose mother refers to his penis as *la porquería* (that dirty thing) learns important information about the meanings of sex. Although respect for and understanding of culture are vital to developing effective HIV-prevention strategies for the Latino community, such strategies may sometimes need to challenge established cultural norms and ingrained standards.

Targeting Interventions

As men and women from Latin America adjust to life in the United States, they learn English and slowly take on beliefs and customs of the mainstream culture. This process of acculturation can continue for several generations and can have a powerful effect on sexual behavior and the cultural meanings of sex, particularly for women. In one study using a language-based measure of acculturation, only 17% of the less-acculturated Latino women reported carrying condoms, whereas 44% of the highly acculturated women did so (Marín & Marín, 1992). Other work also suggests that less-acculturated women use condoms less than do highly acculturated women (Marín, Tschann, Gómez, &

Kegeles, 1993). Less-acculturated women also reported fewer sexual partners, so the overall sexual risk of women with different levels of acculturation may be difficult to determine. In work done in Los Angeles among adolescent Latino women, the less-acculturated (Mexican-born) women were found to be least likely to have had sex, but if they were sexually active they were less likely to be using any type of birth control, and if they became pregnant they were more likely to carry their pregnancy to term than their U.S.-born counterparts (Aneshensel, Becerra, Fielder, & Schuler, 1990).

In our most recent survey of unmarried Latino adults, acculturation correlated negatively with both traditional gender role (–.29 for men and –.32 for women) and sexual discomfort (–.26 for men and –.32 for women). Thus, as women and men are exposed to mainstream U.S. culture and become English-speaking, they become more likely to endorse more egalitarian attitudes and become more comfortable with sex. They also become less coercive or coerced about sex. Whereas 61% of the highly acculturated men reported insisting on sex in the past 12 months when their partner was not interested, 76% of the less-acculturated men reported doing so. Also, 26% of the highly acculturated and 35% of the less-acculturated men reported lying to get sex in the past 12 months. Highly acculturated women less often reported being coerced sexually in their current relationship—82% of the less-acculturated and 66% of the highly acculturated indicated that their partner had insisted on sex when they were not interested. However, the highly acculturated women were more likely than less-acculturated ones to report having been raped or sexually abused (25% vs. 14%). The same experience of coerced sex is, possibly, more readily labeled rape when a woman has been more exposed to mainstream U.S. culture.

These differences are important to consider when developing interventions in English or in Spanish for Latino populations. Spanish-speaking Latinos, who generally have less sexual comfort and less information, will find direct discussion of sex more difficult and will need more basic information about sex. In addition, they will be more likely to hold traditional beliefs, including the idea that it is acceptable and expected for men to coerce women and to have extramarital liaisons. For these reasons, Spanish-speaking women may often feel less able to directly influence condom use than their English-speaking counterparts. More traditional and Spanish-speaking men may feel freer to perpetrate and to admit physical coercion with their partners.

Sexual Socialization

To socialize children more appropriately about sexuality, Latino parents will need to explore the meanings of sex that they have been taught both formally and informally. In focus groups that we conducted with sixth and seventh graders, many children indicated that their parents never talked to them about sex. The children believed that parents would not talk because they were afraid that if they did, they would somehow be condoning or encouraging sex. Certainly this fear may be common but other reasons such as discomfort with sexuality also play a role. One parent in a focus group indicated that she did not want to talk to her daughter about sex because she feared the daughter would ask her the age at which she lost her virginity, which this mother considered far too young. A parent who has experienced sexual abuse or assault (a not uncommon experience) may have great difficulty talking in a candid way about sex and may be fearful of a child's normal curiosity and exploration.

Many parents express the desire to talk more with their children about sex, but these conversations are not easy to hold. An example can be seen in a study of taped conversations regarding the topics of sex and chores held between 19 parent-child dyads, half of whom were Latino. In both the Latino and non-Latino white dyads, the proportion of words the child spoke (as compared to the parent) decreased dramatically when the topic was sex in comparison to chores (Hall, García, & Marín, unpublished data). Parents tended to talk on and on, in lecture form, rather than attempting to engage the child in the discussion. So, parents will need resources and support before they will be able to talk effectively to their children about sex.

Gender Norms and Sexual Comfort

Talking about sex and having information about sex are crucial components in the struggle to increase sexual comfort. Parents who fail to name sexual body parts but refer instead to "down there" are giving important messages that sex is not talked about in the same way that other bodily functions are. So, parents should be given proper names for sexual parts and functions and told to use them "for the sake of your children." Exercises and games in which parents and children are asked to use sexual words can desensitize them. Such exercises will often be necessary for adults in settings such as STD clinics and family planning clinics as well. Similarly, comfort with buying a condom, carrying one, or using one with the lights on are directly relevant to successful and consistent condom use.

Sexual Gender Norms and Coercion

Many HIV-prevention strategies focus on promoting condom use with women, often because women are more easily accessible in health settings than men. However, there are multiple problems with this strategy: Latino culture defines assertive behavior of women regarding sex as inappropriate, many Latino women do not see themselves as at risk, because they have only one partner, others are aware of the risk but feel hopeless about changing their partner's behavior, and some Latino men may become angry and even violent when their partner suggests condom use. In our survey, 16% of women were afraid that their partner might yell at them, 8% thought he might hit them, and 12% thought he might harm them in some other way during sex. Because of these problems and high levels of sexual discomfort in some Latino women, work with women regarding sexuality will often proceed more slowly than work with men. Women will require support and skills-building not only in how to suggest condoms, but in some cases to leave an abusive relationship. Kelly et al. (1994), in their work with inner-city women, observed that women often offered each other both support and resources to leave abusive relationships.

When providers wish to promote condom use among Latino women, they should include the male partner as an additional target of the intervention. Although men are difficult to reach, their greater openness to sexual messages and the fact that they are the ones who actually use the condom make them an ideal target for condom promotion and for changing sexual norms to support condom use. To change their sexual gender norms men may need to examine and question the common meanings of sexual behavior that they have always accepted. Programs that ask men to question the messages they have received from parents and society and programs that teach skills to help men reduce their coercive behavior and to empathize with victims of assault may be necessary on a widespread basis. Sex education programs for children and adolescents should not simply teach refusal skills but should find ways to reduce coercive behavior, such as emphasizing learning how to set personal limits, and empathy training. Our current work in middle schools is incorporating these ideas, which have not been widely used in other programs to date (Kirby, personal communication). Men and boys should be directly involved in the development and implementation of such programs.

As Amaro (1995) points out, women's unequal status, which impedes their ability to protect themselves successfully, has usually not been addressed in HIV-prevention programs. These programs often ask women to behave in ways that directly contradict their socialization as subordinates to men. One program successfully imparted the negotiation skills that inner-city women needed to increase condom use with their partners (Kelly et al., 1994) but also included a group discussion in which the women actively supported each other to change or leave abusive relationships (Kelly, personal communication).

Consciousness-raising programs are currently being evaluated for Puerto Rican college-age women (Serrano-García, personal communication). Serrano-García and Lopez-Sanchez (1991) have proposed a framework for understanding sexual behavior in Latinos, suggesting that one must begin with the reality of unequal levels of power and work with women to help them ask for what they want. Specifically, they suggest that women may be in any of four levels of consciousness, based on Ander-egg (1980): (1) submissive consciousness, in which social reality is seen as natural, given, and unchangeable; (2) the precritical level, in which feelings of dissatisfaction begin to arise and people begin to search for solutions; (3) the critical-integrative level, in which people begin to analyze the social-historical roots of situations and initiate change efforts; and (4) the liberating level, in which people consider their situation oppressive and demand social transformation. Serrano-García and her colleagues are currently implementing an intervention with sexually active university women in Puerto Rico designed to raise levels of consciousness about the asymmetry of women's situation, particularly regarding condom use, to decrease levels of sexual risk behavior in these women. A telling result of pretests of this intervention was that a high proportion of participants ended their relationships with current partners (Serrano-García, personal communication).

Both men and women are adversely affected by cultural scripts that encourage men to be coercive and women to be submissive. HIV-prevention interventions, to be most effective, must find ways to liberate both men and women from these scripts.

Conclusion

Cultural beliefs among Latinos about the meaning of women's and men's behavior in sexual contexts contribute to lower levels of comfort with the holder's own body and sexual activities and more coercive attitudes and behaviors toward women. These cultural aspects are important to understanding condom use. Current models of behavior that have been used in studying condom use have not paid attention to these cultural components of sexual behavior. Interventions that attempt to challenge the prevailing cultural patterns must take into account the power of beliefs about sexual gender roles and sexual discomfort. But Latino culture is not monolithic and much variation exists in the Latino community regarding meanings of sexual behaviors. Whether our interventions ultimately respect or overthrow culture, they must understand and take account of the powerful meanings of sexual behavior in the Latino context.

Note

1 We used a sampling technique that efficiently identified Latinos but was still random in nature. Initially, 143,984 telephone hundred series (area codes + prefix + two digits) were randomly generated from working area codes and prefixes in the nine states. These were computer-matched with telephone directory information and 27,574 (19.2%) of the hundred series were found to have at least one Spanish-surnamed household. Subsequently, 12,078 telephone numbers were randomly generated from these hundred series using a stratification procedure that oversampled hundred series with more Spanish-surnamed households to increase the probability of reaching Latino households. Calls to these 12,078 numbers produced 372 Latino households. The hundred series corresponding to these 372 telephone numbers were treated as primary sampling units (PSU) and additional telephone numbers from these hundred series were computer-generated. At least six attempts were made during varying days and times to reach unanswered telephone numbers.

References

Amaro, H. (1995). Love, sex and power: Considering women's realities in HIV prevention. *American Psychologist, 50,* 437-447.

Ander-egg, E. (1980). *Metodología del desarrollo de comunidad.* Madrid, Spain: UNIEUROP.

Aneshensel, C. S., Becerra, R. M., Fielder, E. P., & Schuler, R. H. (1990). Onset of fertility-related events during adolescence: A prospective comparison of Mexican-American and non-Hispanic white females. *American Journal of Public Health, 80,* 959-963.

Baier, J. L., Rosenzweig, M. G., & Whipple, E. G. (1991). Patterns of sexual behavior, coercion, and victimization of university students. *Journal of College Student Development, 32,* 310-322.

Bandura, A. (1986). *Social foundations of thought and action.* Englewood Cliffs, NJ: Prentice Hall.

Burgos, N. M., & Díaz-Perez, Y. I. (1986). An exploration of human sexuality and the Puerto Rican culture. *Journal of Social Work & Human Sexuality, 4,* 135-150.

Burt, M. (1980). Cultural myths and supports for rape. *Journal of Personality and Social Psychology, 38,* 217-230.

Carrier, J. (1985). Mexican male bisexuality. In F. Klein & T. Wolf (Eds.), *Bisexualities: Theory and research* (pp. 75-85). New York: Haworth.

Carrillo, H. (1995). *Lifting the veil of silence: Sexuality, social influence, and the practice of AIDS prevention in modern Mexico.* Unpublished doctoral dissertation, School of Public Health, University of California, Berkeley.

Catania, J., Kegeles, S., & Coates, T. A. (1990). Towards an understanding of risk behavior: An AIDS risk reduction model (ARRM). *Health Education Quarterly, 17,* 381-399.

Centers for Disease Control. (1991). Characteristics of parents who discuss AIDS with their children—United States 1989. *Morbidity and Mortality Weekly Report, 40,* 789-791.

Choi, K. H., Binson, D., Adelson, M., & Catania, J. A. (1995). *The prevalence and sexual health consequences of sexual harassment and involuntary sex among U.S. adults 18-49 years.* Manuscript submitted for publication.

Cromwell, R. E., & Ruiz, R. A. (1979). The myth of macho dominance in decision making within Mexican and Chicano families. *Hispanic Journal of Behavioral Sciences, 1,* 355-373.

Cunningham, I., Díaz-Esteve, C. M., Gonzalez-Santiago, M. I., & Rodriguez-Sanchez, M. H. (1994). University students and AIDS: Some findings from three surveys— 1989, 1990 and 1992. In B. Vasquez (Ed.), *Puerto Ricans and AIDS: It's time to act. Centro, 6*(1 & 2), 44-59. (published by Centro de Estudios Puertorriqueños, Hunter College, New York 10021)

Dawson, D., Cynamon, M., & Fitti, J. (1987). *AIDS knowledge and attitudes, provisional data from the National Health Interview Survey: United States* (Vol. 146). Hyattsville, MD: U.S. Public Health Service, Centers for Disease Control, National Center for Health Statistics.

Díaz, R. (in press). Latino gay men in the AIDS epidemic. In M. Levine, J. Gagnon, & P. Nardi (Eds.), *The impact of HIV on the lesbian and gay community.* Chicago: University of Chicago Press.

Finkelhor, D. (1993). Epidemiological factors in the clinical identification of child sexual abuse. *Child Abuse & Neglect, 17,* 67-70.

Fischer, G. J. (1987). Hispanic and majority student attitudes toward forcible date rape as a function of differences in attitudes toward women. *Sex Roles, 17,* 93-101.

Fishbein, M., & Ajzen, I. (1975). *Belief, attitude, intention, and behavior: An introduction to theory and research.* Menlo Park, CA: Addison-Wesley.

Fisher, J., & Fisher, W. (1992). Changing AIDS risk behavior. *Psychological Bulletin, 111,* 455-474.

Fisher, W. A. (1984). Predicting contraceptive behavior among university men: The roles of emotions and behavioral intentions. *Journal of Applied Social Psychology, 14,* 104-123.

Fisher, W. A., Byrne, D., White, L. A., & Kelley, K. (1988). Erotophobia-erotophilia as a dimension of personality. *Journal of Sex Research, 25,* 123-151.

Forrest, K., Austin, D., Valdes, M., Fuentes, E., & Wilson, S. (1993). Exploring norms and beliefs related to AIDS prevention among California Hispanic men. *Family Planning Perspectives, 25,* 111-117.

Frankl, V. (1992). *Man's search for meaning: An introduction to logotherapy* (4th ed.). Boston: Beacon.

Gavey, N. (1993). Technologies and effects of heterosexual coercion. In S. Wildinson & C. Kitzinger (Eds.), *Heterosexuality.* London: Sage.

Goldwert, M. (1985). Mexican machismo: The flight from femininity. *Psychoanalytic Review, 72,* 161-169.

Gómez, C., & Marín, B. (in press). Gender, culture, and power: Barriers to HIV-prevention strategies for women. *Journal of Sex Research.*

Gómez, C. A., Marín, B. V., & Grinstead, O. (1994). Sexual coercion in the face of AIDS: Will Latino men and women challenge it? Paper presented at the 10th annual International Conference on AIDS, Yokohama, Japan. *Published Abstracts,* Vol. I, 23.

Hall, D., García M., & Marín, B. V. (1994). [Ratings of interactions between parents and middle school children in transcribed conversations about sexual and non-sexual topics]. Unpublished raw data.

Kelly, J. A., Murphy, D. A., Washington, C. D., Wilson, T. S., Koob, J. J., Davis, D. R., Ledesma, G., & Davantes, B. (1994). The effects of HIV/AIDS intervention groups for high-risk women in urban clinics. *American Journal of Public Health, 84,* 1918-1922.

Koss, M. P., & Oros, C. J. (1982). Sexual experiences survey: A research instrument investigating sexual aggression and victimization. *Journal of Consulting and Clinical Psychology, 50,* 455-457.

Lane, K. E., & Gwartney-Gibbs, P. A. (1985). Violence in the context of dating and sex. *Journal of Family Issues, 6,* 45-59.

Lefley, H. P., Scott, C. S., Llabre, M., & Hicks, D. (1993). Cultural beliefs about rape and victims' response in three ethnic groups. *American Journal of Orthopsychiatry, 63,* 623-632.

Linton, M. A., & Muehlenhard, C. L. (1985). [Women's ability to refuse unwanted sexual advances, unpublished raw data] cited in C. L. Muehlenhard & M. A. Linton (1987), Date rape and sexual aggression in dating situations: Incidence and risk factors. *Journal of Counseling Psychology, 34,* 186-196.

Marín, B. V., & Marín, G. (1990). Effects of acculturation on knowledge of AIDS and HIV among Hispanics. *Hispanic Journal of Behavioral Sciences, 12,* 110-121.

Marín, B. V., & Marín, G. (1992). Predictors of condom accessibility among Hispanics in San Francisco. *American Journal of Public Health, 82,* 592-595.

Marín, B. V., Gómez, C. A., & Hearst, N. (1993). Multiple heterosexual partners and condom use among Hispanics and non-Hispanic whites. *Family Planning Perspectives, 25,* 170-174.

Marín, B., Gómez, C., & Tschann, J. (1993). Condom use among Hispanic men with secondary female sexual partners. *Public Health Reports, 108,* 742-750.

Marín, B., Tschann, J., Gómez, C., & Kegeles, S. (1993). Acculturation and gender differences in sexual attitudes and behaviors: A comparison of Hispanic and non-Hispanic white single adults. *American Journal of Public Health, 83,* 1759-1761.

Muehlenhard, C. L., & Linton, M. A. (1987). Date rape and sexual aggression in dating situations: Incidence and risk factors. *Journal of Counseling Psychology, 34,* 186-196.

Padilla, A., & Baird, T. (1991). Mexican-American adolescent sexuality and sexual knowledge: An exploratory study. *Hispanic Journal of Behavioral Sciences, 13,* 95-104.

Padilla, E. R., & O'Grady, K. E. (1987). Sexuality among Mexican Americans: A case of sexual stereotyping. *Journal of Personality and Social Psychology, 52,* 5-10.

Pavich, E. G. (1986). A Chicano perspective on Mexican culture and sexuality. *Journal of Social Work and Human Sexuality, 4,* 47-65.

Rapaport, K., & Burkhart, B. R. (1984). Personality and attitudinal characteristics of sexually coercive college males. *Journal of Abnormal Psychology, 93,* 216-221.

Scrimshaw, S., Carballo, M., Ramos, L., & Blair, B. (1991). The AIDS rapid anthropological procedures: A tool for health education planning and evaluation. *Health Education Quarterly, 18,* 111-123.

Serrano-García, I., & Lopez-Sanchez, G. (1991). *Un enfoque diferente del poder y el cambio social para la psicologia social-comunitaria.* Paper presented at Interamerican Congress of Psychology, San Jose, Costa Rica.

Sorenson, S. B., & Siegel, J. M. (1992). Gender, ethnicity, and sexual assault: Findings from a Los Angeles study. *Journal of Social Issues, 48*(1), 93-104.

Soto, E. (1983). Sex-role traditionalism and assertiveness in Puerto Rican women living in the United States. *Journal of Community Psychology, 11,* 346-354.

Stets, J. E., & Pirog-Good, M. A. (1989). Patterns of physical and sexual abuse for men and women in dating relationships: A descriptive analysis. *Journal of Family Violence, 4,* 63-76.

Tedeschi, J. T., & Felson, R. B. (1994). *Violence, aggression, and coercive actions.* Washington, DC: American Psychological Association.

Triandis, H. C. (1994). *Culture and social behavior.* New York: McGraw-Hill.

Vazquez-Nuttal, E., Romero-García, I., & de Leon, B. (1987). Sex roles and perceptions of femininity and masculinity of Hispanic women. *Psychology of Women Quarterly, 11,* 409-425.

Villas, P., Bouvet, M., & Bernal, P. (1992). Acculturation and HIV/AIDS knowledge among Hispanos: Findings from southern New Mexico. *Border Health, 7*(1), 10-17.

9

Using a Theory-Based Community Intervention to Reduce AIDS Risk Behaviors: The CDC's AIDS Community Demonstration Projects

MARTIN FISHBEIN
CAROLYN GUENTHER-GREY
WAYNE D. JOHNSON
RICHARD J. WOLITSKI
ALFRED McALISTER
CORNELIS A. RIETMEIJER
KEVIN O'REILLY
THE AIDS COMMUNITY DEMONSTRATION
    PROJECTS

The Centers for Disease Control and Prevention (CDC) are supporting a number of projects designed to implement and evaluate the effectiveness of interventions to reduce the transmission of the Human Immunodeficiency Virus. This chapter describes one of these projects, the AIDS Community Demonstration Projects

(ACDP). The ACDP is a multisite study involving five U.S. cities: Dallas, Denver, Long Beach, New York City, and Seattle. Generally speaking, the ACDP is evaluating the effectiveness of using community volunteers to deliver a theory-based intervention designed to increase consistent condom use or consistent bleach use in a number of ethnically diverse, traditionally hard-to-reach, high-risk populations: men who have sex with men but who do not gay-identify (MSM-ngi), injecting drug users (IDUs) who are not recruited from treatment programs, female sex partners (FSP) of male IDUs, female prostitutes or sex traders (FST), and youth in high-risk situations (YHR). Each project intervened with one to three of these groups (see O'Reilly & Higgins, 1991).

Researchers from the project sites, the CDC, and expert consultants collaborated to design a common protocol that was adapted to develop site-specific and population-specific community-level interventions. The common protocol included five key elements: (1) the use of theories of behavioral prediction and change as a foundation for the design of a community-level HIV-prevention intervention; (2) formative research within the project communities prior to implementing the intervention; (3) small media materials (e.g., pamphlets, brochures, flyers) with role-model stories of individuals who were changing or had changed their risk behaviors; (4) distribution of these small media materials, along with condoms and bleach kits, through networks of community members who reinforced positive behavior change among individuals who were at risk; and (5) an evaluation protocol that in-

---

AUTHORS' NOTE: Portions of this chapter were initially published in "Community Level Prevention of HIV Infection Among High-Risk Populations: Methodology and Preliminary Findings from the AIDS Community Demonstration Projects," *MMWR Recommendations & Reports* (in press).

The authors are at the Centers for Disease Control and Prevention unless otherwise indicated. Martin Fishbein is also at the University of Illinois, Champaign-Urbana; Richard Wolitski is also at California State University, Long Beach; Alfred McAlister is at the University of Texas, Austin; Cornelis Rietmeijer is at the Denver Department of Public Health; Kevin O'Reilly is at the World Health Organization. The AIDS Community Demonstration Projects are Dallas County Health Department: Ann Freeman, Marty Krepcho; Denver County Health Department: David Cohn, Paul Simons; California State University, Long Beach: Nancy H. Corby, Fen Rhodes; National Development and Research Institute, New York City: Susan Tross, Bea Krauss; Seattle-King County Department of Public Health: Robert Wood, Gary Goldbaum; Behavioral and Prevention Research Branch, CDC: Donna Higgins, Dan Schnell; Conwal, Inc., Virginia: John Sheridan.

cluded both process and outcome measures and was linked to the behavioral theory of the intervention.

Several of the elements in this protocol were adapted from earlier community-level interventions such as the North Karelia Project, a community-level risk-reduction program designed to prevent coronary heart disease (Puska et al., 1985; see also McAlister, 1991; McAlister et al., 1980). To tailor the interventions most effectively to local needs and resources, each project implemented this protocol based on the specific circumstances in their community and on the particular population each intervention was designed to reach.

Theoretical Framework

The ACDP is based on behavioral research and has incorporated elements of several theories: the Health Belief Model (Rosenstock, 1974), Social Cognitive Theory (Bandura, 1986), the Theory of Reasoned Action (Fishbein & Ajzen, 1975), and the Transtheoretical Model of Behavior Change (Prochaska, DiClemente, & Norcross, 1992).

The Health Belief Model (HBM) suggests that individuals will be most likely to engage in a preventive health behavior if they believe that they are susceptible to (or at risk for) a given disease, that getting the disease will lead to severe consequences, that engaging in the preventive health behavior will reduce susceptibility and/or severity, and that the perceived benefits of performing the preventive behavior outweigh the anticipated barriers or costs (Becker, 1974, 1988; Rosenstock, 1974).

Bandura's Social Cognitive Theory (SCT) suggests that self-efficacy (i.e., the belief that one has the skills and abilities necessary to perform the behavior under a variety of circumstances) is a necessary component for behavior change. In addition, the individuals must be motivated to perform the behavior. That is, they must believe that the expected positive outcomes of performing the behavior outweigh the expected negative outcomes (Bandura, 1986, 1992, 1994).

The Theory of Reasoned Action (TRA) suggests that individuals' performance of a given behavior is primarily determined by their intention to perform that behavior. Two major factors influence the intention to perform a given behavior: first, the individuals' attitude toward personally performing the behavior (which is based on the individuals' beliefs about the positive and negative consequences of their performing the behavior); and second, the subjective norm concerning the behavior (i.e., the individuals' belief that "most important others" think that the individuals should—or should not—perform the behavior). The subjective norm, in turn, is determined by beliefs about the normative proscriptions of specific others and the individuals' motivation to comply with those specific others (Fishbein & Ajzen, 1975; Ajzen & Fishbein, 1980; Fishbein, Middlestadt, & Hitchcock, 1991).

Perceived costs and benefits, expected positive and negative outcomes, or beliefs about positive and negative consequences can all be viewed as potential positive and negative reinforcers of a given action. In addition, Social Cognitive Theory suggests that individuals can also be reinforced vicariously through observing a model being rewarded for appropriate behavior.

The theoretical premise of the ACDP draws on these three theories and assumes that there are four factors that may influence individuals' intentions and behaviors: (1) the individuals' perceptions that they are personally susceptible to acquiring a given disease or illness; (2) the individuals' attitudes toward performing the behavior, which is based on their beliefs about the positive and negative consequences of performing that behavior; (3) perceived norms, which include the perception that others in the community are also changing and that those with whom the individuals interact most closely are supportive of the individuals' attempt to change; and (4) self-efficacy, which involves the individuals' beliefs that they can perform the recommended behavior under a variety of circumstances.

The relative importance of these four factors as determinants of intention and behavior is expected to vary as a function of both the behavior and the population being considered (Fishbein et al., 1992). In addition to these four critical factors, the degree to which the environment facilitates or inhibits behavior change and the readiness of individuals to change their behavior are also considered in the ACDP.

As discussed by Fishbein et al. (1992), the presence of environmental constraints may prevent people from acting on their intentions. For example, one cannot use condoms or sterile injection equipment if condoms and sterile needles are not available. Thus, as part of a theory-based approach, the importance of environmental facilitation was recognized and this led to an early decision to include the distribution of condoms and bleach kits as an essential part of the intervention.

Also recognized was that different behavior change interventions (or messages) would be necessary for individuals who had not even thought about adopting a given health-protective behavior than for those who were trying to adopt that behavior. The Transtheoretical Stages of Change Model (SOC) directly addresses this issue.

According to the SOC model, some individuals who are performing risky health behaviors may have no intention to change that behavior or to adopt a given preventive behavior (they are at the Precontemplation Stage). Any one of several events may then lead an individual to consider change and perhaps to form an intention to adopt the preventive behavior at some time in the future (the Contemplation Stage). This may be followed by the formation of an intention to adopt the new behavior in the immediate or foreseeable future and this intention is generally accompanied by initial, perhaps exploratory, attempts to adopt the behavior (Preparation Stage). Then the new behavior is adopted (Action Stage) and ultimately becomes a routine part of one's life (Maintenance Stage). Movement through the stages is assumed to be sequential, although individuals may relapse (at any stage) or cycle back through the stages repeatedly before achieving long-term maintenance (Prochaska et al., 1992).

According to the SOC model, to help people change their behavior one should first determine where each person is on this continuum of behavior change and then develop interventions to help him or her move to subsequent, more advanced stages. By having discrete and immediate objectives for persons at risk of HIV infection, an intervention can be more precisely targeted to the needs of individuals. For example, one can empirically determine which of the theoretical factors (e.g., norms, attitudes, self-efficacy, or perceived risk) needs to be addressed to move an individual from one stage to the next.

Generally speaking, the ACDP intervention used social modeling to encourage changes in one or more of the theoretical factors underlying intention and behavior. More specifically, empirical data guided the development of intervention messages designed to move people along the SOC continuum. Intervention messages were based on stories of community members who were trying to change their behavior (role-model stories) and highlighted specific stages of change and cognitive factors based on data collected in the community.

In summary, the intervention was based on a theoretical foundation that contained elements of several behavioral theories and the transtheoretical SOC model. Providing the projects with a firm theoretical underpinning enhanced the development of the interventions and established a basis for both the implementation of the interventions and the evaluation of their outcomes.

Both intervention and evaluation activities were clearly focused by defining the behavioral goals as specifically as possible. For example, formative research indicated that it was important to distinguish between using a condom with one's main (or steady) partner and using a condom with "occasional" partners (or clients). Similarly, it was important to distinguish between using a condom for vaginal sex and using a condom for anal sex. Thus, we separately considered condom use for vaginal and anal sex with main and occasional partners. In this chapter we will focus primarily on two of these condom-use behaviors: always using a condom for vaginal sex with a main partner and always using a condom for vaginal sex with occasional partners. In addition, for those IDUs who share injection equipment, we will focus on the behavior of "always using bleach to disinfect 'works' before injecting."

Formative Research

With the exception of the New York project, the AIDS Community Demonstration Projects were based in state or local health departments that had traditionally implemented clinic-based HIV prevention interventions. The ACDP attempted to implement a behavioral intervention directly in the community to reach groups participating in high-risk behaviors who were less likely to come to the clinics. To implement this community-level behavioral intervention, the project sites needed to develop a thorough base of knowledge about the groups they sought to reach, including (a) the geographic areas in each city where individuals in the risk groups congregated and where ACDP staff and peer network members could conduct the intervention and evaluation; (b) the specific subpopulations within each population at risk; (c) the risk behaviors taking place; and (d) the theoretical variables underlying "risky" and "safer" behaviors among individuals in the risk groups.

To gather this information, project staff in each city undertook 6 months of formative, ethnographic research (Goldbaum, Perdue, & Higgins, in press; Higgins et al., in press). First, interviews were conducted with health department staff and local AIDS researchers to determine what they knew about the target populations. Interviews were also conducted with other professionals who had contact with these populations, such as staff at drug treatment facilities, mental health facilities, and Women, Infants, and Children (WIC) clinics, in addition to police, judicial system workers, and staff members of community-based organizations and other groups (depending on the city and the target population).

Based on the information gathered through these interviews, potential "gatekeepers" were identified. These individuals often served as the link between the population at risk and the larger community. Although some gatekeepers were members of the populations at risk, others were outside of it, such as a recovering IDU or a storekeeper in an area where a large number of sex traders worked the streets. These potential gatekeepers were also interviewed to gain their perspectives on the target populations.

Based on all of the preceding information, subgroups within these populations were identified and the target community was defined. In addition, project staff identified locations where individuals in the target communities were participating in risk-taking behaviors and also identified other locations where members of these communities might congregate. Using a standard protocol that was modified by the sites based on local circumstances, project workers unobtrusively observed people in the identified locations to gain an understanding of those to whom they intended to direct their behavioral intervention.

Finally, through the ties previously established with the gatekeepers, project staff were able to reach individuals in the target communities. The last step in the formative research process involved interviewing the members of the community who were at risk, both individually and in focus groups. More specifically, members of the target community were asked about the types of risk-taking behaviors they engaged in, the social networks they belonged to, the people or groups who would support or oppose consistent condom use or bleaching, barriers and facilitators to adopting these behaviors, their view of the advantages and disadvantages of performing these behaviors, and what they thought might be useful ways to help people like themselves adopt protective behaviors (Higgins et al., in press).

From these extensive qualitative data we were able to better understand the lives of individuals in all of the target risk groups (including
their behavior and motivations) from the perspective of the individuals
themselves rather than from the perspective of those outside of these
populations (Harris, 1990). These qualitative data enabled the development of a common closed-item evaluation instrument to be used at all
sites. In addition, by using ties to gatekeepers and members of the target
populations, each site began to recruit networks of peers and other
community members who could deliver the intervention and build
overall community support for the intervention (Guenther-Grey et al.,
1992; Guenther-Grey, Noroian, et al., in press; Simons et al., in press).
Finally, the projects used the information collected at each site during
this formative research stage to begin developing intervention materials that addressed the appropriate attitudes, norms, barriers, and facilitators to risk reduction among individuals in the target groups (Corby,
Enguidanos, & Kay, in press).

Implementation

As previously noted, each of the five cities designed and implemented interventions for one, two, or three of the six targeted communities at risk for HIV. Dallas identified a pair of census tracts with high
rates of STDs and randomly assigned one as the intervention area and
the other as a comparison area; a second intervention/comparison pair
was added 4 months later. Denver directed an intervention to IDU, and
17 months later added an intervention for MSM-ngi. Long Beach
worked with IDU, FSP, and FST. New York tailored an intervention to
FSP. Seattle directed interventions to IDU, MSM-ngi, and YHR.

The five project sites followed a common protocol for the implementation of the intervention. The intervention protocol emphasized: (a)
development of small media materials that included stories depicting
positive changes in the beliefs, attitudes, intentions, and behaviors of
local target population members (role-model stories); (b) distribution
of these materials by members of peer networks from the local community who were trained to reinforce acceptance of and attention to the
intervention messages, and to successful and unsuccessful attempts to

change behavior; and (c) environmental facilitation through the distribution of condoms and bleach. These components were chosen so that explicit prevention messages and facilitating materials could be distributed to specific populations.

The use of role-model stories was based on a technique of behavioral journalism (McAlister, in press), and the combination of social modeling in journalistic formats with grass-roots networks to promote and reinforce behavior change was adapted from the North Karelia Project, a community-level intervention to prevent coronary heart disease (Puska et al., 1985, McAlister, et al., 1980). Together, the media modeling and community networking provided a practical and potentially powerful vehicle for influencing the theoretical factors underlying risk-reduction behavior change.

This intervention protocol was adapted for the site-specific and population-specific interventions. Some variation in the application of the intervention protocol was expected and encouraged to more effectively tailor the specific interventions to local circumstances.

Intervention Messages and Materials

The behavioral intervention materials were in the form of small media, defined here as community newsletters, brochures, pamphlets, flyers, or baseball cards that contained role-model stories (Corby, Enguidanos, & Kay, in press). A role-model story is an authentic story about a person within the target community that is told in the person's own language and that describes the person's stimulus or motivation for initiating or considering a behavior change, the type of change begun, how barriers to change were overcome, and the reinforcing consequences of the change.

The role-model stories were drawn from interviews with members of the target populations and communities, and small media materials with new stories were produced approximately once a month. The selection of messages to be emphasized in role-model stories was guided by data collected from the study populations at each site. (Specifics of the data collection process are described in the "Process and Outcome Evaluation" section following). First, these data were used to determine the relative mix of role-model stories to be distributed in a community. For example, if survey data indicated that at one site most community members were in the Precontemplation stage for a particular behavior, most of the site's stories dealing with that behavior highlighted a change from the Precontemplation to the Contemplation stage.

Second, specific theoretical factors or beliefs were highlighted if data analysis indicated they were correlated with intentions to change or a stage of change. For example, if people who were in the Contemplation stage for consistent condom use tended to believe that condom use reduces intimacy, whereas people who were in the Preparation stage did not hold this belief, role-model stories would address intimacy issues. Over time, the relative mix of stories produced changed for each intervention; for example, more stories highlighted the Preparation or Action stages as data from a site indicated that the target population was moving along the SOC continuum.

Thus, each site produced unique media materials with role-model stories for each of its intervention populations. These role-model stories were tailored to the local populations in that they were based on real stories of local residents and written to highlight specific stages of change and theoretical factors based on local data.

In addition to the role-model stories, small media also contained basic AIDS information, instructions on the use of condoms or bleach (to clean needles), biographies of community members participating in the project, notices of community events, or information on other health and social services, such as locations of homeless shelters or needle exchanges, schedules for free meals, mammogram screening, or drug and alcohol treatment services. We believed that community interest in and support of the program would be increased by acknowledging and addressing other relevant community concerns.

Distribution of Materials Through Networks

These small media materials, along with condoms and bleach kits, were delivered one-to-one to people in the community. The intervention materials were distributed in part by networks of peers from the target populations or communities (Guenther-Grey et al., 1992; Guenther-Grey, Noroian, et al., in press; Simons et al., in press). In all sites except New York, a second layer of networks consisted of business people, community leaders, and other persons who were not considered "true" peers but who were trusted by the target groups and interacted with them on a regular basis. These network members were known as "interactors." In addition to delivering the small media materials, condoms, and bleach, all network members focused the attention of the recipients on the role-model stories and reinforced attempts to change and actual change in behavior. The use of role-model stories was a key component of the intervention, and peer network members who had made efforts toward lowering high-risk behavior were encouraged to provide role-model stories in which they shared their personal experiences with other community members.

Network members were recruited through contact with a project outreach worker, referral from another service organization, or referral from current or former network members. Several methods were used for maintaining the networks, including (a) offering material incentives such as small amounts of cash, food or movie coupons, or t-shirts or buttons with the project logo; (b) providing opportunities for recognition of the network members' achievements through awards or certificates of participation, picnics, and parties; and (c) maintaining frequent contact between outreach workers and the network members to provide encouragement and reinforcement for their role. Project records indicate that the sites were able to recruit and retain network members from these disenfranchised communities to intervene with the target populations and to provide HIV prevention messages in their communities (Guenther-Grey et al, 1992; Guenther-Grey, Noroian et al., in press).

Depending on the site, peer network members would distribute materials alone, in pairs, or accompanied by a project outreach worker. In addition, the protocol for the intervention allowed projects to maintain storefronts either within or near the intervention neighborhoods. Three of the project sites chose to use storefronts (Dallas, Denver, and New York). These convenient locations served as a focal point for project activities such as parties for assembling intervention materials, support group meetings for peer network members or for individuals living with HIV, health screening (HIV counseling and testing, sickle cell testing), and community events such as a commemoration of World AIDS Day (Simons et al., in press).

Process and Outcome Evaluation

The multisite joint evaluation protocol included both process and outcome evaluation components. Process evaluation measures examined the implementation and diffusion of the intervention throughout the target community to determine if the intervention was reaching individuals in the targeted groups. The project sites used the following process measures: (a) records of network recruitment and retention and the production and distribution of materials, (b) interviews with key observers about the changes they saw in the community and among individuals in the target populations, and (c) records of daily outreach activities. In addition, the Dallas project obtained unobtrusive measures of discarded condoms, bleach bottles, and small media intervention materials.

As these were "demonstration projects," the primary outcome evaluation question was whether or not the behavioral interventions could facilitate movement toward consistent condom and bleach use in the study areas in which the intervention was implemented. More specifically, we evaluated the effectiveness of the intervention in moving people along one or more of the stages of change (SOC) continua.

A common outcome evaluation design was used in each city. Three basic features of the design were (1) the intervention was implemented in one of two geographic areas, whereas the other area served as a comparison condition; (2) cross-sectional surveys were conducted in both areas before and after the intervention began; and (3) a common set of behavioral and cognitive variables was measured in each area during each survey period. The outcome evaluation design is best viewed as a "quasi-experimental" design (Campbell & Stanley, 1966; Cook & Campbell, 1979) because individuals were not randomly assigned to intervention or comparison conditions. Instead, the assignment to a condition was based on a respondent's location in a given geographic area.

Although the behavioral intervention under study was at the community level, the two primary behavior change objectives involved the behaviors of individuals, namely consistent condom use and consistent cleaning of shared injection equipment with bleach. To assess change in the community, the evaluation design collected data concerning sexual and injection drug behavior from samples of individuals in the study areas. Due to different community structures, the protocols for collecting these data varied somewhat by site. Generally speaking however, "purposive" sampling was used (National Research Council, 1991, p. 326). Locations and times for interviewing were selected to reflect the best available information about the population under study in each community. In most communities, interviewers would go to a randomly determined location within the (treatment or comparison) geographic area identified during formative research. For each community, a sampling protocol was developed to provide for the random selection of respondents and interview sites.

Baseline and outcome evaluation data were collected through periodic cross-sectional surveys, with interviews conducted face-to-face and usually taking place in outdoor locations. Interviewers were not part of the intervention teams but they did know which areas were receiving the intervention. Interviewers received training to assure they were able to follow the sampling protocol and correctly administer the survey instrument.

Data Collection Instruments

To collect data from the study populations, the project sites developed an interview instrument referred to as the Brief Street Interview (BSI). The first section of the BSI screened individuals to determine if they were eligible for the longer interview. They were eligible if they reported engaging in sexual intercourse or sharing injection equipment in the recent past (30 or 60 days). If eligible, the individual received the full BSI. BSI questions assessed where individuals were on the SOC continua regarding consistent condom use for vaginal or anal intercourse with main or other partners and regarding always using bleach to clean needles for injection drug use (Schnell, Galavotti, Fishbein, & Chan, in press). Early results indicated that, with the exception of MSM-ngi, too few respondents in some communities reported anal intercourse with main or occasional partners to yield statistically meaningful results, and most sites dropped this section for non-MSM populations. Additional questions assessed the four key theoretical factors (i.e., attitudes toward the behaviors, perceived norms, perceived risk, and perceived self-efficacy), exposure to HIV/AIDS information, exposure to the project intervention, and indicators of risk-reducing behaviors (e.g., carrying a condom, getting tested for HIV). Names were not collected and confidentiality was assured. Respondents were given small amounts of cash or fast food and grocery vouchers for participating.

Once the early implementation phase began, a second, more detailed interview schedule was developed. This instrument, known as the Coffee Shop Interview (CSI), assessed behavioral beliefs about the advantages and disadvantages of consistently using condoms and bleach, normative beliefs about the proscriptions of specific individuals or groups with regard to these behaviors, and efficacy beliefs concerning one's ability to perform these behaviors under various circumstances. After completing the BSI, respondents were offered an additional small incentive to complete the CSI. Approximately 80% of all respondents agreed to participate in the second (CSI) interview.

Intervention Delivery
and Data Collection

Generally speaking, data collection and behavioral interventions were implemented on the following schedule: Two waves of baseline data were collected from February through June 1991. The intervention began in each city in June or July 1991, following the completion of the baseline surveys. As this behavioral intervention continued, two to three waves of data were collected each year; data collection ended in the summer of 1994. For purposes of this report, we summarized the data into three time periods (phases). The first phase, denoted "baseline," was the baseline period previously discussed. The second phase, denoted "start-up," ran from July 1991 through May 1992 and included data from the first three waves after the intervention began. The third phase, denoted "early implementation," ran from June 1992 through August 1993 and included the next three data collection waves. Although not included in this report, the "full implementation" phase began in September 1993 and included the two final waves of data collection. Thus, in total, there were 10 waves of data collection.

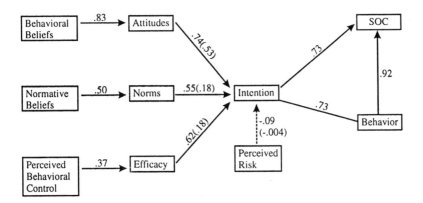

Figure 9.1. AIDS Community Demonstration Projects' theoretical model: Condom use with main partner among men.
Note: Numbers in parentheses are standardized regression weights.

Removal of Repeat Interviews

Data were summarized according to the baseline, start-up, and early intervention phases. Within each community, records within a phase were eliminated if they matched a previous interview within the same phase on gender, race or ethnic group, and location and date of birth.

Preliminary Findings[1]

Test of the Theoretical Model

The theoretical model underlying the ACDP is presented in Figure 9.1. As described earlier, four factors were viewed as potential determinants of intention and behavior: perceived risk, attitudes, norms, and self-efficacy. To test this theoretical model, data from both the BSI and CSI are necessary. For illustrative purposes, data are presented from Wave 7, the first wave of data collection in which both the CSI and the BSI were administered. Figure 9.1 shows the Wave 7 interrelations among the theoretical variables with regard to males' consistent condom use for vaginal sex with their main partner. Consistent with expectations, men's intentions to "always use a condom for vaginal sex with my main partner *from now on*" were predicted with considerable accuracy ($R = .78, p < .001$). More specifically, attitudes ($r = .74, p < .001$; beta $= .53$, $p < .001$), norms ($r = .55$, $p < .001$; beta $= .18$, $p < .001$) and self-efficacy ($r = .62$, $p < .001$; beta $= .18$, $p < .001$) all contributed significantly to an understanding of this intention, although attitudes were clearly the most important determinant. In contrast to expectations based on the HBM, however, perceived risk of acquiring AIDS ($r = -.09$; beta $= -.004$) did not significantly influence the men's intentions to always use a condom for vaginal sex with their main partner.

Three other aspects of Figure 9.1 are worth noting. First, as required by the SOC model, both behavior ($r = .92, p < .001$) and intention ($r = .73, p < .001$) contributed significantly to individuals' stage of change (from Precontemplation $= 1$, to Maintenance $= 5$). Second, intentions were highly correlated with self-reported behavior ($r = .73, p < .001$). Finally, and consistent with expectations, attitudes, norms, and self-efficacy were significantly related to their underlying cognitive determinants. For example, beliefs about the consequences of "always using a condom for vaginal sex with my main partner" were significantly correlated with attitude ($r = .83, p < .001$), normative beliefs were significantly correlated with perceived normative pressure ($r = .50, p < .001$), and perceived control was found to be at least one of the factors underlying self-efficacy ($r = .37, p < .01$).

Data such as the preceding provided guidance for the development of intervention materials. Throughout the 3-year project period, data were collected, analyses similar to the preceding were run in each site, and role-model stories were sought that focused on those variables that had the strongest empirical correlations with intentions and behavior.

Exposure to Project Networks, Staff, and Materials

Effective delivery of the intervention to the target population was crucial to project success. Project efforts were directed toward saturating the community with prevention messages by optimizing the size and effectiveness of the peer network, engaging the cooperation of community businesses, and maximizing the allure of the message and the media through which it was distributed. Other factors that could not be controlled by the project included characteristics of the community such as attentiveness to prevention messages, the total number of people to be reached and their accessibility, and migration into and out of the community. Generally speaking, these characteristics varied widely across the five cities and six types of populations involved in ACDP and were reflected in the proportion of respondents who indicated that they had been reached by project efforts.

Exposure to ACDP networks, staff, and materials was measured by a series of questions at the end of the Brief Street Interview (BSI). Every respondent was asked to describe HIV/AIDS materials they had seen in the community and persons who had spoken to them about AIDS. The time frame for each of these questions was "the last three months," and interviewers recorded information on up to four types of materials and three types of interpersonal contact. Responses were coded into various categories, including specific categories for exposure to ACDP materials, peer or interactor networks, staff, or storefronts (Guenther-Grey, Schnell, & Fishbein, in press).

Respondents who spontaneously reported any exposure to ACDP materials or who reported talking about AIDS with someone who could be identified with the ACDP were classified as "exposed," whereas all others were considered "nonexposed." No distinction is made in this presentation between interpersonal contacts such as talking with ACDP network members or staff, and contact with materials, such as reading a flyer or newsletter, picking up ACDP condoms or bleach kits, or visiting a storefront.

The proportions of respondents within each intervention community who reported any identifiable exposure to ACDP intervention efforts are presented by phase in Table 9.1. Exposure rates ranged from 1% to 17% during the start-up phase, and from 21% to 68% during the early implementation phase. These findings make it clear that community-level interventions such as the ACDP cannot be expected to have significant immediate effects on behavior. Indeed, it took over a year before the intervention reached a substantial proportion of community members. Clearly, if the ACDP had ended after 12 months of intervention, only a small proportion of community members would have been exposed to intervention materials and thus relatively little behavior change could have been expected.

Table 9.1
Exposure to ACDP Intervention by City,
Intervention Community, and Phase

City	Targeted community[a]	Start-up exposure rates	Early implementation exposure rates
Dallas	Two high-STD census tracts	42/392 = 11%	126/414 = 30%
Denver	IDU	4/324 = 1%	60/249 = 24%
Long Beach	IDU	27/348 = 8%	178/322 = 55%
	FST	31/360 = 9%	203/300 = 68%
	FSP	11/162 = 7%	65/143 = 45%
New York City	FSP	36/216 = 17%	92/212 = 43%
Seattle	MSM-ngi	2/124 = 2%	25/119 = 21%
	FST	22/165 = 13%	84/230 = 37%
	YHR	34/262 = 13%	61/263 = 23%

a. IDU = injecting drug users; FSP = female sex partners of IDU; FST = female sex traders; MSM-ngi = men who have sex with men but who do not gay-identify; YHR = youth in high-risk situations.

Behavioral Progress Associated With ACDP

Success of the intervention was determined by the degree to which members of the target community moved along the Stages of Change continua toward the behavioral goals of consistent condom or bleach use. The quasi-experimental design of the ACDP, along with the measurement of exposure in the intervention areas, allowed investigation of two issues:

1. Have intervention-area respondents made more progress toward consistent condom or bleach use than comparison-area respondents?

2. Were intervention-area respondents who reported direct project exposure higher on the SOC scale, on average, than those who did not?

In the following discussion, the first comparison is referred to as the General Intervention Effect, and the second as the Specific Exposure Effect.

Analytical Methods

Following an empirically based algorithm (Schnell et al., in press), each individual was assigned to one of the five stages of change. Specifically, individuals were categorized as shown in Table 9.2. In the following analyses, this stage of change measure (from 1 = Precontemplation to 5 = Maintenance) served as the main behavioral outcome measure (or dependent variable).

Multivariable linear regression models (Kleinbaum & Kupper, 1978) were used to evaluate the effectiveness of the ACDP intervention in moving communities toward consistent condom and bleach use. Three sets of analyses are presented here: (1) consistent condom use during vaginal intercourse with main partners (SOC-VM); (2) consistent condom use during vaginal intercourse with other partners (SOC-VO); and (3) consistent bleach use by IDU to clean shared injection equipment (SOC-Bleach).

To determine whether the movement toward consistent condom use and consistent bleach use occurred more rapidly in the intervention areas than in comparison areas (the General Intervention Effect), time was coded as a continuous variable (0 for baseline, 1 for start-up, and 2 for early implementation). Intervention was coded as 1 for intervention areas and 0 for comparison areas. These regression models included statistical adjustment for gender, race, and ethnicity as categorical main effects. Nine indicator (Yes or No) variables were used to distinguish the 10 pairs of communities (two pairs from Dallas; IDU from Denver; IDU, FST, and FSP from Long Beach; FSP from New York, and MSM-ngi, FST, and YHR from Seattle). Age was treated as a continuous covariate. Statistical significance of the General Intervention Effect across all 10 pairs of communities was assessed by the intervention-by-time interaction term.

To measure the difference between intervention-area respondents who reported exposure to the intervention and those who did not (the Specific Exposure Effect), time was coded as a categorical variable with three levels as previously described. Statistical adjustments for other nuisance variables were managed as described for the General Intervention Effect. Exposure to the ACDP intervention was measured by the dichotomous exposure variable ("exposed" and "nonexposed") previously described. The few respondents reporting exposure at baseline or in comparison areas were reclassified as nonexposed. Statistical

Table 9.2
Algorithm for Assigning Stage of Change for Consistent Condom Use[a]

	Stage of change				
Criterion	Precontemplation	Contemplation	Preparation	Action	Maintenance
Relative frequency of use[b]	—	—	sometimes or almost every time	every time	every time
Duration of "every time" use[c]	—	—	—	less than 6 months	6 months or longer
Immediate intention[d]	—	extremely, quite, slightly sure I will	extremely, quite, slightly sure I will	—	—
Future intention[e]	—	extremely, quite, slightly sure I will	extremely, quite, slightly sure I will	—	—

a. Algorithm applied by starting with criteria necessary for Maintenance, then Action, etc.
b. "When you have vaginal sex with _____, how often do you use a condom?" (every time, almost every time, sometimes, almost never, never)
c. "How long have you been using a condom (every time, almost every time) you have. . .?"
d. "How likely do you think it is that from now on you will use a condom every time. . .?" (extremely, quite, slightly sure I will; undecided; slightly, quite, extremely sure I won't)
e. "In the next 6 months, how likely do you think it is that you will start using condoms every time. . .?" (extremely, quite, slightly sure I will; undecided; slightly, quite, extremely sure I won't)

significance was assessed using this resulting dichotomous exposure term, which represents the time-adjusted difference between respondents in the intervention areas who reported exposure and those who did not.

All mean SOC values referred to in the text and presented in graphs were calculated as population marginal means (Searle, Speed, & Milliken, 1980) in models where time was treated as categorical. These were the mean values that would have been expected if the demographics and community origins of survey respondents had been the same between intervention and comparison areas, and had remained constant across the three phases.

Although linear models are designed for interval-level outcome data, their application to ordinal-level outcomes such as the Stages of Change construct is considered a reasonable strategy if the ordinal nature of the outcome variable is due to crude measurement of an underlying continuous variable (Agresti, 1984, p. 150). Results of analogous logistic models not presented here were similar to those obtained from the linear models.

**Condom Use for Vaginal Sex
With Main Partner**

The overall mean SOC for condom use during vaginal intercourse with main partners (SOC-VM) is presented in Figure 9.2. The total number of respondents represented in this graph is 7,194, and the smallest number used to calculate any given mean value is 156 for intervention-area respondents reporting exposure at the start-up phase. The majority ($n = 4,204$, 58%) of respondents were female, of whom the largest proportion were FSPs ($n = 1,755$, 42%). Among 2,992 male respondents, the largest proportion were IDUs ($n = 1,078$, 36%).

At baseline, the mean SOC-VM value in the intervention area (1.63) was only slightly higher than the mean value in the comparison area (1.59). These values indicate that, on average, respondents were initially between the Precontemplation and Contemplation stages for the adoption of consistent condom use during vaginal intercourse with their main partner. As of early implementation, the mean SOC-VM of 2.03 (the Contemplation stage, i.e., intending to start using condoms consistently in the next six months) among intervention-area respondents was

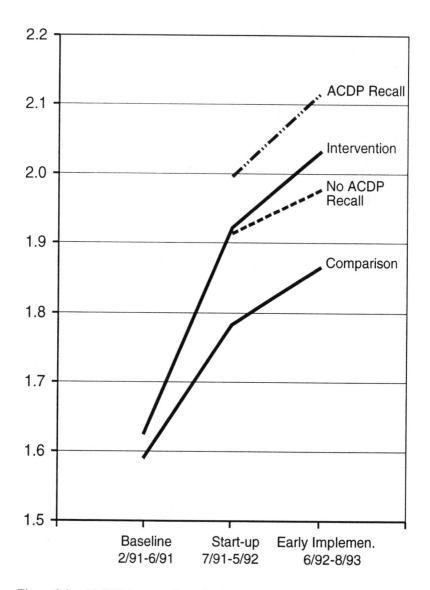

Figure 9.2. SOC-VM mean values: Condom use for vaginal sex with main partner.

Note: Intervention trend > Comparison trend ($p = .095$); ACDP Recall > No Recall ($p = .029$).

higher than the value of 1.87 (slightly below the Contemplation stage) in the comparison areas, but this General Intervention Effect only approached statistical significance ($p < .10$).

Among intervention-area respondents who reported vaginal intercourse with a main partner in the previous 30 days, 9.6% reported exposure to the ACDP during the start-up phase, versus 39.3% as of early implementation. The Specific Exposure Effect was significant ($p < .05$), indicating that, on average, those in the intervention area who were exposed to the intervention (mean SOC = 2.12) were significantly farther along the stages of change scale toward consistent condom use with their main partners than were those not exposed (mean SOC = 1.98).

Condom Use for Vaginal Sex
With Other Partners

The overall mean SOC for condom use during vaginal intercourse with other partners (SOC-VO) is presented in Figure 9.3. The smallest number used to calculate any given mean value was 112 (for intervention-area respondents reporting exposure during the start-up phase), with a total of 6,184 respondents represented in this graph. Respondents were almost evenly split between males ($n = 3,097$, 50%) and females ($n = 3,087$, 50%). The largest proportion of male respondents were IDUs ($n = 1,142$, 37%), whereas the majority of women were sex traders ($n = 2,278$, 74%).

At baseline, the mean values were similar: The mean SOC-VO was 2.80 for the intervention areas and 2.73 for the comparison areas. Note that these means were considerably higher than those for SOC-VM, indicating that even at baseline, respondents, on average, were significantly closer to adopting consistent condom use with occasional partners or clients than they were to adopting consistent condom use with their main partners. On average, respondents were midway between the Precontemplation and Contemplation stages regarding condom use with their main partner but were close to being in the Preparation stage when it came to consistent condom use with occasional partners. One implication of this finding is that although intentional change may be sufficient to move people along the SOC-VM continuum, behavioral change would be required to move people with regard to SOC-VO.

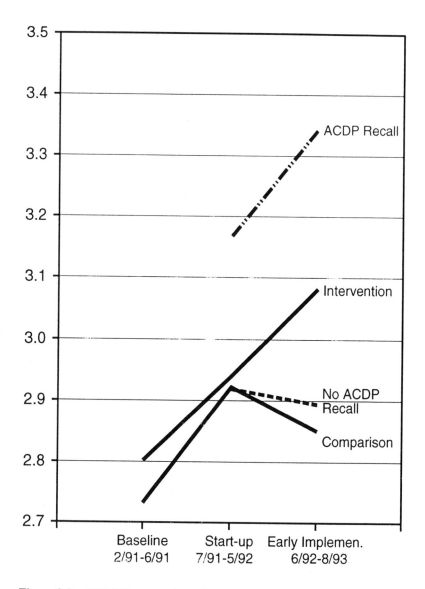

Figure 9.3. SOC-VO mean values: Condom use for vaginal sex with other partners.

Note: Intervention trend > Comparison trend (p = .024); ACDP Recall > No Recall (p = .0001).

As of early implementation, the mean SOC-VO had risen to 3.08 among respondents in the intervention areas, compared to the value of 2.85 in the comparison areas; this General Intervention Effect for SOC-VO was statistically significant ($p < .05$). Among intervention-area respondents who reported vaginal intercourse with a nonmain partner in the previous 30 days, 7.7% reported ACDP exposure during the start-up phase, versus 40.8% as of early implementation.

The Specific Exposure Effect was highly significant ($p < .001$). Once again, within the treatment area, community members exposed to the intervention were significantly closer to adopting consistent condom use for vaginal sex with their "other" partners (mean SOC = 3.34) than were those not exposed (mean SOC = 2.89). As previously indicated, this implies that the intervention had an effect on behavior and on intention.

Bleach Use for Cleaning
Injection Equipment

Figure 9.4 presents results for changes in the mean SOC for the use of bleach to clean injection equipment (SOC-Bleach). Respondents who reported sharing needles or works in the last 60 days were assessed for this behavior regardless of whether they were solicited as part of an IDU intervention community or if they were encountered elsewhere among sex traders, MSM-ngi, street youth, or designated census tracts (by definition, FSPs did not inject). Figure 9.4 represents 3,086 such respondents, of whom 2,028 (66%) were male and 1,058 (34%) were female. As in previous examples, the smallest number of respondents used to calculate a given mean was among start-up respondents reporting exposure ($n = 53$).

The baseline mean value of 2.91 in the intervention areas was greater than the mean of 2.65 for the comparison areas. As of early implementation, the SOC-Bleach mean had increased to 3.11 among respondents in the intervention areas but decreased to 2.53 in the comparison areas; this General Intervention Effect was statistically significant ($p < .005$). In other words, although respondents in the comparison areas, on average, remained between the Contemplation and Preparation stages, those in the intervention areas moved on average to a point slightly above the Preparation stage, indicating an increase in bleach use.

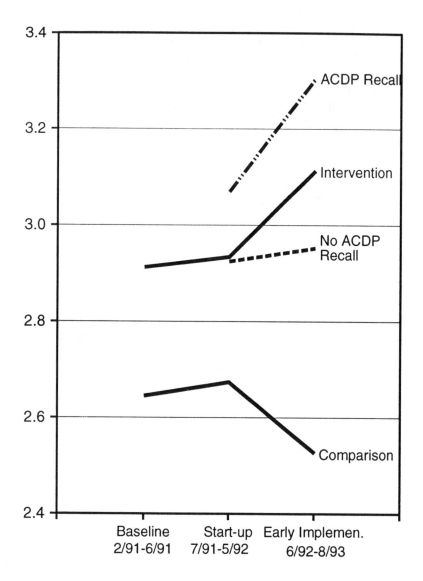

Figure 9.4.   SOC-Bleach mean values: Bleach use to clean injection equipment.

Note: Intervention trend > Comparison trend ($p = .002$); ACDP Recall > No Recall ($p = .001$).

Among intervention-area respondents who reported sharing works or needles in the previous 60 days, 6.7% reported ACDP exposure during the start-up phase versus 45.7% as of early implementation. Similar to the analyses for condom use, intervention-area respondents who reported exposure to project materials (early implementation mean = 3.31) were farther along the SOC continuum toward consistent bleach use than were the group not exposed (early implementation mean = 2.95); this Specific Exposure Effect was also significant ($p = .001$).

Conclusions From Preliminary Data

Contrary to a pervasive pessimism in public health about individuals' ability to change risk behavior (Galavotti & Beeker, 1993), these initial findings indicate that many individuals who are at high risk for sexually transmitted or needle-borne infections can be influenced to form protective intentions and subsequently adopt protective behaviors. The preliminary data presented in this report are encouraging.

The history of recording behavior change in HIV prevention research has typically been that of documenting dichotomous "yes or no" or "all or nothing" measures. Alternatively, the percentage of condom use has been considered but epidemiologic studies suggest that less-than-consistent condom or bleach use with an infected partner results in no reduction in risk of HIV transmission (Saracco et al., 1993). In contrast to these two approaches, the Stages of Change model indicates that behavior change takes time and often occurs in relatively small steps. By using the Stages of Change algorithm to examine these movements, we are able to document important changes that could be overlooked if one were to rely only on assessing behavior as a dichotomous variable. We are able to see more clearly the shifts that occur in a community at large as people respond to an ever-present, medium-intensity intervention, as contrasted with a high-intensity but low-frequency intervention such as an individual HIV-prevention counseling session. As HIV-prevention programs are shifting toward a model of comprehensive intervention strategies, which may include a variety of interventions ranging from those delivered in clinic settings to those delivered on the streets of a community, it is important to note the contribution of a community-level intervention.

The preliminary results presented in this chapter provide only a broad overview of the effect of the interventions on progress toward consistent condom and bleach use. Recall that to promote change in these behaviors the intervention messages focused on cognitive variables such as self-efficacy, perceptions of social norms, and attitudes toward behavioral performance. More in-depth analyses should also reveal an effect on these variables.

Furthermore, although the preceding analyses include adjustments for demographics, city, and type of community, they represent only the comprehensive perspective of the projects. Thorough site-specific and population-specific analyses will be conducted when data are available from the full implementation phase.

In summary, this paper has described the design and methods of the CDC-sponsored AIDS Community Demonstration Projects. Preliminary results were presented for consistent condom use under two circumstances: vaginal intercourse with main partners and vaginal intercourse with other partners. Consistent bleach use for cleaning shared injection equipment was also examined. In each case, individuals in the intervention area who reported specific exposure to the ACDP intervention showed significantly more movement toward consistent protective behavior than those who did not report exposure. For SOC-VO and SOC-Bleach, the exposure effect was strong enough to be significant even when diluted among all intervention-area respondents in contrast to comparison-area respondents. These results clearly indicate that theory-based, community-level interventions using community volunteers can be an effective tool in the fight against HIV transmission.

Note

1. Although the results of the data analyses presented in this chapter are almost identical to those presented in "Community Level Prevention of HIV Infection Among High Risk Populations: Methodology and Preliminary Findings from the AIDS Community Demonstration Projects" (*MMWR Recommendations and Reports,* in press) we have used different subject inclusion criteria for this chapter. Thus, the analyses presented in this chapter are based on slightly different samples of respondents.

References

Agresti, A. (1984). *Analysis of ordinal categorical data.* New York: Wiley.

Ajzen, I., & Fishbein, M. (1980). *Understanding attitudes and predicting social behavior.* Englewood Cliffs, NJ: Prentice Hall.

Bandura, A. (1986). *Social foundations of thought and action: A social cognitive theory.* Englewood Cliffs, NJ: Prentice Hall.

Bandura, A. (1992). Exercise of personal agency through the self-efficacy mechanism. In R. Schwarzer (Ed.), *Self-efficacy: Thought control of action* (pp. 3-38). Washington, DC: Hemisphere.

Bandura, A. (1994). Social cognitive theory and exercise of control over HIV infection. In R. J. DiClemente & J. L. Peterson (Eds.), *Preventing AIDS: Theories and methods of behavioral interventions* (pp. 1-20). New York: Plenum.

Becker, M. H. (1974). The health belief model and personal health behavior. *Health Education Monographs, 2,* 324-508.

Becker, M. H. (1988). AIDS and behavior change. *Public Health Reviews, 16,* 1-11.

Campbell, D. T., & Stanley, J. C. (1966). *Experimental and quasi-experimental designs for research.* Chicago: Rand McNally.

Cook, T. D., & Campbell, D. T. (1979). *Quasi-experimentation.* Boston: Houghton-Mifflin.

Corby, N. H., Enguidanos, S. M., & Kay, L. (in press). Development and use of role-model stories in a community-level AIDS risk-reduction intervention. *Public Health Reports.*

Fishbein, M., & Ajzen, I. (1975). *Belief, attitude, intention, and behavior: An introduction to theory and research.* Redding, MA: Addison-Wesley.

Fishbein, M., Bandura, A., Triandis, H. C., Kanfer, F. H., Becker, M. H., & Middlestadt, S. E. (1992). *Factors influencing behavior and behavior change: Final report.* Rockville, MD: National Institute of Mental Health.

Fishbein, M., Middlestadt, S. E., & Hitchcock, P. J. (1991). Using information to change sexually transmitted disease-related behaviors: An analysis based on the theory of reasoned action. In J. N. Wasserheit, S. O. Aral, & K. K. Holmes (Eds.), *Research issues in human behavior and sexually transmitted diseases in the AIDS era* (pp. 243-257). Washington, DC: American Society for Microbiology.

Galavotti C., & Beeker C. (1993). Changing HIV risk behaviors: The case against pessimism. *American Journal of Public Health, 83,* 1791.

Goldbaum, G., Perdue, K. H., & Higgins, D. L. (in press). Non-gay-identifying men who have sex with men: Formative research results from Seattle, Washington. *Public Health Reports.*

Guenther-Grey, C., Noroian, D., Fonseka, J., Higgins, D. L., & the AIDS Community Demonstration Projects. (in press). Developing community networks to deliver HIV prevention interventions: Lessons learned from the AIDS community demonstration projects. *Public Health Reports.*

Guenther-Grey, C., Schnell, D., & Fishbein, M. (in press). Sources of HIV/AIDS information among female sex traders. *Health Education Research.*

Guenther-Grey, C., Tross, S., McAlister, A., Freeman, A., Cohn, D., Corby, N., Wood, R., & Fishbein, M. (1992). AIDS community demonstration projects: Implementation of volunteer networks for HIV-prevention programs—Selected sites, 1991-1992. *MMWR, 41,* 868-869, 875-876.

Harris, M. (1990). Emics and etics revisited. In N. Thomas, K. L. Pike, & M. Harris (Eds.), *Emics and etics: The insider/outsider debate* (pp. 48-61). Newbury Park, CA: Sage.

Higgins, D. L., O'Reilly, K. O., Tashima, N., Crain, C., Beeker, C., Goldbaum, G., Elifson, C. S., Galavotti, C., Guenther-Grey, C., & the AIDS Community Demonstration Projects. (in press). Using formative research to lay the foundation for community-level HIV prevention efforts: An example from the AIDS community demonstration projects. *Public Health Reports.*

Kleinbaum, D. G., & Kupper L. L. (1978). *Applied regression analysis and other multivariable methods.* North Scituate, MA: Duxbury.

McAlister, A. (1991). Population behavior change: A theory-based approach. *Journal of Public Health Policy, 12,* 345-361.

McAlister, A. (in press). Behavioral journalism: Beyond the marketing model for health communication. *American Journal of Health Promotion.*

McAlister, A., Puska, P., Koskela, K., Pallonen, U., & Maccoby, N. (1980). Mass communication and community organization for public health education. *American Psychologist, 35,* 375-379.

National Research Council. (1991). *Evaluating AIDS prevention programs* (expanded ed.). Washington, DC: National Academy Press.

O'Reilly, K., & Higgins, D. L. (1991). AIDS community demonstration projects for HIV prevention among hard-to-reach groups. *Public Health Reports, 106,* 714-720.

Prochaska, J. O., DiClemente, C. C., & Norcross, J. C. (1992). In search of how people change: Applications to addictive behaviors. *American Psychologist, 47,* 1102-1114.

Puska, P., Salonen, J. T., Koskela. K., McAlister, A., Kottke, T. E., Maccoby, N., & Farquhar, J. W. (1985). The community-based strategy to prevent coronary heart disease: Conclusions from ten years of the North Karelia project. *Annual Review of Public Health, 6,* 147-193.

Rosenstock, I. M. (1974). The health belief model and preventive health behavior. *Health Education Monographs, 2,* 354-385.

Saracco, A., Musicco, M., Nicolosi, A., et al. (1993). Man-to-woman sexual transmission of HIV: Longitudinal study of 343 steady partners of infected men. *Journal of Acquired Immune Deficiency Syndromes, 6,* 497-502.

Schnell, D. J., Galavotti, C., Fishbein, M., Chan, D., & the AIDS Community Demonstration Projects. (in press). Measuring the adoption of consistent use of condoms using the stages of change model. *Public Health Reports.*

Searle, S. R., Speed, F. M., & Milliken, G. A. (1980). Population marginal means in the linear model: An alternative to least squares means. *The American Statistician, 34,* 216-221.

Simons, P. Z., Rietmeijer, C. A., Kane, M. S., Guenther-Grey, C., Higgins, D. L., & Cohn, D. L. (in press). Building a peer network among injecting drug users in Five Points, Denver: Implementation of a community-level HIV prevention program. *Public Health Reports.*

10

HIV Risk Interventions
for Active Drug Users:
Experience and Prospects

FEN RHODES
C. KEVIN MALOTTE

T he cumulative number of AIDS cases
in the United States at the end of 1994
exceeded 440,000 (Centers for Dis-
ease Control (CDC), 1994a). AIDS has become the leading cause of
death for men 25 to 44 years old and it is the fourth leading cause of
death for women in this age bracket (CDC, 1994b). For drug users, the
effect of AIDS has been severe. Almost one-third of the AIDS cases
diagnosed in 1994 occurred among injection drug users (IDUs)—27%
among IDU women and heterosexual men, and another 5% among IDU
men who have sex with men (CDC, 1994a). Injection drug use also was
a factor in two-thirds of the pediatric AIDS cases involving mother-to-
infant transmission reported in 1994 where the mother's risk could be
determined. In 45% of these cases, the mother had been infected
directly through injection drug use; in another 22%, infection had
occurred indirectly as a result of sexual contact with an injection drug
user (CDC, 1994a).

AUTHORS' NOTE: The research on which parts of this chapter are based was supported
by grants from the Community Research Branch of the National Institute on Drug Abuse
(R18-DA05747 and U01-DA07474).

The prevalence of HIV infection among injection drug users varies widely depending on geographic location. Data from the National AIDS Demonstration Research Projects targeting out-of-treatment IDUs (LaBrie, McAuliffe, Nemeth-Coslett, & Wilberschied, 1993) showed HIV infection rates of 58% in New York City, 46%-52% in New Jersey, 46%-54% in Puerto Rico, and 32% in Miami. Rates were considerably lower in Midwest, Southwest, and West Coast cities, for example, 1.4% in Columbus/Dayton, 3.1% in Minneapolis/St. Paul, 8.5% in Houston, 2.2% in Tucson, 5.8% in Long Beach, and 2.4% in San Diego.

HIV infection rates are also high among crack cocaine users. A recent study of young inner-city adults in New York, Miami, and San Francisco found 16% of crack smokers to be infected with HIV, compared with only 5% of nonsmokers (Edlin et al., 1994). Infection rates were highest among crack-smoking women in New York (30%) and Miami (23%), and crack smoking was more strongly associated with HIV infection for women than for men.

This chapter discusses HIV risk interventions for out-of-treatment drug user populations. The chapter begins with a discussion of modes of transmission for IDUs and crack smokers, followed by an overview of collaborative studies sponsored by the National Institute on Drug Abuse (NIDA), a brief account of selected other behavioral investigations, a summary of needle exchange programs, and a comparison of intervention approaches. The chapter then presents a detailed discussion of the NIDA Cooperative Agreement study conducted in Long Beach, California, and concludes with suggestions for improving the effectiveness of HIV risk interventions and a proposed intervention model.

HIV Transmission Vectors

Among injection drug users, HIV infection is transmitted primarily through contaminated injection equipment, specifically needles and syringes, rinse water, cookers (used to mix drugs), and cottons (used to filter the drug solution) (Institute of Medicine, 1994). Drug paraphernalia is frequently shared by one or more individuals at the time drugs are injected. HIV risks associated with sharing injection equipment can be dramatically reduced by proper cleaning of needles and syringes with household bleach before reuse, by not reusing rinse water, and by ensuring that cookers/cottons do not become contaminated by unsterile needles (Haverkos & Jones, 1994; Shapshak et al., 1994; Vlahov, Astemborski, Solomon, & Nelson, 1994). HIV-infected IDUs can also transmit the virus to their sexual partners, who may or may not themselves be IDUs. One-third to one-half of IDUs report having main or casual sex partners who are not drug injectors, with males being more likely than females to have non-IDU partners (Brown & Weissman, 1993; Rhodes et al., 1990).

The HIV risk associated with crack use is an indirect one arising from increased and riskier sexual activity by crack smokers as a consequence of both physiological and social factors associated with crack use (Institute of Medicine, 1994). Characteristically, cocaine acts as a sexual stimulant, especially among men, although there is evidence that it may depress sexual desire and performance in chronic addicts (MacDonald, Waldorf, Reinarman, & Murphy, 1988). The disinhibiting effect of cocaine is reportedly much stronger than that of depressants such as alcohol, Valium, or heroin (Institute of Medicine, 1994), resulting for many individuals in increased sexual desire and enjoyment and causing them to engage in unprotected sexual acts they might not consider under other circumstances. The effects of crack are both intense and short-lived, 3-5 minutes (Ratner, 1993) or possibly as long as 20 minutes (Bowser, 1989), creating an immediate need for more of the drug. A common practice for women, especially in crack houses but also in other settings, is to finance their crack habit by routinely bartering sex for drugs with numerous partners, usually without using condoms (Institute of Medicine, 1994). The tendency of crack users to engage in high-frequency, high-risk sex with numerous and often anonymous partners has been documented in a variety of ethnographic and survey investigations (Booth, Watters, & Chitwood, 1993; Edlin et al., 1994; Inciardi, 1993; Longshore, Anglin, Annon, & Hsieh, 1993; Ratner, 1993; Weatherby et al., 1992). There is also evidence that crack-using IDUs, compared with those who do not use crack, are more likely to have sex partners who are drug injectors (Booth et al., 1993).

Sexual activity serves as a bridge by which IDUs and crack smokers can transmit HIV to other, non-drug-using populations. The importance of this phenomenon is underlined by the statistic that 84% of AIDS cases in 1994 resulting from heterosexual transmission, where partner risks could be determined, involved sexual activity with a person who injected drugs (CDC, 1994). In the 4,802, or 50%, of cases of hetero-

sexual HIV transmission for which partner-risk factors were not identified, it is speculated that a significant number of the partners might be
crack smokers. Transmission of the virus occurs primarily during vaginal or anal intercourse, either from male to female or female to male
(Haverkos & Battjes, 1992; Institute of Medicine, 1994). As with other
STDs, condoms are an effective means of substantially reducing, although not eliminating, HIV infection risk (CDC, 1993).

Overview of Interventions to
Control HIV Transmission in Drug Users

Widely understood is that an urgent need exists to develop effective
interventions to prevent the spread of HIV/AIDS among members of
drug-using populations (Edlin et al., 1994; Fullilove & Fullilove, 1989;
Guinan, 1989; National Research Council, 1989). Specific programs
and strategies to reduce HIV drug-related and sexual risk behaviors
among IDUs and, to a lesser extent, among crack smokers have been
implemented and evaluated in several large-scale collaborative studies
and numerous individual investigations. Intervention efforts have targeted both individuals currently receiving some form of drug treatment
and those not in treatment.

Many of the out-of-treatment drug users who have participated in
these HIV intervention programs report previous involvement in drug
treatment, but a substantial percentage indicate that they have never
received any treatment for their substance abuse. In a nationwide study
of more than 20,000 out-of-treatment drug injectors accessed through
street outreach, for example, it was found that 42% had never participated in any type of drug treatment (Liebman, LaVerne, Coughey, &
Hua, 1993). Findings were similar for all geographic regions of the
country except the South, which had a higher percentage of individuals
who had never been in drug treatment. Compared with drug users in
treatment programs, those not in treatment display more high-risk drug
and sexual behaviors (McCusker, Koblin, Lewis, & Sullivan, 1990) and
have higher rates of HIV infection (Longshore & Anglin, 1994). As a
consequence of these factors, intervention efforts have increasingly
been directed at this very large group of active drug users who are

currently not engaged in drug treatment and whose drug-use and sexual behaviors place them at high risk for becoming infected with HIV or transmitting the virus to others.

NIDA National AIDS
Demonstration Research Project

The National AIDS Demonstration Research (NADR) project was initiated in 1987 by the Community Research Branch of the National Institute on Drug Abuse (NIDA) to implement and evaluate AIDS prevention programs for out-of-treatment injection drug users and their female sex partners. By the time of its conclusion in 1991, the NADR project encompassed 29 comprehensive community-based programs in 27 U.S. cities and Puerto Rico (NIDA, 1994). The NADR effort was characterized by the use of indigenous outreach workers at each site to access target population members, provision of or referral to HIV testing, and use of innovative strategies to modify high-risk behaviors (Brown & Beschner, 1993). A standard structured interview question-naire, the AIDS Initial Assessment (AIA), was employed to assess client demographics, drug treatment history, and STD/HIV history, plus base-line drug use, sexual activity, health status, and HIV/AIDS knowledge. A companion interview instrument, the AIDS Follow-up Assessment (AFA), was used by all sites at 5- to 9-month follow-ups to measure behavior and knowledge change among program participants (NIDA, 1994).

Each of the comprehensive NADR projects implemented standard and enhanced interventions that were evaluated with regard to compara-tive efficacy in reducing HIV risk behaviors. The *standard intervention* consisted of special HIV/AIDS education with referrals to community services and was frequently delivered in the context of HIV counseling and testing. Although the specific content differed somewhat from site to site, all of the standard interventions comprised a maximum of two sessions and emphasized communication of HIV/AIDS information with consideration of methods for reducing personal HIV risk and demonstration of correct techniques for needle cleaning and condom use. The *enhanced intervention* at three-fourths of the sites consisted of the standard intervention plus additional sessions or experiences incorporating one or more of the following components: individual behavioral counseling, couples counseling, behavioral skills training, modification of behavioral and normative beliefs associated with HIV risk reduction, or development of peer support networks. For a minority of sites, the enhanced intervention was not this sort of add-on to the standard intervention, and a small number of sites developed a single experimental intervention that was offered to all clients (Brown & Beschner, 1993; NIDA, 1994). Separate interventions were provided for IDUs and female sex partners. With a few exceptions, enhanced interventions were not based on explicit theoretical models of health behavior change or else used such models only in a very general sense. Activities of the enhanced interventions were selected primarily on the basis of their putative relevance for reducing general or specific needle-related or sexual HIV risk behaviors. Definition and sequencing of intervention activities to ensure consistency with particular theoretical constructs or processes was usually not evident. As a consequence, activities of the different enhanced interventions frequently did not form a coherent whole in theoretical terms.

More than 26,000 IDUs and 5,000 noninjecting sex partners were recruited to participate in the NADR project through street outreach and from shelters, clinics, and other community settings (Brown & Beschner, 1993). Follow-up data were obtained on approximately 13,500 IDUs and 1,600 sex partners located at 28 sites (NIDA, 1994). Demographically, 77% of the IDUs recruited by NADR sites were men; 57% were African Americans, 23% whites, and 18% Hispanics. The mean age of participants was 35 years; 18% lived in shelters or on the street (Liebman et al., 1993). Overall HIV seroprevalence among IDUs was 18%, ranging from less than 1% to 58% depending on site (LaBrie et al., 1993). The characteristics of noninjecting female sex partners were similar to those of IDUs with the exception that female partners averaged 5 years younger (Deren, Davis, Tortu, & Ahluwalia, 1993). HIV seroprevalence data were not available for the female sex partners.

Results for both standard and enhanced intervention IDU clients showed substantial baseline-to-follow-up changes in most drug-related risk behaviors. The overall percentage of individuals reporting use of borrowed needles fell from 48% to 24% and the percentage sharing needles with two or more persons declined from 54% to 23% (Stephens et al., 1993). The reported frequency of drug use also decreased, with the percentage of clients injecting daily falling from 70% to 42%

between intake and follow-up. In addition to decreasing drug use, a substantial fraction (33%) of IDU clients entered drug treatment during the 5- to 9-month period between intake and follow-up, presumably as a consequence of their participation in the risk-reduction interventions. Changes in reported sexual risk behaviors were less marked, however. The percentage of participants reporting more than one sex partner in the past 6 months decreased from 44% at baseline to 36% at follow-up, and the percentage reporting that they always used condoms during sex increased from 10% to 19% (NIDA, 1994; Stephens et al., 1993).

Small differences in HIV risk behaviors were found in favor of the enhanced interventions compared to the standard interventions (NIDA, 1994; Stephens et al., 1993). Interventions at 20 sites were compared on three outcome measures: injection frequency, composite needle risk, and composite sex risk. The percentage of "successful" clients was also calculated for each measure, based on the proportion of individuals whose HIV risks in an area had either decreased or stayed at low levels. Overall injection frequency at follow-up, measured on a scale from 0 to 6, was 2.8 in the enhanced groups compared with 3.0 in the standard groups ($p < .05$), with 51% compared to 48% successful clients. At the individual site level, only one enhanced intervention showed a significantly greater reduction in injection frequency. An overall small difference in favor of the enhanced interventions was also found for composite needle risk, measured on a scale from 0 to 5: 2.2 versus 2.3 ($p < .05$), with 59% versus 55% successful clients for the enhanced compared with the standard interventions. Overall composite sex risk at follow-up, measured on a scale from 0 to 21, was 1.3 versus 1.4 ($p < .05$) in favor of the enhanced interventions, with 73% versus 72% successful clients. Only one site's enhanced intervention, that of Long Beach, was significantly superior to the standard intervention in reducing both composite needle risk in addition to sex risk.

The enhanced intervention conducted by Long Beach employed an individual behavioral counseling model that was formulated in the context of an explicit theoretical framework (Rhodes, 1993; Rhodes, Humfleet, & Corby, 1992). Clients received two standard intervention sessions that incorporated HIV counseling and testing, after which they viewed a videotape employing local drug users to communicate the risks and consequences of HIV infection and ways to minimize risks of HIV exposure. This was followed by two sessions of structured behavioral counseling focused on identifying personal HIV risks, committing to change for a specific risk, and developing and implementing a plan for achieving the risk-reduction objective. Of the initially at-risk clients who participated in this enhanced intervention, 75% decreased their composite injection risk compared with 60% of standard intervention clients (*p* < .03) (Rhodes, Humfleet, & Corby, 1992). However, the differential change in sex risk for the two interventions was modest: 67% of enhanced versus 63% of standard intervention participants demonstrated reductions in composite sex risk or maintained low levels of risk at follow-up (*p* < .05) (Stephens et al., 1993).

In addition to these outcome findings, a significant relationship was found between minutes of intervention exposure and reduction in injection frequency, composite needle risk, and sex risk (*p* < .01), using pooled data from nine sites (NIDA, 1994; Stephens et al., 1993). Interpretation of this finding is confounded, however, by the fact that analyses included data from both standard and enhanced interventions, which differed in average length and also in content.

The special NADR interventions conducted for noninjecting female sex partners of IDUs have not been generally reported in the literature. One intervention for female sex partners that has been described is that of the Long Beach site, which involved a series of four psychoeducational workshops in addition to a standard intervention with HIV counseling and testing (Rhodes, Wolitski, & Thornton-Johnson, 1992). Preliminary findings indicated that the workshops had a positive effect on the personal efficacy of participants and that they were more successful in reducing HIV risks than was the standard intervention alone.

NIDA Cooperative Agreement Program

The Cooperative Agreement for AIDS Community-Based Outreach/Intervention Research Program was initiated in September 1990 by NIDA's Community Research Branch to continue and extend the prevention research efforts with out-of-treatment drug users begun through the NADR project. As of August 1994, there were 21 Cooperative Agreement sites located in the United States plus one site each in Puerto Rico and Brazil (NIDA, 1995). Under the Cooperative Agreement Program, the target population was broadened to include both drug injectors and crack cocaine users, who may or may not also inject drugs.

Although individual sites continued to develop their own enhanced interventions as in the NADR project, all Cooperative Agreement sites used an identical NIDA standard intervention (Coyle, 1993).

As in the NADR Project, a standard structured interview, the Risk Behavior Assessment (RBA), is employed by all sites to obtain client demographic information, drug treatment experience, and STD/HIV history, in addition to baseline drug use, sexual activity, and associated HIV risk behaviors. A standard follow-up interview, the Risk Behavior Follow-Up Assessment (RBFA), is administered by all sites at 5- to 9-month follow-ups. The RBA and RBFA employ a 30-day time frame for self-reported risk behaviors, unlike the 6-month time frame employed by the NADR AIA and AFA interviews. This change was made to increase the sensitivity of the interview at follow-up to the effects of interventions recently completed by clients and also to improve the reliability of baseline and follow-up behavioral self-reports. The RBA and RBFA interviews also obtain information concerning drug use in the past 48 hours; also, urine testing was added in the Cooperative Agreement Program to verify self-reports of recent drug use (NIDA, 1993).

Although most of the Cooperative Agreement studies are still in progress, preliminary outcome data are available for selected programs (NIDA Investigators, 1995). Consistent with the NADR program, these initial findings indicate that the relatively brief two-session NIDA standard intervention leads to substantial changes in drug-related HIV risk behaviors, including reductions in frequency of drug use and significant but considerably smaller changes in sexual risk behaviors. Reductions in HIV risk behaviors have been reported for both drug injectors and crack cocaine users. Relatively few of the site-specific *enhanced* interventions, however, appear at this stage to be successful in demonstrating greater change in risk behaviors than the standard intervention. Six of the original 14 sites of the Cooperative Agreement Program showed significant differential change in composite drug- or sex-related risks for their enhanced interventions versus the NIDA standard intervention (McCoy, Metsch, McCoy & Weatherby, 1995). Three sites, including Long Beach, showed significantly greater change for both categories of risk behavior. A description of the enhanced intervention employed in Long Beach, together with a summary of preliminary findings, is provided in a later section.

Other Behavioral Interventions for Active Drug Users

A number of other behavioral intervention efforts to reduce HIV risk among active drug users, specifically IDUs, have been reported in addition to those of the preceding multisite collaborative studies (e.g., Friedman et al., 1992; Mandell et al., 1994; Neaigus et al., 1990; van den Hoek, Haastrecht, & Coutinho, 1992). All participants in these interventions were active drug users who had been recruited through street outreach or other means not involving treatment programs. Current involvement of individuals in drug treatment was not an exclusionary criterion, however. The intervention content ranged from community organizing (Friedman et al., 1992) to structured individual behavioral counseling (Mandell et al., 1994). All interventions provided HIV counseling and testing as an integral component. The findings from these interventions are largely consistent with those of the other studies reviewed: that is, that IDUs often reduce their injection-related risks to a substantial degree following intervention and may also reduce their sexual HIV risks but to a lesser extent. The only study comparing the relative efficacy of a minimal versus enhanced intervention for out-of-treatment drug users (in this instance standard HIV counseling and testing versus counseling and testing plus a one-hour interactive session) found no differences between the two interventions (Mandell et al., 1994).

Needle Exchange Programs

Needle exchange programs, first in Europe and more recently in the U.S. and Canada, have been established in an effort to reduce syringe sharing by providing access to sterile needles and syringes. In a comprehensive review of needle exchange programs in the United States, Canada, and Europe, Lurie and Reingold (1993) found that (a) the majority of studies of needle exchange programs demonstrated decreased rates of drug-risk behavior among their clients, (b) there is no evidence that needle exchange programs increase community levels of drug use, (c) there is no evidence that needle exchange programs increase the number of discarded syringes, and (d) needle exchanges can reach IDUs who do not access drug abuse treatment services and can serve as a bridge to these and other public health services.

More recently, additional reports have supported these findings. An evaluation of a needle exchange program in San Francisco found increased participation in the exchange over time, a decrease in the median number of self-reported daily injections, and a decline in the percentage of persons who reported their first drug injection in the prior year, thus suggesting that the exchange did not encourage initiation or greater levels of drug use. The evaluation further indicated that participation in the exchange decreased needle sharing (Watters, Estilo, Clark, & Lorvick, 1994). An innovative evaluation of the New Haven needle exchange, using tests of systematic samples of returned needles for evidence of HIV DNA, suggested that HIV incidence may have been reduced by 40% among program participants (Kaplan & Heimer, 1994).

Education and involvement of affected community members, including civic and religious leaders, legal authorities, and IDUs, appears to be an important factor in mounting a successful needle exchange program (Schwartz, 1993). Even when the general idea of needle exchange is accepted, many communities oppose locating it in their neighborhood (U.S. Conference of Mayors, 1994). Other problems in implementing needle exchanges include legal barriers, concern about the appropriateness of using limited resources to fund needle exchanges in lieu of providing treatment slots, and concern that such programs communicate tacit approval or at least mixed messages regarding the acceptability of drug use. As a result, fewer than 50 needle exchanges are currently operating in the United States (U.S. Conference of Mayors, 1994).

Comparison of Intervention Strategies

The interventions that have been described can be characterized in terms of their relative emphasis on direct modification of individuals' risk behaviors through mechanisms such as enhancing perception of personal risk, behavioral skills training, and changing attitudes and beliefs, versus influencing risk behaviors indirectly through modifying one or more elements of the physical or social environment. In the latter category, for example, are the needle exchange programs, which facilitate compliance with behavioral recommendations for sterilized needle use by making new needles readily available to drug injectors and removing used needles from circulation. The social organizing strategy of Friedman et al. (1992) is another example of this approach. By contrast, most of NIDA's (1994) NADR and (1995) Cooperative Agreement interventions have emphasized direct modification of individual risk behaviors, with minimal focus on modifying the environmental context of behaviors. The community-level intervention of the CDC AIDS Community Demonstration Project, discussed by Fishbein and colleagues in this volume, contains elements of both approaches.

Both strategies have their particular strengths and weaknesses, leading to a conclusion that neither should be used in isolation. Community-focused interventions are believed to yield more pervasive and perhaps stable behavioral changes because of their emphasis on manipulating the social reinforcers and environmental constraints associated with desired behaviors. However, behavior change may be slow to occur and the magnitude of individual change may fall short of expectations in the near term. With individual-focused interventions, it is possible to accommodate to the needs of different individuals and their unique circumstances and theoretically to engender larger changes in behavior in briefer periods of time. Maintenance of behavior change is often problematic, however, because of the lack of ongoing environmental supports for the new behaviors.

A Behavioral Intervention Example: The Long Beach Enhanced Intervention for Injection Drug and Crack Users

A behaviorally focused, multisession enhanced intervention for out-of-treatment IDUs and crack users was developed in Long Beach as a part of the NIDA Cooperative Agreement Program (Rhodes & Humfleet, 1993). The Long Beach intervention incorporates both structured and unstructured psychoeducational activities that are provided in both group and individual settings. Change in HIV-related behaviors is promoted through guided assessment of clients' personal HIV risk, articulation of achievable risk-reduction goals, and individualized follow-up of clients' progress in achieving these goals. Role-model video-tapes and structured activities are employed, reflecting principles from the Theory of Stages of Behavioral Change (Prochaska & DiClemente, 1992) and the Theory of Reasoned Action (Ajzen & Fishbein, 1980). Social support provided by peer buddies (client-identified individuals who will support HIV risk-reduction efforts) and by outreach staff is a core element of the intervention and monthly lunch socials are offered for clients and their support buddies (Wood & Rhodes, 1995). The intervention is intended to extend over approximately 4 months. Nonmonetary incentives are provided to encourage intervention participation, including a food bank for study clients and food coupons for session attendance. The present intervention is an outgrowth of an earlier individual counseling intervention for injection drug users (Rhodes, 1993) in which behavioral contracting was used to facilitate definition and achievement of personal HIV risk-reduction goals.

Intervention Design

A core activity of the intervention program is HIV testing and counseling, which is offered to all participants at the time of enrollment. HIV-antibody pretest and posttest counseling are combined with basic AIDS education and prevention training emphasizing drug-related risks. For participants in the enhanced intervention, these two sessions are followed by two group workshop sessions plus one individual session addressing salient issues in personal behavior change. After completion of these structured activities, participants are encouraged to attend a minimum of two informal "risk-reduction socials" held on a monthly basis for program participants, their supportive peers, and program staff. Finally, participants receive a minimum of two planned, supportive visits from outreach staff during the 6-month period of their participation in the program. Altogether, the complete intervention program, including HIV testing and counseling, encompasses nine sessions and planned activities.

Group Sessions

The two group sessions involve three to seven clients plus two facilitators and are highly interactive. Activities consist of structured exercises in which group members are asked to relate their own experiences and provide suggestions to other group participants. Although activities are built around structured exercises, facilitators are able to emphasize the specific HIV risks most relevant for particular group members.

The first group session begins with a review of local HIV/AIDS statistics, with emphasis placed on the elevated AIDS risk of individuals who use drugs. Group members then participate in a worksheet exercise in which they identify their own HIV risks. This is followed by a discussion of appropriate prevention methods. Subsequent to this activity, the stages-of-change model is explained as a framework for thinking about HIV risk reduction. To reinforce this metaphor, participants view role-model videotapes in which former clients report their success in reducing HIV risks. These are interpreted by facilitators and considered by the group within a stages-of-change framework. A second worksheet activity is then conducted in which participants determine their readiness and need to change potential HIV risk behaviors by placing themselves on a stages-of-change continuum for each behavior. This exercise provides a means by which relevant personal HIV risk-reduction goals can be identified by participants. Finally, group facilitators lead a discussion of the importance of social support in chang- ing problematic personal behaviors, using HIV-related and other examples. The importance of social support is then related specifically to the role-model videos and participants relate some of their former experiences of receiving social support in accomplishing difficult goals.

During the second group session, participants discuss their personal goals for HIV risk reduction and begin to identify first steps toward behavior change. The stages-of-change worksheet activity from the first session is reviewed to assist participants in focusing on one personal change, either drug-related or sex-related, that they are willing and able to make to reduce their HIV risk. Group discussion addresses potential barriers to the achievement of identified goals and also possible solutions. Participants then view additional videotapes of former clients who have succeeded in changing specific risk behaviors in the face of barriers. Facilitators assist participants in the definition of initial, concrete steps toward HIV risk reduction that can be taken during the next week based on their chosen goal. Group discussion about the importance of social support in changing personal risk behavior follows, at which time participants are asked to identify an individual who they believe will support and encourage them in working toward achievement of their personal risk-reduction goal (a support buddy).

Individual Behavioral Counseling Session

The individual session provides an opportunity for clients to meet one-on-one with a counselor to discuss personal risk-reduction issues in a private setting. Counselors review the personal risk-reduction goal identified by each client during the group session and the initial step to be taken toward goal achievement. Risk-reduction goals are evaluated to ensure that they are realistic, clearly defined, and reasonably capable of achievement during the 4-month period of the intervention. An effort is made to modify unrealistic or poorly defined goals to increase the probability that they can be successfully achieved and to refine and expand action plans for goal achievement. Specific barriers that might be encountered by the client are identified and possible techniques for overcoming them are considered.

In addition, the social support resources of each client are reviewed and an effort is made to assist clients who have not been successful in identifying a risk-reduction support buddy. If necessary, the client's outreach worker is designated to be a support buddy. The counselor also reinforces the perception of the outreach worker as a positive role model and a source of personal support for risk reduction. Finally, the client's referral needs are also assessed and an additional appointment is made if the client is in need of drug treatment, medical, or social services, so that intervention staff can provide direct assistance in contacting local agencies and arranging referrals. At the end of the session, clients are reminded of the next monthly social event and are assured that their outreach worker will be in touch with them soon.

Monthly Social Events

Clients are invited to attend a minimum of two monthly support socials following their participation in the first group session. These events, which are also attended by outreach and intervention staff, are held at local community recreation facilities that have been identified as providing easy access for participants. Described by staff and clients as "picnics at the park" or "parties," the HIV-focused social gatherings provide peer support for risk reduction and opportunities for social modeling by staff and peers. They also serve to influence the perceived social norms of clients and to increase their self-efficacy for reducing

HIV risks. Drug users receive personal invitations and are encouraged to bring their previously identified support buddy as a guest. The events last approximately two hours, include a meal, and are typically attended by 15-25 clients and 10-15 guests.

Group activities and games provide opportunities for informal interaction among clients, support buddies, and program staff. Small-group discussions, skits, testimonials by clients and outreach staff, and structured exercises focus on aspects of personal risk reduction such as overcoming barriers, defining future steps, and obtaining social support. During these events, an effort is made to link clients who still do not have support buddies with individuals who are willing to serve in this role.

Supportive Follow-Up Contacts

Outreach staff are responsible for conducting a minimum of two supportive follow-up visits with each client that are in addition to contacts they may have with the client at scheduled social events or intervention sessions. These contacts typically last 15-20 minutes and are planned in advance by outreach staff in consultation with intervention staff who have worked with the individual client. Topics discussed include progress in reducing HIV risk, problems encountered in implementing the client's personal risk-reduction plan, development of solutions to identified problems, the importance and relevance of HIV risk-reduction, the personal risk profile of the client, and the client's needs for drug treatment, medical, shelter, or social services. These contacts serve to reinforce the client's view of the outreach worker as a positive role model for adopting HIV risk-reduction behaviors.

Preliminary Findings

Preliminary findings based on 896 clients followed to date (78% of current follow-up eligibles) indicate that both the basic and enhanced interventions are having a substantial effect in terms of reducing HIV risk behavior. The study employed a crossover design in which clients were assigned to standard versus enhanced conditions based on their geographic area of recruitment, defined by matched zip-code clusters. Quota sampling was employed to ensure balance with regard to gender, race/ethnicity, type of drug use, and recruitment zip code. Crossover of the standard and enhanced interventions to the matched zip-code area occurred midway during recruitment of the 1,241 total study participants.

Logistic regression analyses compared changes in multiple drug-related and sex-related risk behaviors for clients participating in most or all of the enhanced intervention versus those completing the NIDA standard intervention. The results showed statistically significant differences at the 6-month follow-up, favoring the enhanced intervention. Results for two behaviors, condom use and stopping drug use, are summarized in Tables 10.1-10.3. All analyses controlled for differences in baseline risk level, gender, age, and race/ethnicity. Baseline risk behavior was a significant and strong predictor of change for most behaviors but gender, age, and race/ethnicity were not significantly related to degree of change for any behavior. At the 6-month follow-up, clients in the enhanced intervention demonstrated greater reduction in frequency of drug injection ($p < .03$), frequency of stopping injection ($p < .001$) and crack use ($p < .01$), and increase in condom use ($p < .03$). Enhanced intervention participants were also more likely to have entered or tried to enter drug treatment ($p < .02$). In addition, follow-up urine testing showed fewer crack users in the enhanced intervention to be positive for cocaine compared with those in the standard intervention ($p < .05$).

Risk behavior changes tended to be greatest in areas that were consistent with clients' personal risk-reduction goals. Among enhanced intervention completers, goal-congruent changes, expressed as the percentage of clients showing positive behavior change at follow-up, were substantially greater than changes made by clients under the NIDA standard intervention. Enhanced versus standard comparisons were 74% vs. 35% for condom use, 33% vs. 22% for stopping drug injection, 35% vs. 16% for stopping crack use, and 55% vs. 35% for entering or trying to enter drug treatment (injectors only).

Improving the Effectiveness of HIV Risk Interventions

Analyses of existing HIV behavioral interventions that target active drug users, in conjunction with previous advice concerning intervention

**Table 10.1
Logistic Regression for Improvement in
Relative Frequency of Condom Use (Past 30 Days)**

Variable	Odds Ratio	p
Race/Ethnicity		
African American	.92	.88
Hispanic	.87	.82
White	.88	.83
Gender (female)	1.29	.29
Age (older)	1.00	.99
Drug use (noninjector)	1.58	.07
Intervention group (enhanced)	1.73	.03
Condom use at baseline (> 0%)	2.43	.001

NOTE: Analysis is based on 344 participants who were sexually active at baseline and follow-up and who reported at baseline less than 100% condom use for vaginal or oral sex in the past 30 days. Odds ratios are adjusted for multivariate effects. All variables are dichotomous; "Other" was the reference category for race/ethnicity.

design articulated by other behavioral science researchers (Booth & Watters, 1994; Fisher & Fisher, 1992; Kelly & Murphy, 1992; Kelly, Murphy, Sikkema, & Kalichman, 1993; Lewis & Kashima, 1993; Sechrest, West, Phillips, Redner, & Yeaton, 1979), have led to the following recommendations or guidelines for developing improved and more powerful interventions:

1. Identify a theoretical framework to serve as a foundation for the intervention and that can be used to guide the development of intervention activities and the definition of outcome behaviors.

2. Ensure that intervention activities are consistent with theoretical components and that they are clearly linked to well-defined behavioral outcomes. Conduct preliminary studies as necessary to ascertain preintervention levels of behavioral determinants such as beliefs, skills, self-efficacy, and social support, and also current levels of outcome behaviors.

3. Conduct preliminary studies to identify demographic, cultural, and other personal and contextual factors that are likely to influence individuals' responses to the intervention, and to determine how the intervention can be structured to address these factors.

Table 10.2
Logistic Regression for
Stopping Injection Drug Use (Past 30 Days)

Variable	Odds Ratio	p
Race/Ethnicity		
African American	1.56	.39
Hispanic	.73	.56
White	.79	.64
Gender (female)	.90	.69
Age (older)	.68	.12
Intervention group (enhanced)	1.88	.01
Frequency of injection at baseline (>19 days past month)	4.23	.001

NOTE: Analysis is based on 439 participants who reported at baseline injection of drugs during the past 30 days. Odds ratios are adjusted for multivariate effects. All variables are dichotomous; baseline drug frequency was split at the median, and "Other" was the reference category for race/ethnicity.

4. Maintain a specific rather than a global focus with regard to risk behaviors targeted for intervention. Focusing on one or two specific risk behaviors or several closely related behaviors is preferable to focusing on a broad range of different behaviors.

5. Ensure that the intervention has sufficient strength to reasonably achieve its intended purpose. Are there a sufficient number of sessions or interactions? Do they extend over a long enough period of time?

6. Pretest intervention components to verify their effectiveness in modifying individuals' beliefs, attitudes, perceptions, and behavioral predispositions associated with behavior change.

7. Create an incentive structure and format for intervention activities that will assure an adequate level of participation by members of the target population. Preintervention studies addressing this issue are highly recommended.

8. Develop an appropriate system for monitoring the intervention process to ensure integrity and strength of the intervention over time.

9. Maintain continuity of exposure to intervention activities. Long intervals of time between intervention activities during the period that behavior change is taking place can result in unnecessary decay of the intervention effect. If the interval between scheduled intervention activities will exceed approximately 3 weeks, it can be beneficial to provide relevant activities that participants will engage in on their own initiative.

Table 10.3
Logistic Regression for
Stopping Crack Use (Past 30 Days)

Variable	Odds Ratio	p
Race/Ethnicity		
African American	1.35	.71
Hispanic	.98	.98
White	3.48	.16
Gender (female)	.78	.45
Age (older)	.80	.46
Intervention group (enhanced)	2.21	.01
Frequency of crack use at baseline (> 23 days past month)	1.23	.49

NOTE: Analysis is based on 297 participants who reported at baseline use of crack and no drug injection during the past 30 days. Odds ratios are adjusted for multivariate effects. All variables are dichotomous; baseline drug frequency was split at the median, and "Other" was the reference category for race/ethnicity.

10. Plan strategies for maintaining behavior changes after the intervention has concluded. Development of supportive peer norms and personal relationships can be quite effective for this purpose. Postintervention booster activities may also provide some benefits.

An Intervention-Oriented Model of Health Behavior Change

As previously noted, basing an intervention on an explicit theoretical framework is likely to improve the effectiveness of the intervention. The remainder of this chapter is devoted to a description of a proposed intervention-oriented model of health behavior change that has evolved from the preceding studies and that we plan to use in future studies. The model is based primarily on three theoretical models: the Theory of Reasoned Action (Ajzen & Fishbein, 1980), the Theory of Planned Behavior (Ajzen, 1991), and the transtheoretical Stages-of-Change Model (Prochaska & DiClemente, 1992).

These three theoretical models, which have closely interrelated constructs, have been linked together in a single framework that emphasizes those cognitive and environmental components that might be directly manipulated in a behavioral intervention. Each of the existing models has particular strengths. The Theory of Reasoned Action is precise in terms of its definition of causal variables and their linkage to behavior, and it has demonstrated predictive validity in a variety of health behavior contexts, including condom use. The Theory of Planned Behavior extends the Reasoned Action theory by explicitly allowing for situations in which the behavior of interest may not be entirely under volitional control—the theory recognizes perceived and actual behavioral control as determinants of behavior in addition to personal intention, with indirect and direct linkages to behavioral action. The theory's subjective component of behavioral control is similar to Bandura's (1994) construct of self-efficacy.

The transtheoretical model of behavior change expresses both cognitive and overt components of personal behavior on a single stage-of-change dimension and relates each of the individual stages to specific intervention processes. The stages represented in the model are: (1) Precontemplation—when the person is not thinking about changing the problem behavior in the next six months; (2) Contemplation—when the person is seriously thinking about changing the behavior but has not made a commitment to act in the next 6 months; (3) Preparation—when there is a firm intention to change in the immediate future, often accompanied by some attempt to change the behavior; (4) Action—the first 6 months after overt behavior change has occurred; and (5) Maintenance—the period beginning 6 months after behavior change has occurred and during which the person continues to work to prevent relapse. According to the model, transition from stage to stage is mediated by stage-specific processes of change that are the strategies and techniques that individuals use in their attempts to change problem behaviors (DiClemente et al., 1991; Prochaska, DiClemente, & Norcross, 1992). Use of a particular strategy, although highly relevant for persons in the Contemplation stage, for example, may be inappropriate for individuals in the Maintenance stage. Most intriguing for the purposes of HIV prevention work is the model's suggestion that the effectiveness of intervention efforts can be increased when intervention processes are matched to the person's stage of change.

The influence of the social context on individual behavior is recognized by all of the theories and models of health behavior change cited previously. Perceived social norms, for example, are assigned a key role in both the theories of reasoned action and of planned behavior. Other aspects of social influence, however, are dealt with less explicitly and systematically in these two theories and in the transtheoretical stage model. In addition to considering social norms, it is also desirable to articulate and integrate the variables of social support and social networks as factors in the process of individual behavior change.

Social support is an important element of social influence. According to Albrecht and Adelman (1987), social support is fundamentally an interactive communication process that alters the receiving individual's "affective, cognitive, or behavioral state" (p. 20) concerning a particular situation, including his or her perception of social norms. Supportive social relationships serve to "reduce uncertainty about the situation [and] the self . . . and function to enhance a perception of personal control" (p. 19). The influence of peers can be especially significant in determining the degree to which individuals perceive given behaviors as normative and how much support they perceive for performance of these behaviors. The effects of social support extend beyond its effect on perceived social norms and normative beliefs. Supportive interactions can also have a large effect on individuals' perceived self-efficacy, attitudes, and behavioral beliefs.

Social network structures can also influence individual behavior through several pathways. One such pathway is provided by social support, the effects of which can be enhanced by certain network structures. In addition to enhancing social support, social network structures can directly affect environmental facilitators and barriers to behavioral performance, for example, by making condoms more or less readily accessible to network members. Network structures can also influence the strength of normative beliefs by enhancing or inhibiting the individual's willingness to comply with the perceived behavioral preferences of significant others. An example of the effects of network structures is provided by Seeman and Berkman's (1988) study of social network characteristics and social support in the elderly. Respondents' network size, proximity of ties, and frequency of contacts were all related to the perceived effectiveness of instrumental and emotional support in their ego-oriented networks. From a theoretical perspective, it would also be anticipated that network density (number of actual to possible ties) and relative centrality of the individual would mediate in the influence of social support (Walker, Wasserman, & Wellman, 1994).

Proposed Model

We propose an intervention-oriented model of health behavior change that incorporates within a single framework all or most of the components that might be directly manipulated in a behavioral intervention. To be of greatest use, such a model should (a) have the precision and specificity of the theories of reasoned action and planned behavior, (b) possess a high degree of heuristic usefulness in terms of suggesting strategies and mechanisms for facilitating adoption of condom use and other risk-reducing sexual practices, and (c) articulate meaningfully Prochaska's stages of behavioral change both in conceptual and measurement terms. A model that meets these conditions is shown in Figure 10.1. The proposed model has as its core the Theory of Reasoned Action (behavioral beliefs, behavioral attitude, normative beliefs, subjective social norm, intention) and it incorporates significant additional elements (self-efficacy) from the Theory of Planned Behavior. Explicit linkages are indicated in the model for barriers and facilitators, social supports, social network characteristics, and processes of behavior change (facilitating processes). Although each of these components is implicit in the theories of reasoned action and planned behavior, making them explicit in the current expanded model enhances the model's usefulness for designing real-world interventions. For clarity of presentation, only latent variable paths are shown in Figure 10.1; correlations between observed measures of variables are not presented.

In addition, the model recognizes the contextual influence of cultural and personal history factors on behavior change and the facilitating influence of Prochaska's stage-related processes of change (DiClemente et al., 1991; Prochaska et al., 1992). In Figure 10.1, these are indicated with dotted lines leading to specific intervention components. Cultural, demographic, and personal history factors are significant contextual determiners and mediators of behavior in addition to the factors specified in the model. Although these elements represent essentially fixed effects within individuals and, as such, are not directly manipulated in the intervention process, the power of an intervention

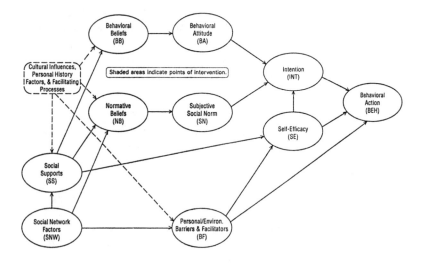

Figure 10.1.   Intervention-oriented model of behavioral action.

Note: Incorporates elements of the theory of reasoned action, theory of planned behavior, and trans-theoretical stage model.

is substantially increased by appropriately recognizing these factors in the intervention structure, so as to create cultural and personal congruence of both content and process.

The rationale for recognizing directly the roles of barriers and facilitators, social supports, social network factors, and processes of change relates to their importance in providing a frame of reference for the generation of specific strategies and mechanisms that may be used in behavioral interventions. Together with behavioral and normative beliefs, these represent the focal points of intervention activity. Therefore, it is useful to understand the relationships of these factors to one another and, through intention and self-efficacy, to behavior, to correctly assess the probable ultimate effects of particular intervention approaches.

Barriers and facilitators may be either personal (internal) or environmental (external) in nature. Examples of personal barriers/facilitators are behavioral skills and emotionality (a strong affective physiological response toward a behavior). Examples of environmental barriers/ facilitators are condom availability and partner willingness to use condoms. Barriers and facilitators are seen as having indirect effects on behavior through their influence on individuals' perceived self-efficacy and direct effects through objective limitation of behavioral options available to individuals. Social support that is received for engaging in a new behavior may act to modify individuals' behavioral and normative beliefs and also to influence their perceived self-efficacy with regard to performing specific behaviors. The characteristics of individuals' social networks can also influence personal behavior change by affecting the strength of social supports, normative beliefs, and environmental barriers and facilitators.

All of the preceding factors have linkages with the facilitating processes identified by Prochaska et al. (1992) as being associated with successful change of problem behaviors. As described earlier, these processes of change refer to techniques and strategies for modifying behavioral beliefs, reducing internal and external barriers, and providing social supports. They represent identifiable mechanisms for bringing about change in each of these areas. By defining the role of facilitating processes in the expanded intervention-oriented model of behavioral action, the relationship of the present model to the stages-of-change model is clarified and the stage-focused processes of change may be understood in terms of their action as enablers of change.

Intention and self-efficacy are the drivers of behavior in the intervention-oriented model portrayed in Figure 10.1. Empirically, these variables have also been found to relate strongly to movement across the five stages of change (Rhodes & Malotte, in press). When behavioral intention was defined and measured to include current and future behavior, strength of intention was related to the stage of change for persons in the nonbehavioral stages (i.e., Precontemplation, Contemplation, and Preparation) in addition to the behavioral stages (i.e., Action and Maintenance). This indicates that increasing the strength of individuals' intentions can result in either initiation of new behaviors or better maintenance of existing behaviors. A similar association was found between the stage of change and perceived self-efficacy, with self-efficacy being an important driver of change at all stages. From both theoretical and empirical perspectives, therefore, it is reasonable to expect that positive changes in the personal intentions and self-efficacy of individuals will be accompanied by progressive movements in their stage of change.

Conclusion

There is an urgent need for effective interventions to reduce HIV risks among out-of-treatment drug users. Relatively brief interventions incorporating HIV testing have proven efficacious in reducing drug-related risks but have been less successful in reducing sexual risk behaviors. Experience to date with more intensive, longer-term interventions has been generally disappointing in terms of demonstrating any incremental effectiveness beyond that of brief interventions. Adherence to a well-defined set of principles for designing interventions holds promise for improving intervention effectiveness and power. In this chapter, an intervention-oriented model of behavior change has been suggested that can be of practical value in guiding the development of interventions.

References

Ajzen, I. (1991). The theory of planned behavior. *Organizational Behavior and Human Decision Processes, 50,* 179-211.

Ajzen, I., & Fishbein, M. (1980). *Understanding attitudes and predicting social behavior.* Englewood Cliffs, NJ: Prentice Hall.

Albrecht, T. L., & Adelman, M. B. (1987). Communicating social support: A theoretical perspective. In T. L. Albrecht & M. B. Adelman (Eds.), *Communicating social support* (pp. 18-39). Thousand Oaks, CA: Sage.

Bandura, A. (1994). Social cognitive theory and exercise of control over HIV infection. In R. J. DiClemente & J. L. Peterson (Eds.), *Preventing AIDS: Theories and methods of behavioral interventions* (pp. 25-59). New York: Plenum.

Booth, R. E., & Watters, J. K. (1994). How effective are risk-reduction interventions targeting injecting drug users? *AIDS, 8,* 1515-1524.

Booth, R. E., Watters, J. K., & Chitwood, D. D. (1993). HIV risk-related sex behaviors among injection drug users, crack smokers, and injection drug users who smoke crack. *American Journal of Public Health, 83,* 1144-1148.

Bowser, B. P. (1989). Crack and AIDS: An ethnographic impression. *Journal of the National Medical Association, 81,* 538-540.

Brown, B. S., & Beschner, G. M. (1993). Introduction: At risk for AIDS—Injection drug users and their sexual partners. In B. S. Brown, G. M. Beschner, & the National AIDS Research Consortium (Eds.), *Handbook on risk of AIDS: Injection drug users and sexual partners* (pp. xxxi-xl). Westport, CT: Greenwood.

Brown, V., & Weissman, G. (1993). Women and men injection drug users: An updated look at gender differences and risk factors. In B. S. Brown, G. M. Beschner, & the

National AIDS Research Consortium (Eds.), *Handbook on risk of AIDS: Injection drug users and sexual partners* (pp. 173-194). Westport, CT: Greenwood.

Centers for Disease Control and Prevention. (1993). Update: Barrier protection against HIV injection and other sexually transmitted diseases. *Morbidity and Mortality Weekly Reports, 42,* 589-591, 597.

Centers for Disease Control and Prevention. (1994a). U.S. HIV and AIDS cases reported through December 1994. *HIV/AIDS Surveillance Report, 6*(2), 1-39.

Centers for Disease Control and Prevention. (1994b). Annual summary of births, marriages, divorces, and deaths: United States, 1993. *Monthly Vital Statistics Report, 42*(13), 1-35.

Coyle, S. (1993). *The NIDA HIV counseling and education intervention model: Intervention manual* (NIH Pub. No. 93-3508). Rockville, MD: National Institute on Drug Abuse.

Deren, S., Davis, R., Tortu, S., & Ahluwalia, I. (1993). Characteristics of female sex partners. In B. S. Brown, G. M. Beschner, & the National AIDS Research Consortium (Eds.), *Handbook on risk of AIDS: Injection drug users and sexual partners* (pp. 195-210). Westport, CT: Greenwood.

DiClemente, C. C., Prochaska, J. O., Fairhurst, S. K., Velicer, W. F., Velasquez, M. M., & Rossi, J. S. (1991). The process of smoking cessation: An analysis of precontemplation, contemplation, and preparation stages of change. *Journal of Consulting and Clinical Psychology, 59,* 295-304.

Edlin, B. R., Irwin, K. L., Faruque, S., McCoy, C. B., Word, C., Serrano, Y., Inciardi, J. A., Bowser, B. P., Schilling, R. F., Holmberg, S. D., & Multicenter Crack Cocaine and HIV Infection Study Team. (1994). Intersecting epidemics—crack cocaine use and HIV infection among inner-city young adults. *New England Journal of Medicine, 331,* 1422-1427.

Fisher, J. D., & Fisher, W. A. (1992). Changing AIDS-risk behavior. *Psychological Bulletin, 111,* 455-474.

Friedman, S. R., Neaigus, A., Des Jarlais, D. C., Sotheran, J. L., Woods, J., Sufian, M., Stepherson, B., & Sterk, C. (1992). Social intervention against AIDS among injecting drug users. *British Journal of Addiction, 87,* 393-404.

Fullilove, M. T., & Fullilove, R. E. (1989). Intersecting epidemics: Black teen crack use and sexually transmitted disease. *Journal of the American Medical Women's Association, 44*(4), 146-147, 151-153.

Guinan, M. E. (1989). Women and crack addiction. *Journal of the American Medical Women's Association, 44*(4), 129.

Haverkos, H. W., & Jones, T. S. (1994). HIV, drug-use paraphernalia, and bleach. *Journal of Acquired Immune Deficiency Syndromes, 7,* 741-742.

Haverkos, H., & Battjes, R. (1992). Female-to-male transmission of HIV. *Journal of the American Medical Association, 268,* 1855.

Inciardi, J. A. (1993). Kingrats, chicken heads, slow necks, freaks, and blood suckers: A glimpse at the Miami sex-for-crack market. In M. S. Ratner (Ed.), *Crack as pipe pimp: An ethnographic investigation of sex-for-crack exchanges* (pp. 37-68). New York: Lexington.

Institute of Medicine. (1994). *AIDS and behavior: An integrated approach* (J. D. Auerback, C. Wypijewska, H. Keith, & H. Brodie, Eds.). Washington, DC: National Academy Press.

Kaplan, E. H., & Heimer, R. (1994). A circulation theory of needle exchange. *AIDS, 8,* 567-574.

Kelly, J. A., & Murphy, D. A. (1992). Psychological interventions with AIDS and HIV: Prevention and treatment. *Journal of Consulting and Clinical Psychology, 60,* 576-585.

Kelly, J. A., Murphy, D. A., Sikkema, K. J., & Kalichman, S. C. (1993). Psychological interventions to prevent HIV infection are urgently needed: New priorities for behavioral research in the second decade of AIDS. *American Psychologist, 48,* 1023-1034.

LaBrie, R. A., McAuliffe, W. E., Nemeth-Coslett, R., & Wilberschied, L. (1993). The prevalence of HIV infection in a national sample of injection drug users. In B. S. Brown, G. M. Beschner, & the National AIDS Research Consortium (Eds.), *Handbook on risk of AIDS: Injection drug users and sexual partners* (pp. 16-37). Westport, CT: Greenwood.

Lewis, V. L., & Kashima, Y. (1993). Applying the theory of reasoned action to the prediction of AIDS-preventive behaviour. In D. J. Terry, C. Gallois, & M. McCamish (Eds.), *The theory of reasoned action: Its application to AIDS-preventive behaviour* (pp. 29-46). New York: Pergamon.

Liebman, J., LaVerne, D. K., Coughey, K., & Hua, S. (1993). Injection drug users, drug treatment, and HIV risk behavior. In B. S. Brown, G. M. Beschner, & the National AIDS Research Consortium (Eds.), *Handbook on risk of AIDS: Injection drug users and sexual partners* (pp. 355-373). Westport, CT: Greenwood.

Longshore, D., & Anglin, M. D. (1994). *HIV transmission and risk behavior among drug users in Los Angeles County: 1994 update.* Los Angeles: University of California, Drug Abuse Research Center.

Longshore, D., Anglin, M. D., Annon, K., & Hsieh, S. (1993). Trends in self-reported HIV risk behavior: Injection drug users in Los Angeles. *Journal of Acquired Immune Deficiency Syndromes, 6,* 82-90.

Lurie, P., & Reingold, A. L. (1993). *The public health impact of needle exchange programs in the United States and abroad: Summary, conclusions, and recommendations.* San Francisco, CA: University of California Press.

MacDonald, P. T., Waldorf, D., Reinarman, C., & Murphy, S. (1988). Heavy cocaine use and sexual behavior. *Journal of Drug Issues, 18,* 437-455.

Mandell, W., Vlahov, D., Latkin, C. A., Carran, D., Oziemkowska, M. J., & Reedt, L. (1994). Changes in HIV risk behaviors among counseled injecting drug users. *Journal of Drug Issues, 24,* 555-567.

McCoy, C. B., Metsch, L. R., McCoy, H. V., & Weatherby, N. L. (1995, August). *The effectiveness of community-based outreach and HIV prevention programs.* Paper presented at National Institute on Drug Abuse Third Science Symposium on HIV Prevention Research, Rockville, MD.

McCusker, J., Koblin, B., Lewis, B. F., & Sullivan, J. (1990). Demographic characteristics, risk behaviors, and HIV seroprevalence among intravenous drug users by site of contact: Results from a community-wide HIV surveillance project. *American Journal of Public Health, 80,* 1062-1067.

National Institute on Drug Abuse. (1993). *Cooperative agreement for AIDS community-based outreach/intervention research program: Policies and procedures manual* (Community Research Branch Publication). Rockville, MD: Author.

National Institute on Drug Abuse. (1994). *Outreach/risk reduction strategies for changing HIV-related risk behaviors among injection drug users: The National AIDS Demonstration Research (NADR) Project* (NIH Pub. No. 94-3726). Rockville, MD: Author.

National Institute on Drug Abuse. (1995). *Cooperative agreement for AIDS community-based outreach/intervention research program: 1990-present* (Community Research Branch Publication). Rockville, MD: Author.

National Research Council. (1989). *AIDS, sexual behavior, and intravenous drug use* (C. F. Turner, H. G. Miller, & L. E. Moses, Eds.). Washington, DC: National Academy Press.

Neaigus, A., Sufian, M., Friedman, S. R., Goldsmith, D., Stepherson, B., Mota, P., Pascal, J., & Des Jarlais, D. C. (1990). Effects of outreach intervention on risk reduction among intravenous drug users. *AIDS Education and Prevention, 2,* 253-271.

NIDA Investigators. (1995, May). *Preliminary report of study findings: Initial sites.* Presented at NIDA Cooperative Agreement Steering Committee Meeting, Vienna, VA.

Prochaska, J. O., & DiClemente, C. C. (1992). Stages of change in the modification of problem behaviors. In M. Hersen, P. M. Miller, & R. Eisler (Eds.), *Progress in behavior modification* (Vol. 28, pp. 184-218). New York: Wadsworth.

Prochaska, J. O., DiClemente, C. C., & Norcross, J. C. (1992). In search of how people change: Applications to addictive behaviors. *American Psychologist, 47,* 1102-1114.

Ratner, M. S. (1993). Sex, drugs, and public policy: Studying and understanding the sex-for-crack phenomenon. In M. S. Ratner (Ed.), *Crack as pipe pimp: An ethnographic investigation of sex-for-crack exchanges* (pp. 1-36). New York: Lexington.

Rhodes, F. (1993). *The behavioral counseling model for injection drug users: Intervention manual* (NIH Pub. No. 93-3597). Rockville, MD: National Institute on Drug Abuse.

Rhodes, F., Corby, N., Wolitski, R., Tashima, N., Crain, C., Yankovich, D., & Smith, P. (1990). Risk behaviors and perceptions of AIDS among street injection drug users. *Journal of Drug Education, 20,* 271-288.

Rhodes, F., & Humfleet, G. L. (1993). Using goal-oriented counseling and peer support to reduce HIV/AIDS risk among drug users not in treatment. *Drugs & Society, 7,* 185-204.

Rhodes, F., Humfleet, G. L., & Corby, N. H. (1992, July). *Efficacy of an individual counseling intervention in reducing AIDS risk among injection drug users.* Paper presented at VIII International Conference on AIDS, Amsterdam.

Rhodes, F., & Malotte, C. K. (in press). Using stages of change to assess intervention readiness and outcome in modifying drug-related and sexual HIV risk behaviors of IDUs and crack users. *Drugs & Society.*

Rhodes, F., Wolitski, R. J., & Thornton-Johnson, S. (1992). An experimental AIDS intervention program for female sex partners of injection drug users. *Health and Social Work, 4,* 261-272.

Schwartz, R. H. (1993). Syringe and needle exchange programs: Part II. *Southern Medical Journal, 86,* 323-327.

Sechrest, L., West, S. G., Phillips, M. A., Redner, R., & Yeaton, W. (1979). Some neglected problems in evaluation research: Strength and integrity of treatments. In L. Sechrest, S. G. West, M. A. Phillips, R. Redner, & W. Yeaton (Eds.), *Evaluation studies review annual* (Vol. 4, pp. 15-35). Thousand Oaks, CA: Sage.

Seeman, T. E., & Berkman, L. F. (1988). Structural characteristics of social networks and their relationship with social support in the elderly: Who provides support. *Social Science and Medicine, 26,* 737-749.

Shapshak, P., McCoy, C. B., Shah, S. M., Page, J. B., Rivers, J. E., Weatherby, N. L., Chitwood, D. D., & Mash, D. C. (1994). Preliminary laboratory studies of inactivation of HIV-1 in needles and syringes containing injected blood using undiluted household bleach. *Journal of Acquired Immune Deficiency Syndromes, 7,* 754-759.

Stephens, R. C., Simpson, D. D., Coyle, S. L., McCoy, C. B., & the National AIDS Research Consortium. (1993). Introduction: At risk for AIDS—Injection drug users and their sexual partners. In B. S. Brown, G. M. Beschner, & the National AIDS

Research Consortium (Eds.), *Handbook on risk of AIDS: Injection drug users and sexual partners* (pp. 519-556). Westport, CT: Greenwood.

U.S. Conference of Mayors. (1994). Needle exchange: Evolving issues. *HIV Capsule Report.* Washington, DC: Author.

van den Hoek, J. A. R., Haastrecht, J. J. A., & Coutinho, R. A. (1992). Little change in sexual behavior in injecting drug users in Amsterdam. *Journal of Acquired Immune Deficiency Syndromes, 5,* 518-522.

Vlahov, D., Astemborski, J., Solomon, L., & Nelson, K. E. (1994). Field effectiveness of needle disinfection among injecting drug users. *Journal of Acquired Immune Deficiency Syndromes, 7,* 760-766.

Walker, M. E., Wasserman, S., & Wellman, B. (1994). Statistical models for social support networks. In S. Wasserman & J. Galaskiewicz (Eds.), *Advances in social network analysis.* Thousand Oaks, CA: Sage.

Watters, J. K., Estilo, M. J., Clark, G. L., & Lorvick, J. (1994). Syringe and needle exchange as HIV/AIDS prevention for injection drug users. *Journal of the American Medical Association, 271,* 115-120.

Weatherby, N. L., Schultz, J. M., Chitwood, D. D., McCoy, H. V., McCoy, C. B., Ludwig, D. D., & Edlin, B. R. (1992). Crack cocaine use and sexual activity in Miami, Florida. *Journal of Psychoactive Drugs, 24,* 373-380.

Wood, M. S., & Rhodes, F. (1995). *Using social gatherings to reduce HIV risks among drug users.* Unpublished manuscript, California State University, Long Beach.

11

Educational Policy, Adolescent Knowledge of HIV Risk, and Sexual Behavior in Zimbabwe and the United States

MICHELLE H. WIERSON
JENNIFER L. BRIGHT

One of the most controversial issues in the history of the AIDS epidemic has involved the dissemination of HIV-related information to the public. As the 1980s began, very little information was publicly available, for not until January 1982 was the first newspaper article on AIDS published in the United States. Even though the U.S. Public Health Service has mandated a policy that scientific information should be translated quickly and clearly to the U.S. population, there has been little enforcement of this policy. Thus, the media have continued to serve as the primary source of information about AIDS in the U.S. (Panem, 1992). Unfortunately, this has often left

AUTHORS' NOTE: This research was supported by a grant from the Hewlett Foundation. The authors would like to thank Neil Steers, James Gonzales, Ana Garcia, Chris Nelson, Melissa Ober, Melissa Paul, Elias Guerrero, Leigh Ann Sabicer, Rob Short, and Craig Thomas for their contributions to this project.

citizens insufficiently informed about AIDS transmission and risk or, worse, misinformed in a manner that has promulgated fear and distress in the general public. As Panem asserted, "a mechanism for collating and distilling research data for public consumption is essential to dispel public confusion and suspicion" (1992, p. 143). Even so, U.S. policy makers continue to argue about how, when, and even *whether* to make information about HIV/AIDS publicly available.

Nowhere has this debate been more heated than in the arena of educating the nation's youth. In 1986, Surgeon General C. Everett Koop called for all schools to offer explicit sex education programs with the goal of preventing AIDS transmission among youth ("Future Directions," 1993-1994). The response to this challenge has been mixed. Although since that time nearly all 50 states have at least recommended the implementation of AIDS education programs, there also exists great fear that such programs will "cause adolescents to become more sexual or will produce a social environment that promotes sexual activity in opposition to the norms or values" of society (Coates, 1992, p. viii). Political arguments in the Congress, media, and within state and local school jurisdictions have focused on the morality rather than the usefulness of educational programs (Panem, 1992). This focus has often diverted policy makers from remembering that the single best way to stem the AIDS epidemic is through behavior change (Kirby, 1993-1994). That is, the real argument should be over how best to target behavior change that will facilitate AIDS prevention (National Commission on AIDS, 1993).

Surveys indicate that adolescents in particular know very little about HIV/AIDS, and because they are especially likely to engage in risky behaviors such as drug use and unprotected sexual activity (Hingson & Strunin, 1992), it is clear that adolescents need to be taught to modify their behavior. Moreover, as only half of adolescents report that they receive sexual and AIDS-related information from their parents (Centers for Disease Control, 1988), it appears that systematically informing youth can best be done through the school system (Wells, 1992). Unfortunately, however, although international organizations recommend comprehensive AIDS education (World Health Organization, 1989) and general guidelines for implementing AIDS education are provided by U.S. governmental agencies (CDC, 1988), most program developers and teachers do not even know where to start in the AIDS education process. If, as the National Commission on AIDS (1993)

asserts, the goal of national prevention policy is to interrupt the transmission of the virus by improving educational efforts, then seeking
information about how to establish and develop effective educational
programs is imperative.

Background of Our Research

One of the ways for the U.S. to gain information about AIDS education is to investigate other countries that have begun to implement
comprehensive programs. That was the purpose of a project begun by
our research group in the spring of 1994. Based on a review of available
health policy literature, we chose two countries as sources of information: Sweden and Zimbabwe. These countries were chosen for two
reasons. First, they represent regions differentially affected by the AIDS
virus. Zimbabwe, a sub-Saharan African country, is part of a region
most affected by AIDS. Conservative estimates of HIV infection are
7-10% of the total population (Pitts & Jackson, 1993). As of 1993, the
official rate of AIDS cases was .001% of the population (WHO, 1993)
but such official statistics are considered to reflect gross underreporting
(Barnett & Blaikie, 1992; Pitts, Jackson, & Wilson, 1990). Sweden, in
comparison, has one of the lowest rates of AIDS cases in any Western
country, affecting a small .00009% of the total population —less than
one case per million people (WHO, 1993).

A second reason that we chose Zimbabwe and Sweden as sources of
information is that they have health-related policies at very different
stages. Sweden has a well-developed, centralized, and comprehensive
national health policy, historically well-known around the world for
excellence (Peters, 1993). In contrast, Zimbabwe has a centralized
health policy that is in an earlier stage of development than either the
U.S. or Sweden (Peters, 1993), but much of the policy development has
been in direct response to the advent of AIDS ("National HIV Action
Agenda," 1994).

The plan of our project was to examine policy effects on adolescents'
understanding of HIV/AIDS in the context of a stress and coping paradigm. This chapter presents some of the early findings from Zimbabwe
and the United States and focuses specifically on AIDS risk knowledge
and sexual behavior. Subsequent papers will incorporate information

gathered from Sweden and will include measures that examine AIDS-related fear and coping strategies.

The purposes of comparing the United States and Zimbabwe were threefold. First, we intended to compare the educational policies that control the development and implementation of AIDS education programs in each country. Second, we attempted to compare the specific curricula of the educational programs that were being implemented. Third, we intended to provide an evaluation of the effect of these programs via a survey of adolescents who were receiving them. All of these purposes were toward the general goal of evaluating policy effectiveness in the two countries in the hope, ultimately, of informing policy-making decisions regarding AIDS education in the United States.

Policy making and policy evaluation are not familiar arenas for most psychologists. Recently, however, more attention has been focused on the role of psychological data in general policy-making decisions. Brooks-Gunn (1995), for example, argued that research can contribute to policy discussions in a proactive way, particularly in regard to policies that affect children and families. Sexual education of adolescents certainly fits this category. Further, since the mid-1980s, social scientists have been specifically challenged to provide data that might inform governmental policy about HIV/AIDS (Batchelor, 1984). Most recently, the National Commission on AIDS (1993) published a report mandating the training of behavioral and social scientists for AIDS prevention research. This report not only called for research data to contribute to the *development* of policy but also for social and behavioral scientists to participate in the policy *evaluation* process itself. Policy evaluation examines whether the stated goals of a particular policy have been achieved (Wells, 1992)—in this case, increased knowledge of the risk factors associated with HIV disease and subsequent reduction of behaviors that increase the risk of HIV infection. If educational policies are going to be carried out with any effect, evaluation data must be provided so that initial policies are strengthened, dropped, or modified, as deemed appropriate.

This study had two components, one qualitative and one quantitative. The qualitative component compared the HIV/AIDS educational policies in Zimbabwe and the United States as they were manifested in educational programs offered in their respective school systems. To obtain this information, individuals from governmental policy organizations, governmental and nongovernmental research organizations, and service/advocacy organizations were interviewed. Subsequently, the quantitative component examined the fruits of these policies— specifically, how much knowledge adolescent samples had about HIV/AIDS risk, how much risky and safer sexual behaviors the adolescents were engaging in, and whether a relationship between knowledge and behavior was present for youth in either sample. We predicted that the country with more systematic and comprehensive educational programs would have adolescents with higher knowledge, lower risky behavior, higher safer-sex behavior, and a stronger relationship between knowledge and behavior. The purpose of the qualitative component was to aid in the generation of specific hypotheses about which country, the U.S. or Zimbabwe, should have significantly better quantitative results. Finally, we hoped that the combination of qualitative and quantitative data would provide suggestions for improving the U.S. system of educating youth about HIV/AIDS.

Qualitative Component Methods

The purpose of qualitative interviews was to describe the educational programs in each country and to highlight their similarities and differences in the following areas: (a) governmental policies regarding education of adolescents about HIV/AIDS, (b) general educational systems, (c) content and process of established AIDS education curricula, and (d) problems encountered in implementation of AIDS education programs. Both authors traveled to Zimbabwe and conducted personal interviews, primarily in Harare, the nation's main urban center. In total, information from 15 different agencies was gathered in Zimbabwe over an intensive two-week period. In the U.S., both personal and phone interviews were conducted over the course of a one-year period. Individuals from 10 different agencies in Atlanta, Washington, DC, and Los Angeles were interviewed.

In both countries, individuals interviewed were those whose work focused on one or more of the following: educating the general public about HIV, treating infected individuals, advocating or lobbying for policy development or changes, researching the epidemic, educating adolescents, or making policies regarding education and HIV/AIDS. These individuals included employees of *governmental agencies* such as the Centers for Disease Control in the United States and the Ministry of Health in Zimbabwe, *nongovernmental organizations* such as AIDS Project Los Angeles, or Women and AID Support Network in Zimbabwe, and *service organizations* such as Mashambazou in Zimbabwe, a program providing support for women with AIDS, and Foothill AIDS project, which offers hospice services for individuals dying from AIDS in Southern California.

Each interview lasted from 45 minutes to 2 hours; when possible, interviews were audiotaped and later transcribed. Notes were transcribed following all interview sessions. To supplement the interview information, written material provided by agencies in both countries was also evaluated and summarized.

Qualitative Results

Based on the qualitative interviews and the reading of national policy information, we found that the educational policies of the United States and Zimbabwe differ in four important ways: in sense of urgency, systematization, relational context, and comprehensiveness. These differences seem to have positively affected the quality and content of Zimbabwe's AIDS education programs. In contrast, the quality of educational programs in the United States is much less promising.

Sense of Urgency

Epidemiological data estimate that sub-Saharan Africa has 64% of the global total of AIDS cases (Barnett & Blaikie, 1992). In Zimbabwe specifically, mortality rate projections suggest that between the years 1991 and 2000 up to 15.8% of the population ages 15 to 50 will die from AIDS (Lewis, 1991). These statistics not only underscore the seriousness of the epidemic in Zimbabwe but also highlight why a sense of urgency for AIDS education is higher in Zimbabwe than in the United States. There, rather than arguing over whether or not it is moral to educate their youth, governmental and nongovernmental agencies, including religious organizations such as the Catholic church, have recently mobilized to develop educational programs for nationwide implementation. Most of this development has occurred since 1989, when government officials in Zimbabwe first acknowledged the catastrophic proportions of AIDS cases in the population in general and the growing number of AIDS cases in the adolescent population specifically. Until that time, an official "policy of silence" existed in the country and little was done to acknowledge the crisis or educate citizens about HIV prevention and treatment. As more and more people died, however, a greater sense of urgency developed.

In contrast, although most policy hearings in the U.S. agree that AIDS education is a good idea, the implementation of many programs is being slowed by debates about how explicit the curriculum should be. Even diffuse, nonexplicit programs for youth are protested and, thus, sent back to committees for revision before implementation ("New York's," 1995). These delays are probably influenced by a tendency to believe that very few U.S. adolescents have AIDS. However, as only minuscule percentages of at-risk adolescents have ever been included in any time-of-HIV seroprevalence study, the actual incidence and prevalence of HIV among American youth are unknown (Hein, 1992). The United States should learn a valuable lesson from Zimbabwe's initial denial of the danger and eventual promotion of AIDS education and prevention: It will pay to develop and implement explicit curricula before the crisis reaches catastrophic proportions.

Unfortunately, many indicators suggest that, for U.S. adolescents, the transmission of AIDS already is increasing dramatically. The number of reported U.S. cases for 13-to 21-year-olds is doubling every 14 months and AIDS is the fifth leading killer of adolescents in this country (Hein, 1992). Given that heterosexual transmission is accounting for more and more HIV prevalence, particularly in adolescents (Vermund, Hein, Gayle, & Thomas, 1989), and given that over half of adolescents are sexually experienced by the age of 19 (Hein, 1992), we must develop the same sense of urgency about educating our youth that exists in countries such as Zimbabwe.

Systematization

Zimbabwe has implemented a standardized AIDS education curriculum in all schools from fourth grade through high school graduation. By 1989, Zimbabwe's government, through the Ministry of Education, had mandated HIV education in all schools, and since 1993 a fully standardized curriculum has been implemented nationwide for junior high school and high school age adolescents. During the 1994-95 academic year, all students from Form 4 (approximately equivalent to fifth grade) and up received systematic AIDS education (Wang, personal communication, June, 1994). The structured programs ensure that students receive a curriculum that is consistent across geographical locations. Moreover, teachers are required to be trained in implementation of the program before administering it, thus strengthening the quality of implementation. A standard text has been developed (Makawa, Ota, Hatendi, & Vera, 1993) that consists of weekly modules emphasizing developmentally relevant topics. To present these systematic materials, teachers lead small group discussions with students. Currently, evaluation methods are being developed to provide data regarding the effectiveness of these educational programs in Zimbabwe.

In contrast, the United States has no standardized or mandated curricula for AIDS education programs. In fact, no federal mandate for educating youth exists (Flamer et al., 1993). In 1987, President Reagan established a set of principles regarding the education of youth in the country that included the following: the decision on whether or not to educate youth and on the content and scope of any programs would be "locally determined," and *no* school curriculum would be mandated by the federal government so that "the American people" could use educational information in a manner appropriate to their community's needs. Therefore, instead of being systematized, AIDS curricula in the U.S. are fragmented and unmonitored.

Although Reagan's principles were in direct opposition to the Surgeon General's views at the same time and although most states have adopted some sort of AIDS curriculum since 1987, the content of the programs still differs greatly by district and state (Wells, 1992). Moreover, a recent survey in California, a state that "requires" AIDS education, indicated that many school districts are not in compliance with the mandate. In addition, few teachers are trained in how to implement the programs that do exist (Forest & Silverman, 1989), further exacerbating the problem. Thus, it is likely that many U.S. students fail to receive the information they need to reduce their chances of contracting sexually transmitted diseases of all kinds. Furthermore, because there is no established system of evaluation for programs that do exist, it is unclear how widespread this problem is.

One of the reasons why it may be easier for Zimbabwe to mandate national education decisions than for the U.S. to do so is because of differences in governmental structure. Zimbabwe's government is centralized, with all educational decisions made at the highest level. Educational policy in the United States is determined by federal, state, and local decision-making strategies (Peters, 1993) and thus is more complicated in implementation. Even so, some federal standards for general curricula do exist in the U.S. and thus it should be possible for the United States to set standards for AIDS-related curricula. Some policy advocates (e.g., Hein, 1992; Panem, 1992) have suggested that, although the specific scope and content of standards could be determined by state and local school boards, U.S. federal funding to support education should be linked to a demonstration that each school district is implementing a program that meets minimal federal standards. Systematic requirement of certain topical coverage (e.g., condom use) could even be included in such minimal standards. In this way it could be assured that every U.S. adolescent receives AIDS education in school. Currently, no such assurance exists.

Relational Context

Another factor that distinguishes Zimbabwe's educational policy from the United States' is that the standard curriculum in Zimbabwe emphasizes the discussion of HIV in the context of other socially and personally relevant issues for students. Thus, self-esteem, dating, friendships, family relationships, communication skills, and spirituality are discussed in general as part of the educational curriculum (Makawa, Ota, Hatendi, & Vera, 1993). Contained *within* these discussions is HIV educational information; for example, when the topic of self-esteem is discussed, teachers and students talk about how feeling good about themselves may relate to protecting their bodies from HIV transmission (Makawa, Ota, Hatendi, & Vera, 1993). When AIDS information and prevention techniques are related to topics appropriate for students at different developmental stages, the HIV information becomes more personalized and thus more valuable. When students understand that engaging in sexual activity, for example, may also involve discussing with potential partners sensitive topics such as sexually transmitted diseases, pregnancy, and emotions, the decision to have sex takes on a more profound meaning.

Unfortunately, AIDS education programs in the U.S. neglect the social and emotional issues that make the topics of HIV, other sexually transmitted diseases, and sexual behavior in general more personally relevant to the youth getting this information (Kantor, 1993-1994). In fact, few programs incorporate self-esteem or communication skills into their curricula even though both factors have been found to affect adolescents' willingness to engage in risky behaviors (Hernandez & DiClemente, 1992). For example, only five states (Maine, Massachusetts, New Jersey, South Carolina, and Wyoming) implement a curriculum that encourages youth to explore their own attitudes and views about sexuality and HIV ("Sexuality," 1993-1994). Typically, the focus of programs in the U.S. is the biological transmission of HIV, presented in a factual, lecture-based manner and covered over only 1 or 2 weeks out of a school year (Gonzales, 1995).

Comprehensiveness

A recent report by the Sex Education and Information Council of the United States (SEICUS—Flamer et al., 1993) asserted that, for HIV education programs to be successful, they must address in depth the following domains: (a) the *cognitive* domain, which incorporates the facts about HIV/AIDS, including statistics on epidemiology and modes of HIV transmission; (b) the *affective* domain, which highlights attitudes about sexuality and HIV and the emotions that accompany sexual relationships; and (c) the *skills* domain, which stresses responsibility and decision-making strategies about sexual behavior. Given Zimbabwe's commitment to AIDS education, it is not surprising that qualitative interviews and an examination of the Zimbabwean AIDS curriculum revealed that all three of these domains are covered in educational programs for their youth. Factual information about AIDS transmission and prevention is presented, feelings about sex are discussed, and skills for negotiating sexual interactions and suggesting the use of condoms are incorporated.

In contrast, the SEICUS study, which evaluated existing educational programs in the United States, found that U.S. curricula usually focus on the cognitive domain but neglect the affective and skills domains (Flamer et al., 1993). Also, though many programs include sexual refusal skills as a component, they tend to concentrate on the possible negative consequences of sexual intercourse rather than promoting thoughtful decision making and communication about a range of sexual feelings and behaviors (Kantor, 1993-1994). U.S. HIV education programs often focus on sexual abstinence rather than on teaching students to manage specific sexual encounters effectively (Haffner, 1993). Therefore, rather than providing comprehensive AIDS information covering multiple domains of importance, U.S. AIDS curricula tend to be limited in both scope and content.

Overall, then, the qualitative comparison of U.S. and Zimbabwean educational policies and programs revealed a stronger and more thorough system for educating youth about HIV in Zimbabwe. However, the effectiveness of comprehensive programs such as those in Zimbabwe is not well-established (Henriksson & Ytterberg, 1992). Although the goal of policies and curricula is to increase adolescent knowledge about HIV/AIDS and reduce risky sexual behavior, no data are available that evaluate whether these goals are being accomplished.

The quantitative portion of our study was designed as an indirect evaluation of policy effectiveness in the U.S. and Zimbabwe. Based on the qualitative interview data, the following hypotheses were generated: (1) Because Zimbabwean curricula are more standardized and more comprehensive, quantitative comparisons would show higher AIDS risk knowledge for Zimbabwean youth; (2) because their educational programs are provided in a more personally relevant context, the Zimbabwean youth would be engaging in fewer risk behaviors than U.S. youth; and (3) because Zimbabwean curricula emphasize cognitive, affective, and skills domains, thus connecting knowledge with tools needed to follow through on safer sexual behavior, the relationship between knowledge and behavior would be stronger for the adolescents from Zimbabwe than for the U.S. sample.

Quantitative Component Methods

Sample

Ninety-one adolescents from the United States (46 males and 45 females) and 89 Zimbabwean youth (60 males and 29 females) participated in this study.

The U.S. sample was recruited through an urban high school in Southern California that agreed to help the researchers with the study. In Zimbabwe, the sample was recruited from a secondary school in Harare, the country's main urban center.

Respondents' ages ranged from 15 to 17, with a mean age of 16 for the U.S. sample and a mean age of 15 years, 10 months for the Zimbabwean sample. Ethnicity of the Zimbabwean students was 85 black Zimbabwean, 1 Caucasian, and 3 unknown. The U.S. participants were more ethnically diverse: 16 Caucasians, 5 African Americans, 52 Hispanics, 5 Native Americans, and 5 other. For both samples, mean parental educational level was graduation from high school. Because of a centrally mandated educational system, this educational level is typical of most Zimbabwean citizens, particular in an urban area such as Harare (Kebokile Dengu-Zvobgo, personal communication, April, 1995). Thus, the educational status of the two samples was roughly equivalent and this provides an approximate indicator of socioeconomic status (SES). Given the vast economic differences between the two countries, a two-factor index of SES (i.e., one incorporating income) was not possible to calculate.

Exposure to HIV-related material was different across the two samples. For the group from Zimbabwe, every youth had received a standardized course of AIDS education in the school setting. This program was integrated into the traditional curriculum throughout the entire school year during which they participated in the study. Moreover, because these AIDS education programs have been administered to youth beginning with Form 7 (roughly equivalent to eighth grade in the U.S.), most of the participating youth already had previous exposure to the material. The material included information about HIV transmission, prevention behaviors, implementation of prevention behaviors (e.g., how to use a condom), sexual negotiation skills (e.g., how to discuss condom use), and personal and relationship issues (e.g., self-esteem, dating, sexual feelings).

In contrast, the U.S. sample received a 2-week program on sexually transmitted diseases and pregnancy that also included a discussion of HIV/AIDS. This module was presented in biology classes for all of the students during the year that they participated in the study. In addition, because similar 2-week modules are included in many junior high school courses in Southern California, most of these students had some previous exposure to this type of AIDS education. The specific content varied according to the discretion of the biology teacher, as no curriculum was provided for them to follow; however, the focus of most modules was on the modes of HIV transmission.

Measures

All participants completed a packet of measures containing demographic items, an AIDS knowledge test, and reports of sexual behavior frequency for the previous 12 months. Additional items asked about other factors that are associated with increased risk of HIV/AIDS in addition to unprotected sexual intercourse. All youth completed the measures anonymously; no identifying information was collected. Special emphasis was placed on the voluntary nature of responding so that participants were encouraged to skip items if they felt uncomfortable answering them.

The AIDS Risk Knowledge Test (Kelly, St. Lawrence, Hood, & Brasfield, 1989) is a 24-item, true-false inventory assessing practical knowledge of AIDS and AIDS risk behavior. Sample items include "A person can get the AIDS virus in one sexual contact," and "The AIDS virus doesn't go through unbroken skin." The test originally was developed for use with gay men but also has available normative data for Caucasian and African American college students. With an adjustment to the reading level, the instrument has been used with a sample of African American adolescents (St. Lawrence, 1993), demonstrating reasonable reliability (Cronbach's alpha =.68) and successfully discriminating between adolescents who engaged in protected versus unprotected sexual intercourse. This modified form of the survey was employed in the present study. The number of items answered correctly was used as a measure of AIDS risk knowledge. Cronbach's alpha was .60 for the Zimbabwean youth and .57 for the U.S. youth, reliabilities similar to those reported with previous adolescent samples.

The Risk Behavior Survey, developed by St. Lawrence (1993) and based on AIDS prevention surveys used by previous researchers (e.g., Darrow, 1983), served as a retrospective report of sexual behavior. The survey asks respondents to report the frequency of protected and unprotected vaginal, oral, and anal intercourse over a specified time period and the number of different sexual partners. Although the original survey used a 6-month time frame, the current study asked respondents to consider the previous 12 months. The time was expanded to gain a broader time frame yet still provide reliable information, based on evidence that retrospective reporting periods of no more than one year seem to be the most reliable when evaluating sexual behavior (Kauth, St. Lawrence, & Kelly, 1991). More importantly, because all of the youth had received at least some form of AIDS education in the year prior to participating in the study, this time frame allowed an assessment of risky behaviors that probably occurred following exposure to some educational material.

Additional items assessed the presence of 12 other factors that have been associated with risk of HIV transmission, many of which are also relevant to sexual activity. Specifically, respondents were asked whether they had ever had sex with a suspected or known IV drug user, had injected drugs intravenously themselves, had a blood transfusion, had sex with someone who had multiple sex partners, had sex as a "one night stand," had sex when drinking alcohol or using drugs, or had sex when pressured. They also were asked if they had ever traded money for sex, traded drugs for sex, or been treated for a sexually transmitted disease. Finally, they were asked whether they had ever had a "sugar daddy" (i.e., an adult male who provides financial support in return for sex) and if they had ever had sex with a long-distance truck driver. These last two variables were added because they are considered to be HIV risk factors in Zimbabwe (Sunanda Ray, personal communication, June 1994).

Finally, all respondents were asked how many people they knew who had HIV and how many individuals they knew who had died of AIDS.

Procedure

For the United States, letters describing the study and meeting the guidelines of informed consent were sent home to parents in four ninth- and tenth-grade classes. A passive assent procedure was employed in which all adolescents were offered a chance to participate unless their parents returned the form denying permission for them to do so. Few parents refused, with the range of refusals in each class being 2-5, roughly 15% of the targeted sample. After the parental assent procedure, the surveys were distributed by classroom teachers during a regular class session; participants were required to sign an informed consent form and turn it in to the teacher before beginning. The actual questionnaires were completed anonymously; the Risk Knowledge Survey and the Risk Behavior Survey were part of a set of measures that took approximately 30 minutes for the adolescents to complete.

In Zimbabwe, a student from the University of Zimbabwe who was a paid research assistant went to high school classes and described the study; letters to parents were sent home with interested students along with consent forms to be signed by their parents. Those who returned the forms were administered the survey packet after school in small groups. They also were required to sign informed consent forms and return them to the research assistant although the questionnaires themselves were completed anonymously.

Most of the Zimbabwean surveys were administered in English. However, if the students preferred, surveys were made available in Shona, a dialect spoken in the region surrounding Harare. Fifteen of the 89 respondents completed a Shona survey, which was translated from English to Shona by a language professor at the University of Zimbabwe.

Quantitative Results

Age of First Sexual Experience

This dependent variable was analyzed by 2 x 2 analyses of variance (ANOVAs) with Sample (Zimbabwe vs. U.S.) and Gender as the independent variables. Youth who had never had sexual intercourse were excluded from these analyses. A main effect emerged for Sample, as the average age of first intercourse for the Zimbabweans was 14 years, 7 months, compared to 13 years, 5 months for the U.S. adolescents, $F(1,75) = 5.97$, $p < .02$. A main effect also emerged for Gender, with males reporting a younger mean age (13 years, 5 months) than females (14 years, 5 months), $F(1,75) = 4,32$, $p < .04$. The interaction term in this analysis was not significant.

Current Levels of General Sexual Behavior

First, the two samples were compared for number of sexually active individuals; a chi square analysis was conducted that yielded a nonsignificant result, $X^2 = 1.46$. Specifically, 40% of the sample from Zimbabwe reported being sexually active, as compared to 45% of the U.S. sample. A similar analysis for gender was statistically significant, $X^2 = 4.27$, $p < .05$; 34% of females were sexually active versus 45% of the males. When sample and gender were considered together, it appeared that Zimbabwean females were less likely to be sexually active (31%) than females from the U.S. (40%); the chi square comparison was not statistically significant but this was largely due to a low sample size and thus it should not be ignored. Similar percentages of males from the two countries were sexually active (Zimbabwe 43%, U.S. 46%).

Next, the *level* of current sexual activity was compared across the two samples, including all respondents and using two different procedures. First, a series of 2 (Sample) x 2 (Gender) ANOVAS was conducted in which dependent variables were the total number of male and female partners over the past 12 months. As can be seen in Table 11.1, the two country samples were nonsignificantly different with regard to their number of sexual partners, for both male and female partners. However, the main effect was significant for gender, showing that males had more female partners and females had more male partners. This effect provided an indirect test of sexual orientation in the sample, showing that the sample was almost exclusively engaging in heterosexual sexual activity. When the interaction term was examined, a significant effect was found, $F(1,161) = 10.92$, $p < .001$. A post hoc analysis revealed that the major source of this interaction was the Zimbabwean females, who reported significantly fewer male partners than did the females from the United States, $F(1,160) = 24.98$, $p < .0001$.

Next, 2 (Sample) x 2 (Gender) ANOVAS were conducted, in which the dependent variables were frequency of vaginal, oral, and anal sex over the past 12 months. Table 11.1 shows that the U.S. adolescents reported higher rates in all three categories than did the Zimbabwean adolescents. No main effects for gender were found but there was a marginally significant gender by sample interaction for vaginal sex $F(1,144) = 3.27$, $p < .07$. A post hoc exploratory examination of means indicated that girls in the U.S. sample were engaging in significantly more vaginal sex than those in Zimbabwe, $F(1,144) = 9.41$, $p < .01$.

Taking these findings together, it appears that the overall level of sexual activity was higher in the United States than in Zimbabwe but that this might be a result of there being fewer sexually active females in the Zimbabwean sample. Therefore, in the following analyses of

Table 11.1
Comparisons of General Sexual Behavior
Over Past 12 Months: Sample and Gender Effects

Variable	U.S. mean	Zimbabwe mean	df	F	p
No. of male partners	1.12	.15	1,149	1.12	ns
No. of female partners	1.69	2.69	1,149	0.05	ns
Frequency of vaginal sex	6.23	1.64	1,147	6.65	.01
Frequency of oral sex	1.62	.54	1,147	5.83	.02
Frequency of anal sex	.80	.11	1,147	5.10	.02

Variable	Male mean	Female mean	df	F	p
No. of male partners	.00	1.96	1,149	41.49	.0001
No. of female partners	3.28	.13	1,149	11.18	.001
Frequency of vaginal sex	2.54	5.10	1,147	1.31	ns
Frequency of oral sex	1.07	.89	1,147	0.48	ns
Frequency of anal sex	.48	.11	1,147	0.75	ns

sexual behavior only sexually active youth are included so that scores are not artificially deflated due to zero frequencies.

Protected Versus Unprotected Sexual Behavior

When the sample was restricted to only those youth who were sexually active, the power for conducting 2 x 2 ANOVAS was greatly decreased (e.g., power indices dropped from .99 to .28 for examining one main effect); therefore, two sets of one-way ANOVAS were conducted in which sample and gender were examined separately. Overall sexual activity was divided into safer versus unsafe sexual behaviors, and the results of comparisons between the U.S. and Zimbabwe are presented in Table 11.2. In examining the frequency of unprotected sexual activity (i.e., without use of a condom), small differences were found between the two samples, except for the frequency of unprotected vaginal sex, which was higher in the U.S. sample with an average

Table 11.2
Protected and Unprotected Sexual Behavior
Over Past 12 Months: Zimbabwe vs. U.S.,
for Sexually Active Sample Only (*N* = 79)

Variable	Zimbabwe mean	U.S. mean	df	F	p
Frequency, without condoms					
Vaginal sex	2.14	7.12	1,52	2.51	.11
Oral sex	1.16	2.19	1,51	.97	ns
Anal sex	.22	.84	1,48	1.26	ns
Frequency, with condoms					
Vaginal sex	4.17	4.21	1,52	.01	ns
Oral sex	1.21	.93	1,50	.19	ns
Anal sex	.28	.38	1,48	.09	ns
No. of partners, without condoms					
Vaginal sex	1.28	1.33	1,52	.01	ns
Oral sex	1.33	.87	1,49	.87	ns
Anal sex	.28	.49	1,48	.47	ns
No. of partners, with condoms					
Vaginal sex	1.78	1.37	1,52	1.07	ns
Oral sex	1.15	.38	1,48	4.43	.04
Anal sex	.27	.34	1,48	.06	ns
Frequency refused, due to not wearing condom					
Vaginal sex	7.33	3.03	1,50	1.02	ns
Oral sex	1.66	.03	1,45	10.16	.002
Anal sex	.63	.09	1,48	3.58	.06
No. of partners refused, due to not wearing condom					
Vaginal sex	1.56	.87	1,48	2.37	.13
Oral sex	1.41	.31	1,44	6.19	.02
Anal sex	.68	.25	1,51	1.43	ns
Proportion of condom use, all sexual interactions	75%	45%	1,44	8.37	.005

around 7 occasions compared to 2 in the Zimbabwean sample; this effect was marginally significant, $F(1,52) = 2.14$, $p < .11$.

Yet when safer-sex behavior was considered, the Zimbabweans reported more oral sex partners who used condoms, $F(1,48) = 4.43$, $p < .04$, a higher frequency of refusing to engage in oral sex without using a condom, $F(1,45) = 10.16$, $p < .002$, and refusing more oral sex partners who would not use a condom, $F(1,44) = 6.19$, $p < .02$. Similar trends emerged for frequency of refusal to engage in unprotected anal sex, $F(1,48) = 3.58$, $p < .06$, and for refusing more partners for vaginal sex who would not use a condom, $F(1,48) = 2.37$, $p < .13$. When all of the cell means are examined, it appears that the U.S. sample engaged in more unprotected, unsafe sexual acts with more partners over the past 12 months, whereas the Zimbabwean sample engaged in more safer sexual acts with more partners. Though this trend is often slight and nonsignificant, its consistency is interesting and may be important.

Given that the U.S. sample was engaging in more overall sexual activity, the proportion of protected sexual activity was also examined. For the Zimbabwean sample, 45.8% reported condom use for *every* sexual interaction over the previous year, compared to only 14.7% of the U.S. sample, a significant difference, $F(1,76) = 7.74$, $p < .01$. The mean reported condom use was 75% of the time for adolescents in Zimbabwe versus 45% for U.S. respondents, also significantly different, $F(1,76) = 8.37$, $p < .005$.

The results of comparisons between males and females are presented in Table 11.3. The most significant difference that emerged indicated that females were reporting a much higher frequency of unprotected vaginal sex, $F(1,52) = 8.27$, $p < .006$. Strikingly, they also reported a significantly lower proportion of condom use over all sexual interactions (39%), compared to 67% reported by males, $F(1,76) = 4.40$, $p < .04$. When safer sex was considered, there were significant differences in males reporting more oral sexual interactions in which condoms were used, and a higher likelihood of refusing oral sex if condoms were not used.

Other Risk Factors

Other HIV risk factors also were examined by creating a composite sum of adolescent responses to the 12 additional risk factors associated

Table 11.3
Protected and Unprotected Sexual Behavior
Over Past 12 Months: Females vs. Males,
for Sexually Active Sample Only (*N* = 79)

Variable	Female mean	Male mean	df	F	p
Frequency, without condoms					
Vaginal sex	10.65	1.97	1,52	8.27	.006
Oral sex	2.39	1.48	1,51	.75	ns
Anal sex	.53	.68	1,48	.08	ns
Frequency, with condoms					
Vaginal sex	4.40	4.08	1,52	.03	ns
Oral sex	.44	1.36	1,50	2.25	.14
Anal sex	.42	.29	1,48	.18	ns
No. of partners, without condoms					
Vaginal sex	1.27	1.34	1,52	.03	ns
Oral sex	.53	1.35	1,49	3.04	.08
Anal sex	.16	.55	1,48	2.04	.15
No. of partners, with condoms					
Vaginal sex	1.24	1.74	1,52	1.56	ns
Oral sex	.21	.97	1,48	4.26	.04
Anal sex	.16	.44	1,48	1.02	ns
Frequency refused, due to not wearing condom					
Vaginal sex	5.89	3.84	1,50	.23	ns
Oral sex	.22	.93	1,45	1.62	ns
Anal sex	.06	.44	1,48	1.72	ns
No. of partners refused, due to not wearing condom					
Vaginal sex	1.00	1.20	1,48	.20	ns
Oral sex	.16	1.11	1,44	4.68	.03
Anal sex	.11	.61	1,51	2.04	.15
Proportion of condom use, all sexual interactions	39%	67%	1,44	4.40	.04

with the transmission of HIV. The entire sample was included in this analysis. No significant effects were found and all groups reported, on average, the presence of less than one additional HIV risk factor.

AIDS Knowledge

In a 2 x 2 ANOVA, Sample and Gender were compared on percentage of correct answers for the 24-item AIDS knowledge questionnaire. The Zimbabwe sample had, on average, 76% correct answers (mean = 17.7), compared with 82% correct answers (mean = 19.8) for the U.S. sample. This difference was significant, $F(1,177) = 7.79$, $p < .001$, indicating significantly more accurate knowledge in the U.S. sample. There was no main effect for gender, but there was a significant sample by gender interaction, $F(1,177) = 5.24$, $p < .05$. Post hoc analysis revealed that the females in the United States had significantly higher knowledge than the females in Zimbabwe (mean = 19.9, 82%, vs. 17.1, 71%), $F(1,177) = 13.37$, $p < .0001$. No other significant post hoc differences emerged.

Knowledge-Behavior Relationship

Although the samples exhibited differences on AIDS knowledge and on some behavioral indices of risky behavior, the most important question was whether or not knowledge was related to behavior in either group, given that the ultimate goal of all AIDS educational programs is to affect behavior through increasing knowledge. Before investigating this question, however, other variables that could influence this relationship were examined—specifically, the number of individuals whom the respondent knew personally who had HIV and the number who had died of AIDS were compared across the two samples. Not surprisingly, both of these comparisons were significant, with Zimbabwean adolescents knowing significantly more individuals with HIV, $F(1,172) = 22.08$, $p < .0001$, and significantly more individuals who had died of AIDS, $F(1,173) = 98.36$, $p < .0001$. These differences become even more meaningful when frequencies are considered—only 25% of the Zimbabwean sample knew no one who had died of AIDS, versus 86% of the U.S. sample. Most Zimbabwean adolescents (51%)

knew two or more individuals who had HIV or had died from AIDS, whereas 47% of the U.S. sample knew none.

To examine whether these differences might have an effect on the knowledge-behavior relationship, correlations were computed between the number of acquaintances with HIV, number of acquaintances who had died from AIDS, scores on the AIDS knowledge survey, number of sexual partners, proportion of condom use, and other AIDS risk behaviors. Both acquaintance variables were significantly, though not highly, negatively correlated with knowledge (HIV acquaintances: $r = -.24$, $p < .01$; acquaintances who died: $r = -.18$, $p < .05$) and the number of acquaintances who died from AIDS was significantly negatively correlated with the number of sexual partners ($r = -.22$, $p < .01$).

Given these patterns, it seemed best to consider the acquaintance variables in some manner in subsequent analyses. However, the two variables were significantly correlated ($r = .67$, $p < .01$); therefore, to avoid problems of high collinearity, the number of acquaintances who had died of AIDS was selected as a single control variable.

To examine the knowledge-behavior relationship, three sets of multiple regression analyses were computed. The first two examined the U.S. and Zimbabwe samples separately and the third examined the samples together to compare the strength of the knowledge-behavior relationship. Three composite scores served as dependent variables in all of these analyses: (1) number of sexual partners (the sum of vaginal, oral, and anal sex partners in the previous 12 months), (2) proportion of safer sex behaviors (computed by summing the total reported vaginal sex, oral sex, and anal sex occasions on which a condom was used and dividing it by the total number of reported vaginal, oral, and anal sex occasions), and (3) number of other risk factors (the sum of the 12 additional HIV risk factors, such as using IV drugs or trading sex for money).

Tables 11.4 and 11.5 present the results of the regression analyses for the Zimbabwean adolescents and U.S. adolescents, respectively. For each sample, a series of hierarchical regressions was performed in which the number of acquaintances who had died of AIDS was entered first and then the HIV Risk Knowledge scores were entered at the next step, to determine their unique relationship to the dependent variable.

For the Zimbabwean youth, several interesting relationships emerged. Specifically, the number of acquaintances who had died from AIDS significantly predicted the proportion of condom use in sexual activity, the presence of additional HIV risk factors, and (marginally)

Table 11.4
Regression Analyses on Three Risk Behaviors, With Number of Acquaintances Who Died of AIDS and AIDS Risk Knowledge as Predictor Variables (Zimbabwe Sample Only, N = 89)

Step	Predictor variable entered	Dependent variable	beta	F	p
1	Acquaintances	No. of partners	−.35	3.26	.07
2	Knowledge	No. of partners	−.17	1.84	.16
1	Acquaintances	% of condom use	.37	7.93	.01
2	Knowledge	% of condom use	.25	4.55	.02
1	Acquaintances	No. of other risk factors	−.22	4.08	.04
2	Knowledge	No. of other risk factors	−.18	2.06	.13

Table 11.5
Regression Analyses on Three Risk Behaviors, With Number of Acquaintances Who Died of AIDS and AIDS Risk Knowledge as Predictor Variables (U.S. Sample Only, N = 91)

Step	Predictor variable entered	Dependent variable	beta	F	p
1	Acquaintances	No. of partners	−.07	.76	ns
2	Knowledge	No. of partners	−.05	.88	ns
1	Acquaintances	% of condom use	.12	1.12	ns
2	Knowledge	% of condom use	.19	2.28	.11
1	Acquaintances	No. of other risk factors	−.49	21.10	.0001
2	Knowledge	No. of other risk factors	−.39	14.24	.0001

the number of sexual partners. Directionally, the more people who had died from AIDS that the Zimbabwean youth knew, the greater was their proportion of condom use, the fewer their additional risk factors, and the fewer their sexual partners during the past 12 months. When the level of AIDS risk knowledge was added, it independently predicted greater condom use and it showed nonsignificant trends toward predicting fewer sexual partners and fewer other risk factors.

For the U.S. sample, neither the number of acquaintances who had died from AIDS nor the AIDS knowledge score predicted their number of sexual partners. Higher AIDS knowledge did marginally predict a higher proportion of condom use. However, a strong relationship emerged for other risk behaviors; both the number of acquaintances who had died from AIDS and AIDS risk knowledge strongly predicted having fewer additional risk factors.

To test whether the knowledge-behavior relationship was stronger for the Zimbabwean sample than for the U.S. sample, a third set of multiple regression analyses was conducted. First, the number of acquaintances who had died from AIDS was entered into the equation for each dependent variable; at the next step, Sample (Zimbabwe vs. U.S.), AIDS knowledge, and the interaction between Sample and Knowledge were entered. The interaction term served as a test of the strength of association between knowledge and behavior across the two groups. The results of these analyses showed that the interaction term was significant for the proportion of condom use ($F = 8.64$, $p < .004$), for the number of other risk factors ($F = 9.61$, $p < .001$), and was marginally significant for the number of sexual partners ($F = 2.27$, $p < .06$). Examination of Tables 11.4 and 11.5 shows that the knowledge-behavior relationship was stronger for the Zimbabwean sample than for the U.S. sample on two of the three factors but stronger for the U.S. on the third. Specifically, higher AIDS knowledge was more closely related to having fewer partners and a higher proportion of condom use for the Zimbabwean youth but higher AIDS knowledge was more strongly related to the presence of fewer other risk factors for the U.S. sample.

Discussion

This study has some limitations, such as differences in sample demographics and plausible alternative explanations, that are discussed later. Nevertheless, it offers several unique contributions to the AIDS literature. First, it incorporates international data; very few AIDS risk studies have been able to apply the same methodology to samples from different countries (Flamer et al., 1993). Second, it includes both qualitative and quantitative data and attempts to draw a link between the two; most studies on AIDS education rely on one or the other. Finally, this study is an effort to evaluate, albeit indirectly, educational policies for adolescent populations. Although such evaluation has been recommended (e.g., Wells, 1992), very little of this type of research has been conducted. Therefore, the results presented here have meaning for the development and implementation of educational programs for youth.

The qualitative analysis revealed some important differences between educational policies and curricula in the United States and Zimbabwe. From this analysis it was possible to generate hypotheses for the quantitative component of the study. With some exceptions, the quantitative data supported these hypotheses. Specifically, adolescents from Zimbabwe were engaging in a significantly higher number of safer-sex behaviors than adolescents from the United States and the relationship between knowledge and sexual behavior was stronger and more consistent for the Zimbabwean youth on the behaviors of number of sexual partners and proportion of times they used condoms. However, the knowledge-behavior relationship was stronger for the U.S. sample for the variable of additional HIV risk behaviors and AIDS risk knowledge itself was higher for the U.S. sample; both of these patterns contradicted our initial hypotheses.

The implication of the higher percentage of AIDS risk knowledge in the U.S. group is not clear. On one hand, it might suggest that educational programs in the United States do a better job of increasing absolute levels of knowledge. Given that these programs tend to focus only on the cognitive domain (Haffner, 1993), perhaps they make information about risk factors and modes of transmission more salient for U.S. adolescents. Indeed, many studies have shown that AIDS risk knowledge for adolescents in the United States is fairly high and has been on the increase since the early 1980s, before any AIDS education programs were in place in the school system (Hingson & Strunin, 1992). St. Lawrence (1993), for example, who employed the same measure that we used in this study, found accuracy rates to be 65% in a sample of youth who may or may not have received AIDS education in school. The fact that the rates for both the samples studied here (Zimbabwe = 76%; U.S. = 82%) were higher is encouraging, because both samples did have some type of AIDS education.

Another possibility that might explain the higher U.S. knowledge is that exposure to factual information from sources other than the educational system may be stronger or more frequent in the United States that in Zimbabwe. For example, media exposure regarding HIV/AIDS has been on the rise in the United States since 1985 and is present in print, television, and film (Panem, 1992). Given that there are only three television channels available in Zimbabwe, it is plausible that media exposure is lower there. However, our travels in Zimbabwe suggest that factual information is distributed in forms and at levels not present in the United States. For example, AIDS-related posters in English and Shona are posted all over the country, particularly in Harare. Posters regarding transmission, risk factors, symptoms of HIV, and myths regarding HIV are present in airports, on street signs, in shops, in schools, and in clinics. Brochures and informational material are frequently distributed by service organizations in the country. Thus, Zimbabweans have an almost daily exposure to some form of AIDS information. We believe that U.S. citizens have less frequent exposure. Consequently, it is even more puzzling that the knowledge difference emerged, and we need to consider possible sources of bias.

Perhaps the difference in knowledge between the two samples was due to bias in the surveys or to cultural or general educational variations (e.g., differences in interpretations of word meaning or differences in reading and comprehension competence) that were not measured in this study. The fact that the measures were developed and standardized on U.S. samples (Kelly et al., 1989) provides possible support for this theory. Or, the difference may be an artifact of the higher number of girls in the U.S. sample, for other U.S. surveys have shown higher knowledge accuracy among girls than boys (Hingson & Strunin, 1992). This possibility is supported by the significant interaction effect of gender and sample on knowledge, which showed that U.S. girls had higher knowledge scores than did girls from Zimbabwe.

Though one goal of AIDS educational programs is to increase knowledge, this is only in service to a second, more critical goal—to reduce the frequency of unprotected sexual activity. Relevant to this, our second hypothesis predicted that sexually active Zimbabwean youth would engage in more protected sexual behavior than U.S. youth due to experiencing more comprehensive educational programs. This hypothesis was generally supported. The most striking results were seen in the proportion of condom use, which averaged 75% for Zimbabwean youth versus 45% for U.S. youth. The percentage of adolescents from Zimbabwe who reported using a condom for every sexual intercourse occasion in the previous 12 months was 46%, compared to 15% of U.S. adolescents. Clearly, then, sexually active youth in the Zimbabwean sample were more committed to a course of safer-sex behavior than those in the U.S. sample. This is consistent with previous quantitative data from the U.S. that have shown that AIDS education is a predictor of knowledge (Durant et al., 1992) but that a majority of sexually active adolescents in this country continue to engage in unprotected sex despite learning about the principle modes of HIV transmission (Hingson & Strunin, 1992).

The gender differences in unprotected and protected sexual activity should be mentioned. There was an indication that girls were engaging in more sexual interactions without condoms; however, we believe that this finding was largely due to the girls from the United States, who were engaging in the highest rates of vaginal intercourse, whether unprotected (U.S. mean = 6.63, Zimbabwe mean = .48) or protected (U.S. mean = 2.33, Zimbabwe mean = .62). Testing the significance of this interaction was not possible, given the severely restricted statistical power of analyses using only the sexually active respondents, but it probably had an effect on our gender results. If this is true, however, it leads to an interesting implication. For U.S. AIDS education programs in particular, it seems critical to target sexually active girls when teaching sexual negotiation skills and condom use; this group may be especially likely to participate in sexual interactions that are unsafe. Moreover, because the sexual mores in the U.S. still often emphasize a girl's responsibility to "say no" to sexual activity, whereas boys are encouraged to seek it, girls probably experience more pressure from sexual partners to have sex that is unprotected. Reinforcing and empowering young women to negotiate sexual interactions so that they are not unsafe or unwanted should be a goal of AIDS educational programs in the U.S. Of course, these emphases may be useful in Zimbabwe as well, but given the sexual conservatism in that country, girls may be less likely to be sexually active in general and thus less at risk for the transmission of AIDS via sexual contact. This certainly was true for the sample in this study.

Our third hypothesis, that the relationship between knowledge and behavior would be stronger in the sample from Zimbabwe, also was generally supported, except in relation to having additional HIV risk factors. The pattern was strongest for proportion of condom use; higher AIDS risk knowledge levels significantly predicted more condom use in Zimbabwe, whereas this relationship was only marginally significant for the U.S. adolescents. Similar findings have been obtained with samples of U.S. college students (Roscoe & Kruger, 1990), showing that only a small subgroup reports an increase in condom use as a function of AIDS information. Because the relationship was present in the sam-

ple from Zimbabwe, this lends some credibility to the belief that comprehensive, systematized educational programs presented in a relational context are likely to result in the behavior change that is the target
of most HIV/AIDS educational policy. At least for these Zimbabwean
youth, all of whom had participated in such an educational program,
AIDS knowledge and protective sexual behavior were related over and
above the effect of knowing individuals who had died of AIDS. In
contrast, however, AIDS knowledge scores were more strongly related
to the dependent variable of having other HIV risk factors for the U.S.
sample. Perhaps the emphases on fear-related information and modes
of transmission in U.S. AIDS programs (Kantor, 1993-1994) does help
deter youth from low-frequency, atypical risk behaviors such as IV drug
use and prostitution. However, because unprotected heterosexual contact with multiple partners is the most common risk factor for adolescents (Hingson & Strunin, 1992), it is particularly discouraging that
knowledge was not significantly related to the number of partners and
was only marginally related to condom use in the U.S. sample. Thus, it
seems that the strategies employed in Zimbabwean educational programs may be more effective for deterring unprotected sexual activity.

Of course, it must be acknowledged that these results offer only
indirect support for a relationship between the quality of AIDS educational programs and their effect on sexual behavioral practices. First,
because no baseline measure of knowledge or behavior was taken in
either country, it is possible that these reports do not represent an actual
change in knowledge and behavior since the implementation of AIDS
education programs. Perhaps Zimbabwean youth always have been
more likely to use condoms than youth from the U.S. However, the
qualitative interviews cast great doubt on this notion, for a consistent
comment that arose in interviews in Zimbabwe was how sexually
conservative the country is and how few sexually active couples use
birth control measures of *any* kind, let alone condoms, due to mores
about the significance of childbirth and child rearing. This suggests that
condom use in Zimbabwe is more likely to be due to the introduction
of new information about HIV/AIDS prevention in that country, which
is suffering staggering levels of AIDS.

Another possibility is that the sexual behavior differences and differences in the knowledge-behavior relationship found here between
the U.S. and Zimbabwe are due to other, more powerful differences
between the two samples than just the nature of their educational programs. In this study it was possible to examine one obvious variable—

knowing individuals who had died of AIDS—but other more subtle cultural differences could not be evaluated, and this limits the strength of our conclusions. In particular, it must be remembered that our samples may not be representative of the general adolescent population (or even of urban adolescents) in the U.S. and Zimbabwe. This fact raises questions about the generalizability of our findings that can only be answered by further research.

A related issue that should be noted is that the stronger relationships found in the Zimbabwean sample when compared to the U.S. sample could be an artifact of sample demographics. First, the samples were unequal in their gender distribution, with the U.S. having a higher proportion of females. Because more U.S. females than Zimbabwean females were sexually active, it is possible that this affected the results. Specifically, perhaps the knowledge-behavior relationship is more pronounced for boys than for girls, thus manifesting itself more clearly in the adolescents from Zimbabwe. However, a series of post hoc regression analyses suggested that this was not the case. Specifically, Knowledge, Gender, and the Knowledge x Gender interaction term were entered into regression analyses in which number of partners, condom use, and other risk factors served as dependent variables. The interaction term served as a test of the strength of association between knowledge and behavior across males and females, and results showed that this interaction term did not significantly predict sexual behavior on any dimension.

A final alternative explanation for the findings in this study may be the heterogeneity of the two samples. Specifically, the Zimbabwean sample was not only more homogeneous in gender, it also was very homogeneous in ethnic distribution. In contrast, the U.S. sample was ethnically heterogeneous, with a majority of Hispanics. The lack of significant relationships between knowledge and behavior for the U.S. adolescents was possibly due to ethnic variations that affected the data. Some support for this possibility comes from examinations of ethnicity effects in other U.S. samples that have found differences in AIDS risk knowledge level between groups of white, African American, and Latino adolescents (DiClemente, Zorn, & Temoshok, 1986). Moreover, higher rates of infection have been found among African American and Latino populations when compared to white populations (DiClemente, Boyer, & Morales, 1988), suggesting that these ethnic groups may be more likely to engage in risky sexual behaviors. Because over half of the U.S. sample was Hispanic, and the rest of the sample varied widely, it is possible that relationships existing for certain ethnic subgroups were obscured in our analyses. Unfortunately, insufficient sample size made it impossible to examine this issue within the U.S. sample; however, as part of our larger study, additional samples from the U.S. also have been surveyed and these ultimately will allow for this type of ethnic comparison.

Conclusion

Despite its limitations, the results of this study are valuable. They indicate that there may be differences between adolescents from the U.S. and Zimbabwe in terms of sexual knowledge, risky sexual practices, and the knowledge-behavior relationship. Further, based on qualitative analysis of national educational policies and programs, these differences may be at least partially due to the higher quality of educational curricula in Zimbabwe. This suggests that the U.S. should learn from the Zimbabwean educational system and make the following policy changes: (a) federally mandate the implementation of AIDS educational programs; (b) require that the content of programs must meet minimal federal standards for being comprehensive, so that they incorporate factual information, skill-related training, discussion of attitudes and feelings related to HIV and sexuality, and training about how to negotiate and communicate with sexual partners regarding the use of condoms in sexual interactions; and (c) provide this curriculum in the context of other interpersonal topics relevant to adolescence, so that the HIV information will have more personal relevance for students who receive it.

References

Barnett, T., & Blaikie, P. (1992). *AIDS in Africa*. New York: Guilford.
Batchelor, W. (1984). AIDS. *American Psychologist, 39*, 1277-1278.
Brooks-Gunn, J. (1995, Spring). Research briefs to inform policy. *SRA Newsletter.*
Centers for Disease Control, Center for Health Promotion and Education. (1988, April). Guidelines for effective school health education to prevent the spread of AIDS. *Journal of School Health, 58*(4), 142-148.

Coates, T. J. (1992). Foreword. In R. J. DiClemente (Ed.), *Adolescents and AIDS: A generation in jeopardy* (pp. vii-x). Newbury Park, CA: Sage.

Darrow, W. W. (1993). *Acquired immune deficiency syndrome in a cohort of homosexual male clinic patients.* Unpublished paper, Centers for Disease Control, Atlanta, GA.

DiClemente, R. J., Boyer, C. B., & Morales, E. (1988). Minorities and AIDS: Knowledge, attitudes, and misconceptions among Black and Latino adolescents. *American Journal of Public Health, 1,* 55-57.

DiClemente, R.J., Zorn, J., & Temoshok, L. (1986). Adolescents and AIDS: A survey of knowledge, beliefs, and attitudes about AIDS in San Francisco. *American Journal of Public Health, 76,* 1443-1445.

Durant, R., Ashworth, C., Newman, C., McGill, L., Rabun, C., & Baranowski, T. (1992). AIDS/HIV knowledge level and perceived chance of having HIV among rural adolescents. *Journal of Adolescent Health, 13,* 499-505.

Flamer, M. G., Brick, P., McCaffree, K., Richards, D., Schreiner-Engel, P., & Vasbinder, S. (Eds.). (1993). *SEICUS report, 21*(1), 1-30.

Forrest, J. D., & Silverman, J. (1989). What public school teachers teach about preventing pregnancy, AIDS, and sexually transmitted diseases. *Family Planning Perspectives, 21,* 65-72.

Future directions: HIV/AIDS education in the nation's schools. (1993-1994, December/January). *SEICUS Report, 21*(2), 31-33.

Gonzales, J. (1995). *AIDS education: Comparing classical and group learning methodologies on AIDS knowledge and attitudes.* Unpublished manuscript, Pomona College, Claremont, CA.

Haffner, D. W. (1993). Toward a new paradigm on adolescent sexual health. *SEICUS Report, 21*(1), 26-30.

Hein, K. (1992). Adolescents at risk for HIV infection. In R. J. DiClemente (Ed.), *Adolescents and AIDS: A generation in jeopardy* (pp. 3-16). Newbury Park, CA: Sage.

Henriksson, B., & Ytterberg, H. (1992). Sweden: The power of the moral(istic) left. In D. L. Kirp & R. Bayer (Eds.), *AIDS in the industrialized democracies* (pp. 55-64). New Brunswick, NJ: Rutgers University Press.

Hernandez, J. T., & DiClemente, R. J. (1992). Self-control and ego identity development as predictors of unprotected sex in late adolescent males. *Journal of Adolescence, 15,* 437-447.

Hingson, R., & Strunin, L. (1992). Monitoring adolescents' response to the AIDS epidemic: Changes in knowledge, attitudes, beliefs, and behaviors. In R. J. DiClemente (Ed.), *Adolescents and AIDS: A generation in jeopardy* (pp. 17-31). Newbury Park, CA: Sage.

Kantor, L. M. (1993-1994). Scared chaste? Fear-based educational curricula. *SEICUS Report, 21*(2), 1-15.

Kauth, M. R., St. Lawrence, J. S., & Kelly, J. A. (1991). Reliability of retrospective assessments of sexual HIV risk behavior: A comparison of biweekly, three-month and twelve-month self-reports. *AIDS Education and Prevention, 3,* 207-214.

Kelly, J. A., St. Lawrence, J. S., Hood, H. V., & Brasfield, T. L. (1989). An objective test of AIDS risk behavior knowledge: Scale development, validation, and norms. *Journal of Behavior Therapy and Experimental Psychiatry, 20,* 227-234.

Kirby, D. (1993-1994). Sexuality education: It can reduce unprotected intercourse. *SEICUS Report, 21*(2), 19-25.

Let's talk: An AIDS action programme for schools. (1993). Harare, Zimbabwe: Ministry of Education and Culture in association with UNICEF.

Lewis, P. (1991, April). *AIDS and AIDS in Africa*. Unpublished paper, Monsomer Norton, Bath, UK.

Makawa, J., Ota, C., Hatendi, F., & Vera, A. (1993). *Methods and AIDS education*. Harare, Zimbabwe: UNICEF and Ministry of Education and Culture.

National Commission on AIDS. (1993, July). *Behavioral and social sciences and the HIV/AIDS epidemic*. Washington, DC: Author.

National HIV action agenda. (1994, April). *National AIDS Policy Coordinator Report*. Harare, Zimbabwe.

New York's watered-down AIDS curriculum doesn't please critics. (1995, February). *AIDS Policy and Law*.

Panem, S. (1992). *The AIDS bureaucracy*. Cambridge, MA: Harvard University Press.

Peters, B. G. (1993). *American public policy: Promise and performance*. Chatham, NJ: Chatham House.

Pitts, M., & Jackson, H. (1993). Press coverage of AIDS in Zimbabwe: A five year review. *AIDS Care, 22*, 223-230.

Pitts, M., Jackson, H., & Wilson, P. (1990). Attitudes, knowledge, experience and behavior related to HIV and AIDS among Zimbabwean social workers. *AIDS Care, 2*, 53-61.

Roscoe, B., & Kruger, T. (1990). AIDS: Late adolescents' knowledge and its influence on sexual behavior. *Adolescence, 25*, 39-47.

Sexuality, education, and sexual rights. (1993-1994). *SEICUS Report, 21*(2), 33-35.

St. Lawrence, J. (1993). African-American adolescents' knowledge, health-related attitudes, sexual behavior, and contraceptive decisions: implications for the prevention of adolescent HIV infection. *Journal of Consulting and Clinical Psychology, 61*, 104-112.

Vermund, S. V., Hein, K., Gayle, H., Cary, J., & Thomas, P. (1989). AIDS among adolescents in NYC: Case surveillance profiles compared with the rest of the U.S. *American Journal of Disease in Children, 143*, 1220-1225.

Wells, J. A. (1992). Public policy perspectives on HIV education. In R. J. DiClemente (Ed.), *Adolescents and AIDS: A generation in jeopardy* (pp. 233-248). Newbury Park, CA: Sage.

World Health Organization. (1989). *AIDS education in schools: Report on a European workshop*. Copenhagen: Author.

World Health Organization. (1993). *AIDS: Images of the epidemic*. Geneva: Author.

Author Index

Subject Index

About the Authors

NANCY E. ADLER earned her PhD in social psychology from Harvard and is Professor of Medical Psychology in the Departments of Psychiatry and Pediatrics at the University of California, San Francisco. There she is Director of the Health Psychology Program and Vice-Chair of the Department of Psychiatry, and she also heads a planning initiative on Socioeconomic Status and Health for the John D. & Catherine T. MacArthur Foundation. Her work has focused on applying social psychological models to understanding and changing health behaviors, particularly in the area of adolescent contraceptive use and nonuse, and sexual risk behaviors resulting in unwanted pregnancy and sexually transmitted diseases.

JENNIFER L. BRIGHT is a PhD candidate in social psychology at Claremont Graduate School. She received her B.A. in psychology from Mount Saint Mary's College in 1992 and her M.A. in social psychology from Claremont Graduate School in 1994. Her current research interests include the effect of public policy on AIDS education for adolescents, and her future goals involve using psychological research to help nonprofit agencies run effectively.

LESLIE F. CLARK received her PhD in social psychology in 1985 from UCLA and is currently Associate Professor in the Health Behavior Department, School of Public Health, at the University of Alabama, Birmingham. Recently she earned an M.P.H. degree from Emory University while working in an NIMH/CDC postdoctoral program in the Division of HIV/AIDS at the Centers for Disease Control and Prevention. Her research focuses on adaptation to HIV, prevention of mother-to-child HIV transmission, cognitive processing of HIV prevention messages, and perceptions of partner safety.

RALPH J. DiCLEMENTE is an Associate Professor at the University of Alabama at Birmingham, with appointments in the Department of Health Behavior in the School of Public Health, the Department of Pediatrics in the School of Medicine, the Social Medicine Program, and the Health Psychology Program; and he is Co-Director of the Prevention Sciences Research Program at the Center for AIDS Research. He earned an M.S. in social epidemiology at the Harvard School of Public Health and a PhD in health psychology at the University of California at San Francisco. His research has centered on epidemiological and survey studies of sexual and contraceptive practices and AIDS risk behavior, particularly among adolescents.

MARTIN FISHBEIN received his B.A. from Reed College and his PhD in psychology from UCLA in 1961. Since that time he has been a faculty member at the University of Illinois at Urbana-Champaign, where he is currently Professor of Psychology and Research Professor in the Institute of Communications Research. He has served on the NIMH Mental Health AIDS Research Review Committee and in other capacities as a consultant to the NIMH AIDS research program. Most recently, he has become a guest researcher and Acting Branch Chief in the Behavioral Intervention and Research Branch of the Division of STD Prevention at the Centers for Disease Control and Prevention. Within social psychology he is famous as coauthor of the Theory of Reasoned Action.

JEFFREY D. FISHER is Professor of Psychology at the University of Connecticut. He has been a member of the Psychobiological, Biological, and Neurosciences Subcommittees of the Mental Health Acquired Immunodeficiency Syndrome Review Committee of the NIMH, and has served on the editorial boards of several professional journals. He has published widely on determinants and models of AIDS risk behavior change, and is coprincipal investigator (with William A. Fisher) of a major AIDS risk reduction research project funded by NIMH.

WILLIAM A. FISHER is Professor of Psychology and Professor of Obstetrics and Gynecology at the University of Western Ontario in London, Canada. He is on the editorial boards of the *Journal of Sex Research* and the *Journal of Psychology and Human Sexuality.* He has published widely on psychological determinants of reproductive health behaviors and he is coprincipal investigator (with Jeffrey D. Fisher) of a major AIDS risk reduction research project funded by NIMH.

JANET S. HARRISON received a PhD in community psychology from Georgia State University and is currently a researcher at the Centers for Disease Control and Prevention. Her research interests include relationship and gender-role determinants of HIV risk, and community planning approaches to HIV prevention.

JOHN B. JEMMOTT, III received his PhD in Psychology from Harvard University and is currently a Professor of Psychology at Princeton University. His research has centered on social psychological influences on health. During the past 8 years he has conducted a series of studies on the application of social psychology to HIV risk reduction among inner-city African Americans, particularly adolescents. This work has involved development of theory-based, culture-sensitive, behavioral interventions to reduce HIV risk-associated sexual behavior.

KELLY L. KAY received a B.A. degree in psychology and a M.P.H. degree from Emory University and is currently a researcher at the ORKAND Corporation in Atlanta. Her research interests include determinants of HIV-risk behavior in women, gay men, and adolescents.

C. KEVIN MALOTTE is Associate Director of the Center for Behavioral Research and Services at California State University, Long Beach. He earned M.P.H. and Dr.P.H. degrees from the UCLA School of Public Health, and an M.A. in social psychology from Claremont Graduate School. His current work includes studies of compliance with medical regimens and drug and sexual risk reduction among drug users and other high-risk populations.

BARBARA VANOSS MARÍN is an Associate Adjunct Professor in the Department of Epidemiology and Biostatistics and a coinvestigator at the Center for AIDS Prevention Studies at the University of California, San Francisco. She earned her PhD in applied social psychology from Loyola University of Chicago and was a postdoctoral fellow at UCSF in health psychology. Her long-standing interest in promoting healthy behaviors for Latinos in culturally appropriate ways began during years she spent living in Bogota, Colombia, in the 1970s. Her research topics have included smoking cessation, breast-feeding promotion, and HIV prevention among Latinos, and she has written on methodological issues of doing cultural research and coauthored *Research with Hispanic Populations*.

KIM S. MILLER earned a PhD in sociology from Emory University. She is the Coordinator of Youth Activities in the Division of HIV/AIDS Prevention at the Centers for Disease Control and Prevention. Her research interests include determinants of sexual risk behaviors in adolescent populations and family communication processes.

JANET MOORE earned a PhD in social psychology from the University of Georgia, Athens, and is the Acting Chief of the Behavioral and Social Studies Section, Epidemiology Branch, of the Centers for Disease Control and Prevention. Her research interests include the quality of life for HIV-infected women and HIV risk behavior in women.

KATHRYN A. MORRIS received her B.A. from Gettysburg College and her M.A. in psychology from the University of Texas at Austin, where she is currently a doctoral candidate in social and personality psychology. Recently she was awarded a dissertation research grant from NIMH to investigate denial as a coping mechanism to deal with the threat of HIV infection.

✳ **STUART OSKAMP** is Professor of Psychology at Claremont Graduate School. He received his PhD from Stanford University and has had visiting appointments at the University of Michigan, University of Bristol, London School of Economics and Political Science, University of New South Wales, and University of Hawaii. His research interests include a wide variety of social issues where findings concerning attitude and behavior change are important to the formation of public policy. His books include *Attitudes and Opinions* and *Applied Social Psychology*. He has served as president of the American Psychological Association's Division of Population and Environmental Psychology and the Society for the Psychological Study of Social Issues (SPSSI) and as editor of the *Applied Social Psychology Annual* and the *Journal of Social Issues.*

FEN RHODES is Director of the Center for Behavioral Research and Services and Professor of Psychology at California State University, Long Beach. He earned his B.S. degree from Georgia Institute of Technology, an M.S. from George Washington University, and a PhD from Ohio State University. Since 1988, he has developed and evaluated HIV-risk interventions for out-of-treatment drug users, and currently he is also investigating the effect of alternative HIV counseling and testing strategies for STD clinic patients.

CYNTHIA ROSENGARD received her PhD in clinical psychology from the University of Connecticut and is currently completing a post-doctoral fellowship in health psychology at the University of California, San Francisco. Her interests include influences on health-related decision making and the development, implementation, and evaluation of health-promotion interventions. She has conducted research on safer-sex behavior in college students and health decisions of adolescents and homeless women.

WILLIAM B. SWANN, JR. received his B.A. from Gettysburg College and his PhD from the University of Minnesota in 1978. Since then he has taught at the University of Texas at Austin, where he is currently a Professor of Psychology. He received a Research Scientist Development Award for his research on self-knowledge and interpersonal relationships, and recently he became interested in studying social-cognitive processes related to the AIDS epidemic.

SUZANNE C. THOMPSON is Associate Professor of Psychology at Pomona College and at Claremont Graduate School. She received her PhD in social psychology in 1983 from the University of California, Los Angeles. Her publications include a coedited journal issue on perceived control in vulnerable populations and articles on perceived control, coping with stressful life experiences, caregiver-patient relationships during chronic illness, and the doctor-patient relationship. Recently her research has focused on safer-sex attitudes and behavior in response to the AIDS crisis.

MICHELLE H. WIERSON is Assistant Professor of Psychology at Pomona College and received her PhD in clinical psychology in 1992 from the University of Georgia. Her empirical, theoretical and clinical work focus on the effect of social and family stressors, including HIV/AIDS, on adolescent development, coping, and psychological adjustment.